INTEGRATING SEX AND MARITAL THERAPY

A Clinical Guide

Edited by

Gerald R. Weeks and Larry Hof

*Marriage Council of Philadelphia and
University of Pennsylvania*

Brunner/Mazel *Publishers* • New York

Library of Congress Cataloging-in-Publication Data

Integrating sex and marital therapy.

   Includes bibliographies and index.
   1. Marital psychotherapy.   2. Sex therapy.
I. Weeks, Gerald R., 1948–   . II. Hof, Larry.
[DNLM: 1. Marital Therapy—methods. 2. Sex Disorders—
therapy.   WM 611 I59]
RC488.5.I514 1987   616.89'156   86-23283
ISBN 0-87630-447-1

Copyright © 1987 by Gerald R. Weeks and Larry Hof

Published by
BRUNNER/MAZEL, INC.
19 Union Square
New York, New York 10003

MANUFACTURED IN THE UNITED STATES OF AMERICA

10 9 8 7 6 5 4 3 2

Dedicated to
Emily H. Mudd, Ph.D.

Co-Founder and Director of
The Marriage Council of Philadelphia
1933 to 1952

Director, The Marriage Council of Philadelphia and
The Division of Family Study in Psychiatry
University of Pennsylvania School of Medicine
1952 to 1967

Pioneer in
Sex Education and Sex and Marital Therapy

Foreword

The behavioral sciences are poised for a breakthrough as the need for a greater integration of theory and therapeutics has become evident. This volume is a valuable contribution to that breakthrough.

The years from 1940 through 1979 saw a rapid expansion of treatment methods and theories with many promises that all too often failed to be fulfilled. The demand for mental health services escalated and treatment theories and techniques proliferated to attempt to meet the need. Some new messiahs added some increment to our understanding of human behavior and therapeutic armamentarium.

As monolithic approaches were forced to soften, daring theoreticians and therapists reached out, at first in an eclectic fashion, to try to incorporate the techniques and information from other systems into the one with which they were most familiar. Pieces from one orientation would often be grafted onto another. Or, in a sense, a therapist would be therapeutically opportunistic, calling on any technique he or she could recall or improvise in order to accomplish an intermediate goal of therapy.

In the 1980s the need for a greater integration of theory and therapeutics has been increasingly obvious. Eclecticism isn't sufficient. A new level of integration is required and a number of individuals and teams have begun to respond of necessity to this challenge. Further proliferation of schools that espouse different nuances of existing theory or practices border on the counterproductive. Unfortunately, it is hard to come by the research money necessary for controlled comparative longitudinal studies. This leaves theoretical and practice integration as the order of the day, backed up by whatever research can be done to test the hypotheses of the theory and the results of the practice.

For example, in at least four large teaching and clinic facilities in different parts of the United States (Wisconsin, Pennsylvania, Massachusetts, and New York), structural, strategic, and psychodynamic family systems approaches are beginning to be integrated into a single program. Others are taking this a step further by beginning to integrate child and family therapies and forms of adult and family modalities. Some behavior therapists, including some of its originators, have come to recognize that multimodal forms of treatment are needed to deal with aspects of clients' reactions in order to fulfill therapeutic goals. They began to include techniques from insight and systems forms of treatment.

Scheflen (1981) provided us with a starting conceptual basis for an integrated theory that is founded on a concept of levels of systems within the individual and those other systems outside of one's own skin that one is part of or interfaces with. These systems range from the genetic and cellular biochemical to the family, community, peer systems, workplace, national, and so forth.

Other workers are utilizing smaller segments of the large picture puzzle as they work on integrating relatively discrete sections of the bigger picture. With the publication of Masters and Johnson's research on the anatomy and physiology of sex and on the definition and treatment of sexual dysfunctions, in the late 1960s and early 1970s, an explosion took place in psychiatry, psychology, and many other fields which is still reverberating. A new interest was generated (not accidently coinciding with simultaneous changes in society such as "the pill," changes in concepts of sexual morality, women reaching for greater equality with men, the sharp increase in the divorce rate, etc.) in studying sex and treating the sexual dysfunctions. Contributions began to pour in from psychiatry, psychology, gynecology, urology, endocrinology, internal medicine, surgery, embryology, neuroanatomy, and physiology — and they are still increasing. Nine scientific journals dealing with one or more aspects of sexology have come into existence since 1968.

Largely as a result of Masters and Johnson's emphasis, sex shifted from being considered to be an individual's problem to being a couple's problem and even a family problem. This shift brought the emphasis on treating the sexual dysfunctions into the arena of couple and marital therapy. In turn, this has led to the need for this volume.

The editors, Gerald Weeks and Larry Hof, recognize the need to integrate sex and marital therapy. They have made an important contribution to filling in one corner of the integrated picture puzzle. Sex and its role in human behavior, in and out of marriage, and intergenerationally within families, have begun lately to receive added attention. We can even speculate that just as Freud recognized sex as a fundamental cornerstone in the development of his theoretical system and therapeusis, so we may find that sex once again emerges as having a central or paradigmatic role in a new integrated understanding of human behavior. That is, if the couple's biological, cultural, psychological, and systemic forces that enter into determining an individual's and/or couple's functioning can be integrated into a unified theory, then perhaps that system might serve as a paradigm for the larger picture of human behavior. This is the added potential I see for this volume, going beyond the immediate one of helping to improve our functioning as therapists of couples with or without sexual problems.

Although sex and marital therapists deal with essentially the same population, many have avoided moving into the others' presumed area of competence. It is a prime example of how "turf" and a touch of insecurity may
blind even conscientious professionals to the obvious. Many sex therapists
still remain focused on treating the sexual dysfunction, even though they
recognize on some level of consciousness that sex is but a part of a particular
couple's relationship. Similarly, significant numbers of marital therapists, if
they take a sex history at all, usually do so in a perfunctory fashion. Some
marital therapists may not be aware after many months of treatment, or even
after termination, that the couple had a sexual dysfunction that they had never
volunteered to mention. Often clients and therapists seem to have a collusive
taboo against dealing with sexual problems. This, of course, reflects on the
therapist, not the client.

Early on in the era of the new sex therapy, several sex and marital therapists
who had developed skills in both subspecialties began to define criteria for
both forms of treatment as if they were entirely disparate and unrelated. When
I first published my thoughts on the subject (Sager, 1974), I was much too
rigid about separating both syndromes, the sexual and the marital. Fortunately, two years later (Sager, 1976), I was able to describe a more flexible and
integrative approach that recognizes how often the two syndromes come from
similar and interrelated sources. Sex therapy is not a discipline or science by
itself but is based on contributions from a wide variety of scientific arenas.
A broad professional and discipline base is necessary for all practitioners.

The editors of this volume recognize the need to integrate sex and marital
therapy, and this volume makes a significant contribution to that task. The
contributors greatly broaden our knowledge of sex in relation to marriage
and families and enable therapists of all schools to succeed in taking that
qualitative leap that integration makes possible.

New York   Clifford J. Sager, M.D.
October 1986

REFERENCES

Sager, C. J. (1974). Sexual dysfunctions and marital discord. In H. S. Kaplan (Ed.),
    The New Sex Therapy (pp. 501–518). New York: Brunner/Mazel.
Sager, C. J. (1976). Sex therapy in marital therapy. *American Journal of Psychiatry,
    133*(5), 555–558.
Scheflen, A. E. (1981). *Levels of Schizophrenia*. New York: Brunner/Mazel.

Contents

Preface

The field of sex therapy has experienced tremendous growth in the last 20 years. The use of the term "sex therapy" for most clinicians brings several well-known therapists to mind and is associated with the treatment of a fairly limited number of sexual problems. "Sex therapy" also refers to an approach to therapy which is brief, problem-focused, has an educational component, involves seeing a couple together, consists of specific treatment formats and techniques, and often involves giving clients specific homework assignments. Many people in this field consider these elements to be so clearly defined that they view sex therapy as a distinct profession.

The view of sex therapy as a profession has had both positive and negative consequences. Sharply focused research has led to an expanded and widely disseminated base of knowledge. Clearly defined ethical and training standards have contributed to the emergence of practitioners who can effectively treat a wide variety of sexual dysfunctions. On the other hand, a case could be made to support the contention that the view of sex therapy as a profession has resulted in isolation and compartmentalization. In their wake, stagnation has emerged in the field of sex therapy, and the evolutionary process has begun to be truncated by theoretical dogma and technological rigidity.

The purpose in writing and editing this book was to build on the work of individually oriented sex therapy by adding the systems perspective. This book, then, represents an attempt at the integration of sex and marital or systems therapy. Such an integration could revitalize the field of sex therapy by expanding the types of problems treated, providing new perspectives for understanding problems, and creating the opportunity for therapists to develop treatment programs for specific problems. To date, the field has been severely restricted to the type of problems usually treated. People experience a variety of sexual problems which do not fall into these few categories. For this reason, the book includes chapters on dealing with family sexuality; love, intimacy, and affection; inhibited sexual desire; geriatric sexuality; effects of rape on the marriage; and infertility. The integration of sex and marital therapy changes the way problems are understood from an individual to a

systems perspective. Not only is such an integration useful for the sex therapists, but marital therapists have generally had little interest or facility in doing
sex therapy. These two fields can thus enhance and enrich each other. Finally, the integration allows for the creation of treatment programs which draw
from several specific approaches to therapy ranging from individual to interactional to intergenerational therapies. This type of integration calls for
a new breed of sex therapist, therapists trained in individual, sex, marital,
and family therapy.

OVERVIEW OF THE BOOK

Part I of this book focuses on the conceptualization of sexual problems
from a systems perspective. The traditional individual behavioral perspective
of sex therapy is broadened to include the contextual and interactional dimensions of relationships. The first two chapters examine the more theoretical
aspects of the systems perspective. Chapter 1 provides a broad, specific, and
current systemic framework for evaluating the marital relationship of clients
with sexual problems and dysfunctions. Chapter 2 examines the theoretical
basis of love, sex, and intimacy. These concepts are differentiated and discussed in terms of our ability to share them with others.

The second part of Part I discusses some of the general applications of
the systems perspective to treating sexual problems. Chapter 3 discusses a process of understanding sexual problems within an intergenerational framework.
This framework also provides a new way of treating sexual problems intergenerationally.

Chapter 4 focuses on in-office techniques that can be helpful in enhancing a couple's sexuality. The use of these techniques is based on understanding a couple's interactions and how these interactions affect the couple's intimate relationship. Chapter 5 shows how therapists may act as educators to
help parents provide sexuality education for their children. Chapter 6 reveals
how sexual problems may result from negative self-hypnosis. Sex hypnotherapy reverses this process by teaching the couple how to develop a positive
stance toward sexuality.

The six chapters that comprise Part II of the book describe how to systematically treat a variety of common sexual problems. Chapter 7 examines
infertility as a life crisis. The couple's reactions, coping mechanisms, and
therapeutic interventions are described in great detail. Chapter 8 reviews the
causes of extramarital sex and gives an overview of the various approaches
therapists use in helping couples resolve this issue. Chapter 9 discusses the
types of marital and sexual dysfunctions that can result from rape and describes treatment approaches for these dysfunctions. Chapter 10 provides a

systematic model for the diagnosis and treatment of inhibited sexual desire. This model systematically integrates the individual, interactional, and intergenerational approaches to treatment.

Chapter 11 discusses how various factors—organic, psychological, and cultural—may contribute to behavior that is labeled as hypersexual. Organic factors are few, insofar as our present awareness is concerned, but cannot be overlooked. Psychological factors are many and complex and include psychoses, personality disorders, and reactive overcompensations. Hypersexual behavior can be effectively treated by conjoint psychotherapy of the individual plus the "significant other."

Chapter 12 shows how traditional therapeutic techniques can be modified to meet the special needs of elderly couples. This chapter gives the reader an understanding of sexual functioning in older couples and gives a number of specific interventions.

Contributors

Daniel L. Araoz, Ed.D.
Professor of Mental Health Counseling, Long Island University

Ellen M. Berman, M.D.
Clinical Associate Professor of Psychiatry, University of Pennsylvania; Senior Consultant, Marriage Council of Philadelphia; Co-Director, Women's Center, Philadelphia Psychiatric Center.

Maggi Ruth P. Boyer, M.Ed.
Manager of Education and Training for Planned Parenthood of Bucks County; Instructor, Clergy Training Program, Marriage Council of Philadelphia; Private Consultant.

Martin Goldberg, M.D.
Clinical Professor of Psychiatry, University of Pennsylvania School of Medicine; Director, Division of Family Study, University of Pennsylvania School of Medicine; Director, Marriage Council of Philadelphia.

Larry Hof, M.Div.
Lecturer in Psychiatry, University of Pennsylvania School of Medicine; Senior Staff Member, Marriage Council of Philadelphia.

Frederick G. Humphrey, Ed.D.
Associate Professor of Family Studies, University of Connecticut; Private Practice in Marital, Sexual and Family Therapy.

Ellen Kalinsky, M.A.
Private Practice in Family and Sex Therapy.

Luciano L'Abate, Ph.D.
Professor of Psychology and Director of Family Psychology Program, Georgia State University.

Patricia P. Mahlstedt, Ed.D.
Private Practice in Psychology; Clinical Instructor, Baylor College of Medicine, Department of Obstetrics and Gynecology, Houston, Texas.

William R. Miller, Ph.D.
Private Practice in Clinical Psychology, Bala Cynwyd, Pennsylvania.

Jacob D. Stone, ACSW
Private Practice, with Specialization in Gerontology, Doylestown, Pennsylvania; Principal in Stone Associates, Inc.

William C. Talmadge, Ph.D.
Private Practice of Marital and Sex Therapy, Atlanta, Georgia.

Stephen R. Treat, D.Min.
Clinical Associate in Psychiatry, University of Pennsylvania School of Medicine; Senior Staff Member, Marriage Council of Philadelphia.

Gerald R. Weeks, Ph.D.
Director of Training, Marriage Council of Philadelphia, Division of Family Study and Joint Doctoral Program, Marriage Council and Graduate School of Social Work, University of Pennsylvania.

Part I

Conceptualizing Sexual Problems from a Systems Perspective

Section I

Theoretical Issues

Chapter 1

Evaluating the Marital Relationship of Clients with Sexual Complaints

Larry Hof

Although the short-term, behaviorally oriented approach to the treatment of sexual dysfunctions has proven to be an effective treatment modality over the last 15 years, couples who experience severe marital distress demonstrate a poorer prognosis for treatment in a variety of forms of sex therapy. The research that supports this conclusion (see Berg and Snyder, 1981, for a listing of studies) confirms the belief that sexual dysfunctions do not occur in a vacuum, and they must be viewed within the context of the total system of the client(s).

The various subsystems (e.g., marital, extended family, individual, biological, social, etc.) interact with each other and impact on one another. The marital relationship impacts on the sexual problem, and, in turn, the sexual problem impacts on the marital relationship, as each of these interacts with a variety of other forces. This being the case, it is obvious that a comprehensive and multidimensional approach to the treatment of sexual dysfunctions must include a thorough evaluation of the marital relationship. This conceptualization enables the therapist to assess and understand the place of forces within the marriage in the etiology and maintenance of the sexual dysfunction; the relative strength of relationship-enhancing forces that could potentially facilitate and support the process of sex therapy; and the relative strength of relationship-diminishing forces that could potentially inhibit and even undermine the process of sex therapy. With this information, the practitioner and client(s) are better able to decide whether sex therapy is appropriate at the time and what strengths might be drawn upon. The therapist can also better anticipate potential problem areas in therapy and thus be prepared for them and plan more effectively to resolve them should they emerge. If sex therapy is contraindicated (because of the presence of severe, rather than moderate, marital distress), the marital evaluation can indicate what needs to be addressed in marital therapy in order to pave the way for the future treatment of the sexual problem.

A review of the literature relevant to sexual assessment and evaluation reveals a significant deficit in the area of information pertaining to the marital evaluation of clients with sexual problems. Masters and Johnson (1970) stressed that the couple is "always" the patient and in so doing noted that a systems perspective was needed when treating sexual dysfunctions. The process and content of the individual and conjoint interviews were discussed in great detail, with the focus on the specifically sexual aspects of the relationship. The broader, nonsexual dimensions of relationship functioning were barely noted. From this early publication, little can be gained regarding the nature and theoretical base of a comprehensive marital evaluation.

In another early publication, the Group For The Advancement of Psychiatry (1973) emphasized the concepts of "marital unit," "mutual responsibility," and "complex multidimensional system based on the way each partner sees the other and sees the marriage itself, on the self-image of each, and on each partner's perception of how he or she appears to the other" (pp. 775–776). Beyond this, little was said to enable the clinician to identify and evaluate the component parts of the marital system and their relationship to sexual problems. The extensive listing of topics covered in a sexual history (pp. 827–836) contained no questions specifically designed to evaluate the marital relationship.

At about the same time, Kaplan's important work on the treatment of sexual dysfunctions appeared (1974). In that work, a systems perspective pervaded the assessment section of the book. Intrapsychic "causes" of sexual dysfunctions were described from a Freudian perspective, along with a brief review of cultural and developmental sources of the kinds of conflict that can lead to sexual dysfunctions. In discussing "The Relationship – Dyadic Causes of Sexual Dysfunctions" (Chapter 9), Kaplan focused on partner rejection, transferences, lack of trust, power struggles, contractual disappointments, and sexual sabotage. She also discussed the need to assess when relationship factors require direct intervention in treatment, and when they can perhaps be bypassed. In addition, there was a strong emphasis on social learning theory (as well as psychoanalytical theory) as providing a helpful base for understanding the etiology and treatment of sexual dysfunctions. In spite of the wealth of material presented, the reader is left without a broad-based, systematic, and detailed format for evaluating the marital relationship of clients with sexual problems.

Some four years later, LoPiccolo and LoPiccolo (1978) edited their *Handbook of Sex Therapy*, to update the reader on the then most current developments in the treatment of sexual dysfunctions. Generally speaking, a systems approach was assumed as a foundation for the book. In the discussion of clinical assessment, Lobitz and Lobitz (Chapter 5) presented their approach to the initial evaluation. They stressed the importance of relationship factors, but there was insufficient breadth and depth in this area. In LoPiccolo and Heiman's discussion of the sexual assessment and history interview (Chapter 6), nine questions pertaining directly to the relationship were included, but without any theoretical framework for the questions.

Kaplan's most recent work, *The Evaluation of Sexual Disorders* (1983), represented the first systematic integration of the biological and psychological aspects of the evaluation process. Relationship factors were given a place of appropriate prominence and were addressed from a conceptual and methodological perspective, with a specific focus on the following: (1) specific problems in the sexual interaction — inadequate techniques, poor communication, and incompatible sexual fantasies; (2) neurotic interactions — power struggles, contractual problems, parental transferences, and ambivalence about intimacy, commitment, and romantic success; (3) psychopathology of the spouse; and (4) incompatible marriage. A few specific questions gave the reader insight into Kaplan's approach. Yet, when this writer finished reading the relationship-oriented sections, he was left with a degree of dissatisfaction. There simply was insufficient depth and systematization to enable the reader to know how to make a comprehensive marital evaluation of clients with sexual complaints or dysfunctions.

In fairness to the above writers, it must be stated that the *marital* evaluation of clients with sexual problems was not their major focus. As the years have progressed, however, the need for more thorough attention to this area has become evident. Students and therapy trainees have continued to ask for more "specifics" in this area. In addition, knowledge regarding the nature and aspects of effective marital relationships and the important role of the extended family/multigenerational context in the etiology and maintenance of some sexual problems has increased dramatically.

The purpose of this chapter, then, is not to replace anything that has been written before. Rather, its purpose is to add more flesh to the skeleton created by those who have previously written, to attempt to provide the clinician with a broader, more specific, and more current systematic framework for evaluating the marital relationship of clients with sexual problems and dysfunctions.

EVALUATING THE MARITAL RELATIONSHIP: AREAS OF FOCUS

When evaluating the marital relationship within the context of sex therapy, four specific areas of focus are indicated: (1) psychometric indicators of marital adjustment; (2) assessment of the current relationship style of the couple; (3) identification and assessment of the original and current marital contract; and (4) exploration of the extended family/multigenerational context.

Psychometric Indicators of Marital Adjustment

A variety of inventories and scales are available to enable the therapist to assess sexual and marital adjustment. A special issue of the *Journal of Sex and Marital Therapy* (5:3, Fall, 1979) was devoted to the subject and described over 50 instruments. A comprehensive and updated review and critique of instruments that assess sexual functioning and adjustment is beyond the scope of this chapter, and the focus here will be on three instruments of practical use to the clinician.

The use of brief, valid, and reliable instruments such as the Locke-Wallace Marriage Inventory or the Dyadic Adjustment Scale can give the therapist a good overall sense of the clients' perceptions of marital adjustment and satisfaction (Locke & Wallace, 1959) and dyadic adjustment (not necessarily marital), the latter with a focus on dyadic satisfaction, dyadic cohesion, dyadic consensus, and affectional expression (Spanier, 1976). Without at least a moderate level of satisfaction, sex therapy is unlikely to be successful.

The Marital Satisfaction Inventory (Snyder, 1979), which focuses on a variety of relationship issues, including affective communication, problem-solving communication, quality of leisure time together, etc., has proved useful in "differentiating couples with generalized marital distress from those with specific sexual dysfunctions" (Berg & Snyder, 1981, p. 294).

Inventories and scales such as these can help the therapist distinguish couples with severe marital distress (poor prognostic indicator for sexual therapy) from those with moderate or less marital stress. The latter group is much more likely to benefit from sex therapy, and, in some cases, successful sex therapy with people in this group may even facilitate resolution of other marital problems (Sager, 1976b).

Assessment of the Current
Relationship Style of the Couple

The assessment of the current relationship style of the couple enables the therapist to identify positive forces and processes within their relationship that could facilitate treatment and to identify relationship-diminishing forces and processes that could disrupt or block desired growth and change in therapy. When evaluating the current relationship style of the couple, the therapist seeks information via questioning and direct observation regarding the following issues:

- How are the inclusion, control, and affection/intimacy issues handled within this relationship?
- What is the balance between feelings, rationality, and behavior in this relationship?

- How effectively do the partners communicate with each other?
- How effective is the couple's problem-solving and decision-making process?
- How effectively do the partners manage conflict?

Inclusion, control, and affection/intimacy issues. Schutz (1966) has stated that all individuals have three basic interpersonal needs, which are manifested in various behaviors and feelings in the individuals' relationships with other people: the need for inclusion, the need for control, and the need for affection/intimacy. Berman and Lief (1975), Hof and Miller (1981), and Doherty and Colangelo (1984) have discussed and developed the relationship of Schutz's concepts to marital and family functioning, emphasizing that these are perhaps the three core issues in relationship functioning.

The key "inclusion" question in a marriage is: What is the extent of each partner's commitment to the other and to the relationship? A continuum from noncommitment or disengagement to extreme enmeshment, where boundaries are virtually nonexistent, expresses the various possibilities. The therapist can inquire directly regarding the extent and nature of commitment (e.g., high versus low level of commitment; commitment out of duty, fear, religious values, financial realities, for the sake of the children or maintaining a family unit; or commitment based on love, shared values, interests, and intimacies). In addition, further insights can be gained as the couple's communication and interaction is observed (e.g., to what extent do they speak of a future together?).

It is important that each partner has a sense of personal identity (versus enmeshment), commitment, belonging or membership (versus disengagement), and a belief that the other person is committed to the relationship at a somewhat similar level. Without some sense of parity in this area, trust will remain relatively low, as will the willingness to risk self-disclosure in potentially vulnerable areas. The implications for the sex therapist are obvious. Without a sufficient level of self-identity and commitment to the relationship, many partners are unable or unwilling to expose their pain, embarrassment, shame, etc., or to risk trying to change behaviors when failure could possibly lead to feared ridicule or abandonment.

Some key "control" questions in a marriage are: How equitably is power distributed and what is the level of satisfaction with the power distribution? How are decisions made and roles renegotiated? To what extent does each partner see himself/herself and the other as a responsible person? The therapist can inquire directly regarding these issues and can observe the interaction of the couple when a decision is required in the therapeutic process on even such a small issue as the day and time of the next appointment (e.g., does each express opinions? do they consult each other in the decision-making process? do they value each other's ideas? can they compromise?).

When one partner believes he/she is somewhat powerless or resents the other's unilateral decision making or role definition, the situation is ripe for the control struggle to spill over into the sexual relationship in overt attempts to control sexual expression, in the withholding of sex, or, even more passive-aggressively, in the inhibition of sexual desire. On the other hand, when both partners believe that they themselves and their partner are powerful and responsible, mutual and satisfying problem solving, decision making, and role renegotiation become real possibilities in many areas, including the area of sexual expression.

The key "affection/intimacy" question in a marriage is: What is the degree of intimacy experienced between the partners and to what extent are they each satisfied with it? Intimacy here refers to the in-depth sharing of core aspects of oneself with one's partner. As with the inclusion and control issues, direct questioning in this area can yield significant information. For example, "what is each partner's perception of the quantity and quality of physical and non-physical affection expressed in the relationship?" "what types of intimacy do they share and what is their satisfaction level with each type?" Direct observation can also give important clues (e.g., to what extent do they employ touch during the sessions? to what extent are supportive, warm, and caring expressions exchanged during the sessions?).

With Clinebell and Clinebell (1970), the author believes that there are at least 12 varieties or facets of intimacy: sexual, emotional, intellectual, aesthetic, creative, recreational, work, crisis, commitment, spiritual, communication, and conflict. Since no one can be intimate with all people in all ways, it is important that a couple define for themselves in what ways they desire intimacy and work to achieve those goals. When in-depth intimacy in one area is desired by one partner to a certain degree, but to a lesser degree or not at all by the other, the potential for deep hurt and diminished satisfaction in the relationship is obvious. When core intimacy needs are not addressed satisfactorily, the potential for sexual problems increases dramatically.

Feelings, rationality, and behavior. In order for an individual and a relationship to function at its optimal potential, it is necessary that there be a balance between feelings, rationality, and behavior. Many therapies emphasize one of these dimensions of the self to the virtual exclusion of the others, encouraging the development of skills in one area as the so-called "key" to effective interpersonal functioning. We thus have behaviorists, cognitionists, and affective expressionists. All, in the author's view, err to the extent that they do not seek a balance between all three of these areas of the self.

Egan (1970) has expressed the need for "total human expression" in relationships, the blending of "thought-full" and "feeling-full" expression in effective communication processes. L'Abate and Frey (1981), with their E-R-A (Emotionality-Rationality-Activity) model, make the same point.

When evaluating the marital relationship with regard to these issues, the therapist seeks to ascertain the extent to which each partner is aware of the full range of human emotions—joy, love, hurt, loneliness, pain, anger, etc.—and to what extent each is able to express those feelings effectively and appropriately to the other. When lack of affective awareness or ineffective or inappropriate expression blocks effective relationship bonding or functioning, skill training may be needed (see Treat, Chapter 4, this volume; Hof and Miller, 1981; and L'Abate and Milan, 1985, for specific exercises). For example, in the treatment of sexual dysfunctions with couples, the effective expression of, and empathic response to, pain, fear, or anger frequently remove blocks to sexual function by diminishing defensive responses or passive-aggressive gambits.

In the area of rationality, the therapist can be most helpful in looking for cognitive distortions and irrational beliefs (Burns, 1980; Epstein & Eidelson, 1981; Epstein, 1982). Cognitive distortions such as the following can be very destructive: (1) overgeneralizations (e.g., "Since it happened once before between us, it will happen over and over again!"); (2) all-or-nothing thinking (e.g., "Since we have this one problem area that is really destructive, our whole relationship is bad!"); (3) magnifying the negative and disqualifying the positive (e.g., "This one problem area has got to be worked on at all costs, because it impacts tremendously on everything we do and makes all the good things between us meaningless!") (4) personalizations (e.g., "The fact that you have this problem proves that you don't love me, that there's something wrong with me, and that I am probably responsible in some way for your problem!"). When applied to oneself, to one's partner, or to the marital relationship, such irrational beliefs can distort reality, leading to erroneous conclusions and contributing to the development of hurt or angry feelings and defensive postures.

Virtually every sex therapist has assigned a sexual task to a couple, only to have them report that it was an unmitigated disaster. Yet, after close scrutiny, the clients and therapist discovered that it was really 80% positive, but the couple had cognitively distorted the evaluation of the experience by overemphasizing the negative and discounting the positive.

Perhaps the most common irrational belief encountered in sex therapy is that "my partner should know what I need and how I feel without me having to tell him/her." Other examples include the following: if you loved me, you would do what I want, always; if I know what you feel, I must do what you want; I should be able to fix anything that is wrong between us; a man should never be weak or vulnerable; a woman should never be sexually aggressive or too opinionated; if we get too close, one of us will lose control, and that will be bad or destructive.

If the marital evaluation can identify the presence of these unhelpful cognitions, appropriate steps can be taken to correct them before the advent of the sex therapy tasks. Or, at the minimum, the clients can be forewarned regarding the potential negative consequences of continuing to use such irrational or distorted cognitive processes. Frequently, the assigned task of specifying strengths regarding oneself, one's partner, and the relationship can point up cognitive distortions rather quickly, as the process is observed and monitored by the therapist. Clients frequently have difficulty with the task if there are significant distortions in their cognitive processes.

In the area of behavior, the marital evaluation focuses on communication skills, problem-solving and decision-making skills, conflict utilization skills (all discussed in subsequent sections), and behavior exchange skills. The therapist needs to know to what extent each partner is able to express positive and specific requests for behavioral change in the other, and to what extent the couple is able to create and carry out appropriate "partitive" (*quid-pro-quo* or tit-for-tat) contracts or "holistic" (good faith) contracts (Stuart, 1980). When these skills are absent, their development frequently becomes part of the treatment process, facilitating the expression of sexual requests in a positive manner and the creation of sexual (and other) behavior exchanges.

Communication skills. In the area of communication, the interviewer is endeavoring to assess the ability of each partner to express clearly and effectively his/her thoughts and feelings in self-responsible "I" statements; to use both verbal and nonverbal means of communication; to confirm/clarify what was heard; to give selective, specific, and timely feedback; and to make constructive and positive requests (Stuart, 1980). When these basic skills are missing, skill training will be needed to overcome the deficits in social learning in this area. (For specific communication exercises, see Treat, Chapter 4, this volume; Miller, Nunnally, and Wackman, 1979; Hof and Miller, 1981; and Guerney, 1977).

When these skills are present, partners are more likely to be aware of the total person, what is being said verbally and nonverbally, and what is not being said, such as unexpressed feelings, hidden messages, etc. They are better able to listen to their partner with ears, eyes, and sometimes touch, and they can listen and attend to the impact of the other on themselves, their thoughts, feelings, and bodies. The implications for sex therapy, in terms of effectively expressing one's wants and needs and empathically and deliberately responding to one's partner, are obvious.

Problem-solving and decision-making processes. In this area of the relationship, the therapist assesses the ability of the couple to define a problem, to explore alternative solutions and the possible positive and negative consequences of each, to reach an effective decision regarding which alternative(s) to explore provisionally, to create an action plan, and to carry out the plan and evaluate it when completed. (The "power" aspects of the decision-making process were discussed above, under "Inclusion, control, and affection/intimacy issues.") Without sufficient problem-solving and decision-making skills, the likelihood of maintaining the ability to change various aspects of the sexual relationship without the aid of third-party intervention is minimal. However, with these skills, partners become effective change agents for themselves.

Conflict management. In the marital evaluation, the practitioner needs to assess how the couple manages conflict. Can they identify and "own" their feelings to themselves and to their partner, accepting them as his/her own feelings and not blaming the partner for the way he/she feels? Can they identify the "real" issue? Can they maintain a present orientation, avoiding the dragging up of past history to "prove a point"? Can they use polarization constructively, to get away from each other when anger has escalated beyond manageable limits, or just to think more clearly, for the purpose of figuring out how to move closer together on the issue at hand? Can they identify areas of mutuality regarding the issue (i.e., what they have in common)? Do they have an effective problem-solving process? Can they celebrate the resolution of a conflict and, when necessary, at least agree to disagree?

Destructive marital conflict can result from deficits in social and skill learning regarding conflict utilization, conflict management, and problem solving. In addition, dysfunctional intrapsychic-interpersonal processes can lead to and contribute to dysfunctional conflict spirals. Narcissistic vulnerability, which can lead to destructive parental transferences upon one's partner and the use of projective identification, can wreak havoc in a relationship.

During the marital evaluation, the therapist needs to assess the amount of narcissistic vulnerability within the system. Feldman (1982) defines this vulnerability as "a weakness or deficiency in the structural cohesiveness, temporal stability, and/or affective coloring of the self-representation" (p. 417). It can lead a person to respond to real or perceived disapproval or rejection with "conscious or unconscious self-fragmentation, identity diffusion, and/or diminished self-esteem" (p. 417). The amount of narcissistic vulnerability present within the system can be gauged by assessing the relative strength and weakness of positive and negative introjects within each partner. When significant vulnerability and sensitivity are present, narcissistic expectations, unempathic behavior, narcissistic rage and anxiety, projective identification, and cognitive distortions can flourish, leading to destructive conflict spirals (Feldman, 1982).

Feldman's (1982) thorough paper on this subject highlights the need for genuine empathy on the part of the therapist to enable individuals and couples to resolve narcissistic vulnerability. In addition, he explains how emotional awareness training, dream work, empathy training, cognitive awareness training, relationship strength specification, self-instruction training, problem-solving training, and behavioral contracting can be utilized to overcome the more destructive outgrowths of narcissistic vulnerability and enable couples to develop more constructive conflict styles.

Without the ability to manage conflict effectively, angry and resentful feelings have a way of remaining unresolved and ever-present, serving as effective means for undermining sex therapy. Yet, with such skills, hope and trust are increased as issues are addressed constructively and resolved.

Identification and Assessment
of the Original and Current Marital Contract

Much of the information gathered in the aforementioned areas gives the interviewer and the couple insight into various dimensions of the current relationship contract (i.e., what are each person's desires and expectations in a variety of areas in the marriage? what is each willing to give? what agreements — verbal, conscious but nonverbalized, unconscious — have been made with oneself and one's partner?) (Sager, 1976a). Open discussion regarding the current and original marital contract enables the therapist and clients to get as much as possible "on the table," where it can be carefully examined, affirmed where it is helpful, and changed where it blocks current desired personal or relational growth and change.

Sager's (1976a) "Reminder List for Marriage Contract of Each Partner" provides a helpful means for exploring the marital contract via (1) categories based on expectations of marriage (e.g., to create a family, to provide sanctioned and readily available sex, etc.); (2) categories based on psychological and biological needs (e.g., independence-dependence, activity-passivity, closeness-distance, etc.); (3) categories that are derivative or the externalized foci of other problems (e.g., energy level, interests, friends, values, etc.). By writing out a summary of what each partner wants in relationship to these areas, and what each is willing to give in exchange, personal responsibility and clarity of expression are likely to increase. Specific statements in the area of sexual expression or desire can help facilitate the development of mutually agreed-upon goals for sex therapy and point out differences in bold relief! (A more popular and very readable trade version of Sager's contract theory and process is available in Sager and Hunt, 1979.)

Exploration of the Extended
Family/Multigenerational Context

Just as the sexual problem does not exist in a vacuum, neither does the marital relationship exist in a vacuum. Therefore, the evaluation of the marital relationship must also include at least a brief look at the extended family/multigenerational context of the couple and the problem. The therapist examines where each person "fits" in his/her extended family, what "messages" have been transmitted as "legacies" across the generations with regard to inclusion, control, and affection/intimacy issues (including messages related to sexuality), and what impact those messages have had on the person as he/she lives within the current relationship.

When a general discussion indicates the need for further exploration, the sexual genogram process developed by the author can be quite facilitative (Hof & Berman, 1986). This process involves (1) an introduction to, and discussion of, the role of early learning and intergenerational processes in the development of individual, couple, and family systems, including potential relationships to the presenting sexual problem; (2) the creation and exploration, by each partner, of a genogram, a "diagram of extended family relationships including at least three generations" (Foley & Everett, 1984, p. 12); (3) the creation and exploration, by each partner, of a sexual genogram, a reconsideration of the multigenerational system with a specific focus on pointed questions relating to sexuality and intimacy; (4) exploration and discussion of genogram material/issues with extended family members, as needed; (5) review of the total process and integration within the treatment plan for the sexual dysfunction. (See Hof and Berman, 1986, Chapter 4, for a detailed discussion of this process.)

The author treated a couple referred with multiple sexual dysfunctions (premature ejaculation and primary orgasmic dysfunction). Prior attempts at sex and marital therapy had been unsuccessful, because of the direct and frontal assault of the therapist on the issues. As the problem unfolded, via the sexual genogram process, a long history of sexual contact between the woman and her grandfather, father, and older brother was exposed. This material had been hidden by the woman in all previous therapies. She expressed how the "gentle process" and the normalization of intergenerational processes had enabled her to confront this difficult material in her own way and time. The systemic and reciprocal implications with her partner (mutual protection) were then able to be explored with rapid resolution of the presenting sexual dysfunctions.

The extended family/multigenerational context also includes the identification of where each partner and the relationship fits with regard to the individual and family life-cycle (Carter & McGoldrick, 1980). Life-stage transitions (e.g., midlife transition) can be traumatic. Normative events (e.g., marriage, birth of a child, retirement) and paranormative events (e.g., miscarriage, divorce, job loss) in the family life-cycle can generate pronounced effects, especially with the first occurrence of an event (e.g., the birth of a first child). Life-style changes, anxieties, resentments, and fears triggered by such transitions and events can impact directly on sexual desire and function.

By being sensitive to such possibilities, as a brief relationship/marital history is taken, the interviewer can often enable the couple to discover previously unrealized forces at work within or beneath the sexual complaint. These forces may be triggered by current life-cycle issues or may be the result of "unfinished business" from the couple's past. The therapist can help the couple explore this area by focusing on how each partner and the couple handles transitions from one life stage to another and copes with the normative and paranormative events of the family life-cycle.

For example, the author treated a couple in which the male experienced secondary impotence. Recent retirement and the move of his daughter, son-in-law, and granddaughter left him "somewhat anxious and blue." When the feelings were normalized and placed within a life-cycle context, a great relief was experienced and the impotence was resolved extremely rapidly. In this instance, behavioral sex therapy was definitely secondary to the resolution of the current relationship/life-cycle issues.

CASE ILLUSTRATION

The following, more detailed case illustration provides an example of how the marital evaluation process can contribute to case formulation and diagnosis and can assist in the planning of the treatment process.

Mr. and Mrs. F. are a middle-aged couple, married for 10 years. They initiated therapy to resolve long-standing sexual dysfunctions. Mr. F. had a long history of premature ejaculation. Mrs. F. presented with inhibited sexual desire and lack of orgasmic experience with her partner. She had been, however, orgasmic through self-pleasuring/masturbation during her teen and young adult years. They decided to enter therapy because they had recently experienced a deepened sense of commitment to each other via participation in a marital enrichment experience. They believed they now had the support each needed to tackle the long-standing problems.

Scores on the Dyadic Adjustment Scale indicated a fairly high degree of perceived dyadic satisfaction and cohesion, with somewhat lower degrees of perceived dyadic consensus and affectional expression.

The individual, sexual, and marital evaluation gave a picture of two rather nonassertive individuals, very much dependent on each other. Neither was able to directly communicate personal needs and desires or feelings of pain or anger. However, low-level expressions of warmth and caring were frequent and were appreciated overtly by both partners. The expression of strong feelings to each other inevitably led to a period of withdrawal from each other. Self-esteem in each of them was low, but there was a clear desire and determination to "solve their problems and feel better" as a couple and as individuals. Problem-solving and decision-making skills were adequate, as long as strong feelings were not involved. Conflict management suffered because of the inability to tolerate painful or angry affect. Commitment to the relationship was, however, high.

An early history of sexual traumatization for Mrs. F. was alluded to, but she dismissed it as irrelevant and resisted further exploration (leaving the therapist with the awareness of a possible future need to explore the extended family/multigenerational context). Although Mrs. F. complained of Mr. F.'s premature ejaculation, she was somewhat relieved that their sexual experience was not of a longer duration. In addition, Mr. F.'s low self-esteem was confirmed by her nonresponsiveness to him (cognitive distortion = personalization) and his continued premature ejaculation (cognitive distortion = all-or-nothing thinking). Thus, both had some investment in maintaining the status quo (i.e., a relationship contract, with some provisions based on preconscious psychological needs, was entered into).

Because of their high motivation and specific request for sex therapy, the decision was made not to initially focus directly on the obvious marital issues or to seek to uncover the early trauma in Mrs. F.'s history. Sex therapy was initiated with the following assumptions: (1) the need for increased assertiveness and communication of thoughts and feelings between them could be facilitated directly through the sensate focus experiences and other behavioral prescriptions; (2) the resulting increased assertiveness and communication would increase pair bonding and positive feelings for each other; (3) the increased pair bonding and positive feelings would offer a secure base from which they could attack related problems outside of the marital dyad (e.g., the inability of both to be assertive at work and Mrs. F.'s inability to become differentiated from her family of origin, despite an expressed desire to do so); (4) successful exploration of, and achievements in, those areas would generate enough increased self-esteem for them to be able to focus directly on individual, intrapsychic issues (e.g., Mrs. F.'s sexual traumatization and Mr. F.'s need to maintain a low self-image); (5) resolution of those issues would permit completion of their goals in sex therapy, namely, a mutually satisfying, orgasmic sexual experience in which Mrs. F. could actively initiate sexual activity and Mr. F. could maintain ejaculatory control.

The early stages of therapy were characterized by increased assertiveness and positive feelings toward each other. Both learned that the experience of sexual pleasure was not tantamount to being "selfish." She learned that she could communicate needs and wants without making her partner angry. He learned that being angry is "normal" and that expressions of anger need not be destructive as they had been in his family of origin. He also realized that he maintained low self-esteem to keep his anger under control, for fear that if it emerged, he would be "killed" by his father. With his new approach to the use of anger and his own power, and with Mrs. F.'s increased responsiveness, Mr. F.'s premature ejaculation was managed quite quickly with the stop/start technique. This was paralleled by reports of increased assertiveness on the job and toward Mrs. F.'s family of origin. As her sexual pleasure increased, however, Mrs. F. became increasingly anxious and was unable to make further gains. The decision was made to cease conjoint sex therapy and to proceed individually with Mrs. F.

In individual therapy, Mrs. F. began to unfold the history of sexual abuse by her father, along with extensive guilt, rage, and fear of rejection. She was able to identify how her inability to enjoy sexual relationships with her husband enabled her to maintain control over those suppressed and repressed memories and feelings. The uncovering and partial working through of those experiences and feelings via the sexual genogram process mentioned above led to the reinitiation of conjoint therapy, with a sharp focus on diminishing her enmeshment with her family of origin and on enabling her to emotionally separate her husband from her sexually abusive father.

Once the trauma was addressed directly, many gains were made in the areas of communication of feelings, wants, and needs; assertive ability within and outside the marriage; and their sexual relationship. Sex therapy was reinitiated and systematic desensitization techniques were employed in a conjoint setting, to enable Mrs. F. to continue the process of working through the early trauma and managing the anxiety and memories raised by an enjoyable sexual relationship with her husband. Another marital enrichment experience enabled both of them to develop more effective conflict management skills.

Therapy lasted for 65 sessions over one and one-half years. At termination, both partners reported increased satisfaction with the marital relationship and with each other. The gains in assertiveness and communications noted above were maintained. Their sexual relationship was experienced as mutually satisfying, with Mr. F. better able to maintain ejaculatory control and Mrs. F. being orgasmic during most of their intercourse experiences. A follow-up evaluation over a year later indicated that all gains were being maintained.

EVALUATING THE MARITAL RELATIONSHIP: PROCESS GUIDELINES

As the practitioner conducts the marital evaluation, several process guidelines need to be present in his/her mind. First, the amount of information to be gathered may appear to be overwhelming at the outset. Yet, when one realizes how much of it can be gathered through the assignment and discussion of one or two small tasks, it can be placed in a proper perspective. An effective evaluation can be accomplished in two to four sessions.

The author frequently assigns R. B. Stuart's Marital Pre-Counseling Inventory and their Sexual Adjustment Inventory to clients presenting with a sexual complaint.* These positively oriented, data-gathering devices are filled out and discussed by the partners. That process is then discussed with the therapist (who observes the clients' interaction in the office setting, attending to his/her own feelings as they are evoked in the interview), giving precise information in virtually all of the areas discussed above in "Assessment of the Current Relationship Style of the Couple." The assignment and discussion of non-demand, nongenital pleasuring can accomplish the same task.

Simple questions such as "What expectations did you have of each other when you married?" open up the discussion of the marital contract. Similarly, questions regarding "How did you learn that?" or "What was it like in your family of origin in that area?" lead into a discussion of the extended family/multigenerational context.

Second, the marital evaluation, like all aspects of the total assessment process, is ongoing. It continues throughout treatment, is affected by the treatment process, and contributes to the ongoing adjustment of the treatment process. The therapist continually scans the couple and the relationship with reference to marital adjustment, current relationship style, the marital contract, and the extended family/multigenerational context. An individual session with each partner can be very helpful in identifying or uncovering relationship secrets (such as a previous or current extramarital affair) and in giving the therapist a sense of how each person's style of interaction is affected by the presence/absence of the partner. Similarly, a total family session or two may reveal much new information regarding interactional styles, family secrets, and potential supports or blocks to the therapeutic process.

Third, the marital evaluation is, in fact, part of the treatment process, insofar as it enables the clients to gain insights, diminish anxiety, increase hope, and plan for change.

Fourth, the marital evaluation process is *with the clients, not just by the therapist*. Preliminary impressions are elicited from the clients, as well as shared by the therapist. Provisional hypotheses regarding how behaviors have been learned, what purpose they have served in the relationship, etc., are suggested by both the clients and the therapist and discussed openly more often than not. (Of course, speculations regarding the nature of unconscious motivations are treated very cautiously.) This demystifies the therapeutic process, increases the sense of a "treatment team" approach to the sexual problem, and is likely to increase the responsible involvement of the clients in the resolution of their sexual problem.

---

*These inventories can be purchased from Research Press Company, 2612 North Mattis Avenue, Champaign, Illinois 61820.

Fifth, the therapist should realize that indications and contraindications are just that. They are not rigid rules to be adhered to without flexibility. For example, the presence of severe marital distress is a contraindication for sex therapy. However, if the "facts" are discussed with the couple, and all agree on a provisional try of sex therapy, with the possible positive and negative consequences considered in advance, some real benefits may occur. The clients may, somewhat paradoxically, succeed and attain their goal. Or they may not succeed and, having given it a try, may then be willing to do the marital work needed to provide a firm base for the future resolution of the sexual problem.

A significant part of the art of sex therapy involves assessing when relationship issues can be or need to be bypassed, and when they need to be confronted or resolved. For example, Charlie and Arlene are genuinely afraid of intimacy, because of a fear of loss, exacerbated by the recent death of a parent. To protect themselves from too much closeness and subsequent loss, she has developed inhibited sexual desire, and they have developed ineffective problem-solving and conflict styles. In one scenario, addressing the latter issues would be counterproductive and simply increase the resistance of the couple. In such an instance, a direct and gentle addressing of the grief/loss issue may be a more productive approach, leading to a reemergence of sexual desire and diminished conflict. On the other hand, with another couple, the addressing of the problem-solving and conflict issues in a structured way might pave the way for the emergence of renewed confidence in the relationship, a sense of accomplishment, increased trust, and gradual movement to the more painful grief/loss issue and resolution of the sexual dysfunction. With a third couple, directly addressing the sexual desire disorder with a brief therapy approach might provide a secure enough environment in which small increments of intimacy could be achieved and shared, leading to greater security and a reduced fear of loss. The direct addressing of the grief/loss issue might thus be obviated by successful sex therapy. In addition, latent problem-solving and conflict-resolution skills used outside of the relationship might now be able to be used within the relationship.

Answers to questions of what to address and when and how to confront or bypass relationship issues frequently emerge as the assessment and treatment process evolves, and they just as frequently change along the way. If the therapist proceeds with hope, respect, and good will, moving slowly with incremental steps, accentuating the positive and managing anxiety along the way, actively involving the clients as therapeutic partners in all phases of the assessment and treatment processes, and viewing everything as a provisional try—then, the likelihood of the clients being able to resolve their sexual problem is greatly increased.

REFERENCES

Berg, P., & Snyder, D. K. (1981). Differential diagnosis of marital and sexual distress: A multidimensional approach. *Journal of Sex and Marital Therapy, 7*, 290-295.

Berman, E., & Lief, H. I. (1975). Marital therapy from a psychiatric perspective: An overview. *American Journal of Psychiatry, 132*, 583-592.

Burns, D. (1980). *Feeling good: The new mood therapy*. New York: New American Library.

Carter, E., & McGoldrick, M. (1980). *The family life cycle*. New York: Gardner.

Clinebell, H. J., & Clinebell, C. H. (1970). *The intimate marriage*. New York: Harper and Row.

Doherty, W. J., & Colangelo, N. (1984). The family FIRO model: A modest proposal for organizing family treatment. *Journal of Marital and Family Therapy, 9*, 19-29.

Egan, G. (1970). *Encounter: Group processes for interpersonal growth*. Belmont, CA: Brooks/Cole.

Epstein, N. (1982). Cognitive therapy with couples. *American Journal of Family Therapy, 10*, 5-16.

Epstein, N., & Eidelson, R. J. (1981). Unrealistic beliefs of clinical couples: Their relationship to expectations, goals and satisfaction. *American Journal of Family Therapy, 9*, 13-22.

Feldman, L. B. (1982). Dysfunctional marital conflict: An integrative interpersonal-intrapsychic model. *Journal of Marital and Family Therapy, 8*, 417-428.

Foley, V. D., & Everett, C. A. (1984). *Family therapy glossary*. Washington, DC: American Association for Marriage and Family Therapy.

Group for the Advancement of Psychiatry (1973). Assessment of sexual function: A guide to interviewing, *8*, Report no. 88, (pp. 755-850).

Guerney, B. G., Jr. (1977). *Relationship enhancement*. San Francisco: Josey-Bass.

Hof, L., & Berman, E. M. (1986). The sexual genogram. *Journal of Marital and Family Therapy, 12*, 39-47.

Hof, L., & Miller, W. R. (1981). *Marriage enrichment: Philosophy, process and program*. Bowie, MD: Brady.

Kaplan, H. S. (1974). *The new sex therapy*. New York: Brunner/Mazel.

Kaplan, H. S. (1983). *The evaluation of sexual disorders*. New York: Brunner/Mazel.

L'Abate, L., & Frey, J. (1981). The E. R. A. model: The role of feelings in family therapy reconsidered: Implications for a classification of theories of family therapy. *Journal of Marital and Family Therapy, 7*, 143-150.

L'Abate, L., & Milan, M. A. (Eds.). (1985). *Handbook of social skills training and research*. New York: Wiley.

Locke, H. J., & Wallace, K. M. (1959). Short marital adjustment and prediction tests: Their reliability and validity. *Marriage and Family Living, 21*, 251-255.

LoPiccolo, J., & LoPiccolo, L. (Eds.). (1978). *Handbook of sex therapy*. New York: Plenum.

Masters, W. H., & Johnson, V. (1970). *Human sexual inadequacy*. Boston: Little Brown.

Miller, S., Nunnally, E., & Wackman, D. B. (1979). *Talking together*. Minneapolis: Interpersonal Communication Programs.

Sager, C. J. (1976a). *Marriage contracts and couple therapy*. New York: Brunner/Mazel.

Sager, C. J. (1976b). The role of sex therapy in marital therapy. *American Journal of Psychiatry, 133*, 555–559.

Sager, C. J., & Hunt, B. (1979). *Intimate partners*. New York: McGraw-Hill.

Schutz, W. C. (1966). *FIRO (the interpersonal underworld)*. Palo Alto, CA: Science and Behavior.

Snyder, D. K. (1979). Multidimensional assessment of marital satisfaction. *Journal of Marriage and the Family, 41*, 813–824.

Spanier, G. B. (1976). Measuring dyadic adjustments: New scales for assessing the quality of marriage and similar dyads. *Journal of Marriage and the Family, 38*, 15–28.

Stuart, R. (1980). *Helping couples change*. New York: Guilford.

Chapter 2

Love, Intimacy, and Sex

Luciano L'Abate and
William C. Talmadge

Writing of such concepts as love, sex, and intimacy is asking for trouble. As psychotherapists we talk around and about these feelings, behaviors, and concepts frequently with our patients. In fact, just recently one of us asked a husband in a couple's interview, "When do you feel most loved by your wife?" He stared for what seemed to be a long time, then proudly stated, "When I hurt my back about a month ago and she rubbed Ben-Gay on it." This husband continued by saying that his wife sometimes got angry when he hurt his back. It was reframed to him that she was probably angry at times like that because she was scared and loved him. While leaving the interview, Mr. Smith commented, "This love thing sure is complicated."

Love, intimacy, and sex *are* complicated, but they are at the basis of primary, intimate, committed relationships, such as marriage, in a most profound and primitive manner. The thesis of this chapter is twofold. First, the ability to share love, negotiate power, and establish an intimate foundation are three of the necessary and sufficient conditions for a satisfactory and fulfilling marital and sexual relationship (L'Abate, 1986; L'Abate & Colondier, in press; L'Abate, submitted for publication; Talmadge & Talmadge, 1985, 1986). Second, the ability to share love, negotiate power, and establish an intimate foundation are colored, shaped, and set in motion by our early primary relationships, primarily the family of origin. This position assumes that both partners are physically healthy, fully functioning individuals.

The chapter is also based on the assumption that love and intimacy can only be *shared* and are not subject to negotiation. This does not mean that couples do not struggle with these issues, but, rather, they represent interpersonal resources which cannot be exchanged like many other interpersonal resources. Money, and its use, for example, can be negotiated in a relationship. Love and intimacy are based on feelings and must be shared—not bargained for other interpersonal resources. Sex in a relationship has multiple functions. Sex as a physical act may be negotiated or exchanged for other resources. However, sex as an act of love cannot be negotiated. It can only be given or shared. Sex manuals have unfortunately fostered the negotiation of sex because of the emphasis on technique and performance rather than love and intimacy.

SEXUALITY

Sexuality is a primary force in the life of every individual. It is a pervasive and integral force, involving physiological and psychological processes. It is an active, dynamic, and organic process with a multiplicity of interrelated and changing variables. It is a force not to be denied without heavy expense to the individual. We think of sexuality more broadly than just penises, vaginas, and intercourse. Sexuality is the process of *being* that we express through our manifestation of *being* male or female, a man or woman, masculine or feminine; it is how we think and feel about and express our gender, our sex organs, our body, our self-images, and our choices and preferences.

A sexual script forms through early developing self-image, sexual experience, culture, parental role models, and peer relationships. Our script continues to evolve over the years of our living. However, the basic foundation of the sexual script is laid in our early development through our *attachment* and bonding with our primary care providers (usually the family of origin) and all that these relationships were and were not (Bowlby, 1969, 1973; Harlow, 1958; Kaplan, 1978). The quality of the attachment in the primary years shapes our ability to love, touch, give, receive, and commit. Our contention is that the quality of attachment and affectional care sets the tone of future intimate sexual relationships (Scharff, 1982; Talmadge & Talmadge, 1985; Wallace, 1981). For instance:

> Jerry was a strong, entertaining, and handsome young man who repeatedly had difficulty getting close to women. He was very capable of starting relationships; however, as these relationships moved toward more intimate forms, he would sabotage them or take flight. He sought therapy for himself after several episodes of being unable to maintain an erection with two different partners. Jerry was frustrated, angry, and ashamed. He did not understand what was happening to him. Shortly after his birth his parents divorced, his mother was institutionalized for depression, his father went broke, became destitute, and the children were divided among relatives and foster homes. Jerry was placed in a number of different foster homes, some of which were good and some bad, during the first 26 months of his life before being returned to his mother's care.
> Developing an intimate sexual relationship had become a tragic problem for this man, which was related to his poor attachment foundation in his first years of life. In the continuing therapy Jerry became increasingly aware of his intense fear of abandonment. His erectile losses served him by preventing him from getting closer to these two women although both were understanding and did not make a fuss when this happened. It was Jerry who was most agitated and

would distance himself from his partner. In therapy he began to find a very frightened and hurt little boy under his presenting frustration, anger, and shame. Jerry was terrified of being left as he had been so many times in his early life.

Sexual expression, especially the act of intercourse, is one of the most vulnerable interactions that a couple undertakes. The experience of lying nude with one's partner in the process of giving and receiving pleasure is a most vulnerable and dependent state. At no other ordinary time in the life of a couple are they more vulnerable. The act of intercourse, of having a portion of another person's body inside another's body cavity, is an extremely vulnerable physiological position. Because of this highly physiological openness and vulnerability, the symbolic reawakening of the unconscious processes is likely. This sexual expression in a committed relationship is a "physical expression of the primary emotional bonds and is best understood in the context of the relationships which govern it, primarily the family of origin and marriage" (Talmadge & Talmadge, 1985, p. 1107). For instance:

Cathy and Harry were referred by her individual therapist, who thought the couple needed conjoint therapy because of their unhappiness with each other, Cathy's inorgasmia, and Harry's premature ejaculation. In the process of therapy they were given the homework assignment of genital sensate focus, which is an erotic touching exercise where both people are nude and one partner touches the erotic and exciting areas of the other partner's body. Up to this point in therapy, Harry had been very successful in controlling his ejaculation. However, in this exercise when Cathy began touching around his genitals, he ejaculated. Cathy became tearful and ran from the room. As the couple talked about this, all they understood was Cathy's deep sense of sadness.

In their next therapy interview, the therapist asked Cathy to picture herself in that same situation and to feel that sadness. When Cathy acknowledged imagining herself there, the therapist asked her to go back in time and report the first memory that came to mind. She slowly started to weep as she reported two incidents. The first was when she was about eight years old and her mother had awakened her in the middle of the night pretending as though it were the next morning and time for school. When Cathy got to the breakfast table, Mom said, "Surprise, I fooled you," at which point Cathy learned it was about 2:00 or 3:00 A.M. The second memory was of a Christmas morning. Cathy and her brother hurried to the living room where Santa Claus was to have left their presents, but nothing was there. The kids were very disappointed. Soon they aroused Mom to explain what had happened, to which she laughingly replied that today was really the day before Christmas. However, shortly thereafter she joked with the kids that she had fooled them as she presented them with hidden presents in another room. Through the sexual exercise, Cathy's unconscious was symbolically triggered in exposing the deep sadness and hurt she had felt in growing up with a sadistic mother.

The sexual interaction of a couple who love one another is one of the most intimate and exciting forms of relating in which they engage. The love drives them to closeness, both emotionally and physically. This desire for closeness is satisfied emotionally through each individual's understanding of her/his self and the sharing of the self with the loved one, while the drive for closeness physically is satisfied through touch, affection, and sexual intercourse (Lowen, 1965). At the same time it is understood that couples do not live in a vacuum of love and intimacy. All the other interactions, roles, and stresses of life impact on the couple's love life. However, it is our belief that those couples who love one another, profess their love, and work at it are among the happiest in their sexual relating. We believe for the marital sexual relationship to fully develop it must be bound in love, intimacy, and negotiated power.

LOVE AND INTIMACY

Issues of love (i.e., nurturance in Parsons' view, Parsons & Bales, 1955) need to be separated sharply from issues of power (i.e., instrumentality in Parsons' view). Love and being are not negotiable resources (except when sex is for sale professionally . . .). Information and services (i.e., doing) or money and possessions (i.e., having) are all negotiable resources (L'Abate, 1986). Love, on the other hand, is not and should not be negotiable because it would be confused, fused, and diffused with issues of power. Love is based on feelings, and feelings can be shared but not negotiated. Power is negotiable, love is not.

Love as a researchable and legitimate area of study has only recently reached its peak (Branden, 1980; Coutts, 1973; Curtin, 1973; Fogarty, 1985; Fromm, 1956; Grant, 1976; Haughton, 1970; Peterson & Payne, 1975; Pope et al., 1980; Swensen, 1985), producing as many definitions as there are sources.

Initially it is the love for one another that draws individuals together in coupling relationships. In the early phase of a relationship this is characterized more as passion, lust, and attraction. However, if the relationship is to continue, a deeper caring must develop. From this deeper sense of caring the couple begins their journey of intimacy. A healthy sexual relationship grows from this intimate connection based on a love for one another. Love in an ongoing sexual relationship requires commitment and discipline. This love is an active, expressed concern for the life, growth, and well-being of one's partner. It is grounded in the knowledge of oneself (the being) and his/her partner (thou). This deeper sense of caring is based on the valuing, understanding, and expressing of self to the loved one. The valuing, understanding, and expressing of self are the primary components of being. We think of the issues of being and intimacy as two of the basic aspects of love. The following case example illustrates the issues of being, discipline, and commitment involved in love.

Mike was in his late forties when he came to therapy with his wife because of their constant arguing and his persistent premature ejaculations. However, both professed to the therapist to love each other dearly. The couple had been married for three years. This was his wife's second marriage and his first. The couple lived with her two children in her home which she owned prior to their marriage, and he paid a modest amount each month for the maintenance of the house. Mike's ideas of loving meant that you cared for that person. However, he had experienced very little care in his growing up with a mother who had been diagnosed as "depressed," "paranoid," "hysterical," and "demented" by those physicians and institutions by whom she was treated.

In Mike's therapy group in his third year of psychotherapy he brought the following problem. When his wife had returned from a tour of Europe she brought him a gift, a beautifully engraved gold wedding ring. Until this point Mike had not worn a wedding ring. When given the gift, he graciously thanked his wife but had not worn the ring. He was in a crisis because he did not know what to do about the ring, although he professed to love his wife dearly. In the group's exploration of this problem, the group confronted Mike with his refusal to symbolically profess his love and commitment to his wife through the wearing of his ring, his unwillingness to purchase a house of their own, and his stashing money in his bank account of which she had no knowledge. Mike had been confronted with his lack of discipline and commitment in his love of his wife. During the next year and a half Mike started wearing his wedding ring, bought a house with his wife, and opened joint bank accounts. Recently Mike told his group that while visiting the country home of a friend, he and his wife were walking near the stables when suddenly horses charged them as the horses were racing back to the barn. Mike jumped out of harm's way. Immediately, he began to question himself because he had done nothing to assure his wife's safety. He was filled with shame and guilt. In discussing this he examined his conflict between the wants of his self and his love of his wife.

Issues of Being

Being is a difficult concept to understand, in spite of various attempts by humanistic writers to define it (May, 1983). It becomes clearer when we are able to separate resources into three different and nonoverlapping channels (L'Abate, submitted for publication). Money and possessions are considered as parts of having. Services and information (i.e., activities) are parts of doing. Love and status are parts of being. This latter concept, then, includes love of self and others as well as a sense of self-importance, understanding of self, and a willingness to express what is known about self to the loved one. Hence, a sense of self-valuing, -understanding, and -expressing is necessary but not sufficient to be able to love and to be loved, i.e., to share love.

What is love and how is it demonstrated, expressed, and shared? Love as a developmental process consists of at least three elements: (a) two behavioral components: received care and caring; (b) two cognitive components: seeing the good and forgiveness; and (c) an emotional component, i.e., intimacy.

Received care means it is enormously difficult, if not impossible, to give care if one has not received care. It is based in the primary caretaker's tasks of feeding, protecting, sheltering, and guiding (Harlow, 1958; Bowlby, 1969; Suomi, 1977).

Caring is the concrete, behavioral expression of love according to definite physical activities, ranging from cooking and earning a paycheck to carrying a bedpan and cleaning up a diaper. We perform services for those we love and expect them to serve us when we are incapacitated. In the sex act, caring is shown by doing and performing those activities that are pleasurable to us and to our partner.

Seeing the good is a cognitive process that represents our ability to see positive qualities in ourselves before we see them in those we love. These qualities may be physical, characterological, temperamental, etc. One of the prerequisite qualities for a "good" sex life consists of seeing oneself as a sexual human being who deserves to give and to receive pleasure. Seeing the sexual good in oneself implies a parallel process of seeing oneself as competent and important (Ford, 1985; Marlowe, 1985). Seeing the good in one's partner implies also listening and learning from him so that feedback is not taken or given as criticism. In Fromm (1956) this quality is described as respect. However, true respect develops from self-respect. In sexual interaction with the loved one this respect means desiring to please the other and oneself, inquiring and stating what is enjoyed. This feedback is crucial in negotiating pleasurable sexual activities, when, more often than not, feedback is given within a context of fears and anxieties about sex, sometimes producing conflict and distress.

Forgiveness is a second cognitive process basic to personal and marital well-being (L'Abate, 1986; L'Abate, submitted for publication) that has been neglected by most individual, marital, and family therapists. Yet, this process seems a *sine qua non* condition for seeing the good. How can we see the good in ourselves and others if we do not forgive our errors, i.e., our trespasses and those of the persons we love? Can we give up our demands for performance or perfection in ourselves? If we cannot do it for ourselves, how can we do it for those we love? Forgiveness becomes a very active issue with couples in which one of the partners has had an affair that is recognized by the couple. The "betrayed" partner can make the other partner pay for the rest of the marriage if forgiveness is not acknowledged.

Issues of Intimacy

In addition to love, intimacy has been found increasingly to be a crucial variable in marriage and family life (L'Abate, 1986; Derlega, 1984; Patton & Waring, 1984; Sloan & L'Abate, 1985). However, intimacy, like love, has as many definitions as there are authors who write about it. Two components

are critical in intimacy, according to Douvan (1977): the ability and cooperation to be dependent and the ability to express, withstand, understand, and
resolve the conflict and hostility that occur in intimate relationships. Others
have discussed intimacy as a composite of identity, expressiveness, affection,
autonomy, cohesion, compatibility, conflict resolution, and sexuality (Waring & Reddon, 1983). L'Abate (1977, 1986) concretely discusses intimacy as
the sharing of hurt and fear of being hurt. Intimacy in marriage means that
each partner brings and participates with ego strength, power, interdependen-
cy, vulnerability, touch, trust, mutuality, an understanding of self, and a sharing of the self as known. As is the case with most of us, the self is wanting,
vulnerable, fallible, and needy. In order for intimacy to progress we must
make room for the regression of the childlike and often scared needy selves
(Dicks, 1967).

Hatfield (1984) has listed some of the reasons why intimacy is a fearful
condition, a position already considered by L'Abate and Samples (1983): (a)
fear of exposure; (b) fear of abandonment; (c) fear of angry attacks; (d) fear
of loss of control; (e) fear of one's own destructive impulses; (f) fear of losing one's individuality or of being engulfed. Many of these fears can be sub-
sumed under the rubric of hurts related to our fallibility, vulnerability, and
neediness (L'Abate, 1986). We think of all of this needing to be integrated
within the relationship. This integration process forms the intimate foundation in the journey of marriage and therefore must continue to be established,
evolved, and developed in order for the sexual relationship to be fulfilling
and growthful.

Thus, we often perceive sexual problems as indicative of intimacy difficulties. The lack of intimate, expressed emotional feeling, affection, interdependence, and vulnerability supports the lack of sexual contact. The intimacy in the life of a couple is one of the major determining factors in a
satisfactory and pleasurable sex life. Only disturbed couples are able to fulfill
each other sexually without intimacy. For most couples satisfactory and enjoyable sexual expression is not an option without intimacy. True orgastic
pleasure reaches its heights in continually evolving intimate marriages. In the
intimate marriages sex may take place for the pure fun of sex and/or the expression of love. However, this position would go a long way in explaining
why most partners who feel unloved often do not want to have sex for the
sake of sex alone. How can we share the high orgastic pleasure if we cannot
share the lows of hurt and fears of being hurt? In fact, sex as an act, i.e.,
performance—doing—can be had relatively easily. It is much more difficult
to share sex within the context of a loving and intimate relationship. In fact,
behaviorally oriented therapists who would emphasize sex as an act without
consideration of its emotional aspects as an act of love may well miss the boat!
Sex as an expression of love is a sharing of feelings, sensations, and ex-

periences related to past and present anxieties, hurts, fears, and frustrations. If and when such a sharing does not take place, sexual performance may be impaired.

We are maintaining, therefore, that sex as an activity, i.e., performance, is negotiable provided attendant feelings to the activity in terms of past experiences are shared beforehand. An example of this process could be found in the following vignette:

> A college professor and his wife plagued by severe depression with frequent hospitalizations, after sessions where they learned to work positively with their depressions (L'Abate, 1986), completed successfully the sharing of hurt exercise (contained in L'Abate, 1986) where they were able to share their past hurts together. After leaving this session, entirely on their own and without any prompting from the therapists, they called their children to check on whether they were all right, telling them that they would be away for the rest of the day but would get home by six o'clock. They checked in a nearby motel and "consummated the honeymoon" that 12 years earlier had been a dismal failure sexually.

ABILITY TO NEGOTIATE POWER

Only recently have we become aware of the importance of the ability to negotiate as the necessary ingredient of satisfactory sexual, marital, and family relationships (L'Abate, 1986; L'Abate & Colondier, in press). In fact, this important and fundamental ability is not mentioned in most texts of family, marital, and sexual therapy. We are aware that if and when this ability is missing or is incomplete, it is practically impossible to hope that a marriage or a relationship will "make it," i.e., be a mutually satisfying relationship. It may "make it" miserably, and often misery loves company. Staying together in a marriage does not necessarily mean that partners love each other or can negotiate issues! Be that as it may, the negotiation of power implies negotiation either of material resources, i.e., having (money and/or possessions), or of services and/or information, i.e., doing. Conflicts over issues of having and doing, more often than not, derive from our inability to share issues of *being* intimate and important together without demands for performance or perfection, as discussed above.

Negotiation is a difficult ability to learn because most of our models (i.e., parents, siblings, in-laws, and relatives) most of the time have failed to show us how to do it. Hence, the ability to negotiate is just as difficult to learn as the ability to love for exactly the same reason. All of us, in one way or another, mostly trial and error, learn eventually. The cost, however, is high and many of us do not make it. By negotiation here is meant a process of bargaining, problem solving, and decision making that follows invariable sequences of: (a) defining the issues, (b) proposing possible solutions (i.e., courses of action) with their rewards and costs; (c) implementing an agreed-upon course of action; (d) evaluating its outcome; and (e) deciding whether to keep that course of action or change it for a fallback or alternative solution.

Power consists of authority, i.e., who makes the decision, and responsibility, i.e., who carries out the task of implementing a course of action. Both authority and responsibility can be shared and negotiated in a balanced and equitable fashion to the satisfaction of both partners, or there can be an imbalanced and, very likely, an unsatisfactory relationship where one partner's status or sense of self-importance is achieved at the expense of the partner with lower status. Under these conditions not only is negotiation impossible, but, as discussed by Stock (1985), intimacy is also impossible, since it can be achieved mainly between partners who regard each other as *equals*.

The ability to negotiate increases multiplicatively under at least three conditions: (a) the level of functionality of the marriage, that is, the higher the level, the better the chances of successful negotiation and outcome; (b) the level of competence of both partners, that is, the higher the level of competence, the better the chances of successful negotiation; and (c) the presence and quality of motivation to negotiate, i.e., obviously one needs to want to negotiate, in addition to a satisfactory level of functionality and a certain degree of competence. These three separate but interactive conditions can be summarized under the equation that negotiation potential (NP) = level of functionality $\times$ skill $\times$ will.

L'Abate (1986) has proposed three different models to specify each of those three conditions. Level of functionality is defined by the A-R-C model that ranges from clearly dysfunctional abusive, apathetic, and atrophied (A) to somewhat more functional reactively repetitive relationships (R). The highest level of functionality is achieved under the condition of conductivity (C), where partners are in charge of themselves and are committed to creative change for the better. In addition to evidence reviewed by L'Abate (1986), a recent review by Ford (1985) cites strong supporting evidence for the existence of these three degrees of functionality.

Competence (skill) can be assessed through the E-R-A-Aw-C model, which makes successful intimate (close and prolonged) relationships, and, of course, negotiations, a function of assets in emotionality (E), rationality (R), activities (A), awareness (Aw), and context (C). As stated earlier, most of our inability to negotiate derives from our inability to share our hurts and our fears of being hurt, a process that starts from how we are in touch with our feelings, i.e., emotionality. Feelings determine how close or how far we are from each other. Hence, E deals with distance, and R determines how we modulate, modify, and moderate that distance through our activities (A). Awareness is seen as feedback originating *after* activities have taken place. On the basis of our evaluation of the outcome and the context (C) we can return circularly back to E and repeat the process. Inability to access E and to use it creatively leads to exaggerations in R (i.e., obsessions) or in A (i.e., impulsive or repetitive addictions) or in both R and A. Hence, this model makes emotionality the cornerstone of interpersonal competence. In addition to the evidence reviewed by L'Abate (1986), Marlowe (1985) has provided a review of the empirical literature that tends to support parts, if not all, of this model.

Motivation (will) to negotiate, the third condition necessary for successful negotiation, has been considered by L'Abate (1986) in terms of priorities, that is, the amount of energy expended in space and time to deal with (a) oneself, (b) marriage, (c) children, (d) parents/in-laws/siblings, (e) work, friends, and (f) leisure (Marks, 1977). In addition to intrafamily priorities, one needs to deal with one's attachments, beliefs, and commitments (the A-B-C model), and the use of resources, such as having, doing, and being, as mentioned at the outset of this chapter. When these priorities are ill defined, mixed up, and vague, it becomes very difficult to "know oneself" and to be clear about what is more or less important or relevant. Stereotypically, we men identify and equate ourselves erroneously with our workselves, that is: we men acquire an occupational definition of self according to our jobs, leaving the women the definition of selves as mothers. Either way, the self is given up either for the job, the children, or the marriage ("I want to make you happy"). How can the bridge of marriage survive when the pillars of the self are inadequate?

Lasch (1984) has condensed well the major qualities that make for the autonomous interdependence that is basic to a satisfactory marital and sexual relationship:

> The achievement of selfhood, which our culture makes so difficult, may be defined as the acknowledgment of our separation from the original source of life, combined with a continuing struggle to recapture a sense of primal union by means of activity that gives us a provisional understanding and mastery of the world without denying our limitations and dependency. Selfhood is the painful awareness of the tension between our unlimited aspirations and our limited understanding, between our original intimations of immortality and our fallen state, between oneness and separation. (p. 20)

CONCLUSION

The ability to reach orgasm is a relatively easy goal. To achieve orgasm with someone who loves us and whom we love is a very difficult task because in order to reach the peak of ecstasy, we also need to share the valleys of despair and hurt. Sex as a physical act is negotiable. Sex as an act of love-being and intimacy can only be shared.

REFERENCES

Bowlby, J. (1969). *Attachment*. New York: Basic Books.

Branden, N. (1980). *The psychology of romantic love*. Los Angeles: J. P. Tarcher.

Coutts, R. L. (1973). *Love and intimacy: A psychological approach*. San Ramon, CA: Consensus.

Curtin, M. E. (Ed.). (1973). *Symposium on love*. New York: Behavioral Publications.

Derlega, V. J. (Ed.). (1984). *Communication, intimacy, and close relationships*. Orlando, FL: Academic Press.

Dicks, H. V. (1967). *Marital tensions*. New York: Basic Books.

Douvan, E. (1977). Interpersonal relationships; Some questions and observations. In G. Levinger & H. Raush (Eds.), *Close relationships; Perspective on the meaning of intimacy*. Amherst: University of Massachusetts Press.

Fogarty, T. F. (1985). The role of romantic love in marriage. In D. C. Goldberg (Ed.), *Contemporary marriage: Special issues in couples therapy*. Homewood, IL: Dorsey Press.

Ford, M. D. (1985). The concept of competence: Themes and variations. In H. A. Marlowe, Jr., & R. B. Weinberg (Eds.), *Competence development: Theory and practice in special populations*. Springfield, IL: Charles C Thomas.

Fromm, E. (1956). *The art of loving*. New York: Harper & Row.

Grant, V. W. (1976). *Falling in love: The psychology of the romantic emotion*. New York: Springer.

Harlow, H. F. (1958). The nature of love. *American Psychologist, 13*, 673–685.

Hatfield, E. (1984). The dangers of intimacy. In V. J. Derlega (Ed.), *Communication, intimacy, and close relationships*. Orlando, FL: Academic Press.

Haughton, R. (1970). *Love*. Baltimore, MD: Penguin Books.

Kaplan, L. J. (1978). *Oneness and separateness: From infant to individual*. New York: Simon & Schuster.

L'Abate, L. (1977). Intimacy is sharing hurt feelings: A reply to David Mace. *Journal of Marriage and Family Counseling, 3*, 13–16.

L'Abate, L. (1986). *Systematic family therapy*. New York: Brunner/Mazel.

L'Abate, L., & Colondier, G. (in press). The emperor has no clothes. Long live the emperor!: A critique of family systems thinking and a reductionistic proposal. *American Journal of Family Therapy, 14*.

L'Abate, L. (Submitted for publication). What is being? Notes toward a clarification of the process.

L'Abate, L., & Samples, G. (1983). Intimacy letters as invariable prescription for closeness-avoidant couples. *Family Therapy, 10*, 37–45.

Lasch, C. (1984). *The minimal self: Psychic survival in troubled times*. New York: W. W. Norton.

Lowen, A. (1965). *Love and orgasm*. New York: Macmillan.

Marks, S. R. (1977). Multiple roles and role strain: Some notes on human energy, time and commitment. *American Sociological Review, 42*, 921–936.

Marlowe, H. A., Jr. (1985). Competence: A social intelligence perspective. In H. A. Marlowe, Jr., & R. B. Weinberg (Eds.), *Competence development: Theory and practice in special populations*. Springfield, IL: Charles C Thomas.

May, R. (1983). *The discovery of being: Writings in existential psychology*. New York: W. W. Norton.

Parsons, T., & Bales, R. F. (1955). *Family: Socialization and interaction processes.* New York: Free Press.

Patton, D., & Waring, E. M. (1984). The quality and quantity of marital intimacy in the marriages of psychiatric patients. *Journal of Sex and Marital Therapy, 10,* 201–206.

Peterson, J. A., & Payne, B. (1975). *Love in the later years.* New York: Association Press.

Pope, K. S., et al. (1980). *On love and loving: Psychological perspectives on the nature and experience of romantic love.* San Francisco, CA: Jossey-Bass.

Scharff, D. E. (1982). *The sexual relationship: An object relations view of sex and the family.* Boston: Routledge & Kegan Paul.

Shapiro, D. (1981). *Autonomy and rigid character.* New York: Basic Books.

Sloan, S. Z., & L'Abate, L. (1985). Intimacy. In L. L'Abate (Ed.), *Handbook of family psychology and therapy.* Homewood, IL: Dorsey Press.

Stock, W. (1985). The influence of gender on power dynamics in relationships. In D. C. Goldberg (Ed.), *Contemporary marriage: Special issues in couples therapy.* Homewood, IL: Dorsey Press.

Suomi, S. J. (1977). Neglect and abuse of infants by rhesus monkey mothers. *Voices, 12*(14), 5–8.

Swensen, C. H., Jr. (1985). Love in the family. In L. L'Abate (Ed.), *Handbook of family psychology and therapy,* Homewood, IL: Dorsey Press.

Talmadge, L. D., & Talmadge, W. C. (1986). Relational sexuality: An understanding of low sexual desire. *Journal of Sex and Marital Therapy, 12,* 3–21.

Talmadge, W. C., & Talmadge, L. D. (1985). A transactional perspective on the treatment of sexual dysfunctions. In L. L'Abate (Ed.), *Handbook of family psychology and therapy.* Homewood, IL: Dorsey Press.

Wallace, D. H. (1981). Affectional climate in the family of origin and the experience of subsequent sexual-affectional behaviors. *Journal of Sex and Marital Therapy, 7*(4), 196–306.

Waring, E. M., & Reddon, J. R. (1983). The measurement of intimacy in marriage: The Waring Intimacy Questionnaire. *Journal of Clinical Psychology, 39*(1), 53–57.

Section II

Practical Applications

Chapter 3

The Sexual Genogram – Assessing Family-of-Origin Factors in the Treatment of Sexual Dysfunction

Ellen M. Berman and Larry Hof

The field of family therapy has had considerable difficulty acknowledging sexuality as an organizing force in family life. In breaking from the Freudian position, with its central focus on Oedipal struggles and sexual drive states, to focus on system and context, family therapy has chosen a neutral, indeed avoidant, attitude toward sexuality in general.

Sexuality is a central binding and organizing force in the life of a couple, enabling them to break from their family of origin to form a dyad. In addition, gender-based sex role behavior contributes greatly to the structure of life within the new dyad. However, a search of three classic texts in the family therapy field (Boszormenyi-Nagy & Spark, 1973; Minuchin, 1974; Framo, 1982), as a representative sample, reveals a total of about four pages devoted to sexuality, most in case examples with no accompanying theoretical discussion. Boszormenyi-Nagy and Spark (1973) did briefly describe a case of sexual dysfunction related to unresolved guilt over disloyalty to parents.

For the authors cited, the lack of a specific focus on sexual issues was primarily because they were interested in developing other salient aspects of their new theories. In addition, sexual dysfunction was viewed in the above texts, at least, as part of a larger, systemic problem. It is notable, and rather discomforting, that as the years progressed, the important issues relating to sexuality as a specific dimension of family functioning were left almost exclusively to the sex therapists.

Sexuality and gender role development are also certainly major concerns in the life of the developing child. The literature on human sexuality educa-

Portions of this chapter are reprinted from Volume 12, Number 1 of *Journal of Marital and Family Therapy*, Copyright 1986, American Association for Marriage and Family Therapy. Reprinted by permission.

tion and child development is extensive, but organized around traditional models of Freudian, cognitive, and behaviorally learned responses. There has also been much work on cross-cultural sexual attitudes and behaviors. Although it is obvious from this work that much sexual learning is from direct interaction between parents and children, the models presented and discussed are basically nonsystemic in nature. There is little sense of how specific patterned behaviors/attitudes are carried from generation to generation, or how different children in a family can embody different aspects of their parents' sexuality.

The concept of sexual scripting as presented by Gagnon (1977) is one apparent exception to this general trend in the human sexuality education literature. Although he primarily emphasizes the concept of cultural scripts, he at least devotes some attention to the interactive nature of scripts between partners and, very minimally, discusses scripts developed and transmitted between familial generations.

It is interesting to note that writers strongly influenced by the transactional analysis school of therapy (e.g., James & Jongeward, 1971; Steiner, 1974), on the other hand, strongly emphasize the interactive nature of scripts between partners and scripts developed and transmitted between familial generations (usually limited to two generations). However, these writers generally fail to develop the sexual aspects of such scripting processes. The one notable exception in this sexual area is Wyckoff's (1974) work, which focuses on sex role scripting in men and women, but does not address the issue of sexual dysfunction at all.

In some ways, Wyckoff's work was representative of the beginning attempts to link sociocultural aspects of human sexuality with intergenerational (two-generation) messages and/or scripts and the consequent effects on male/female interactions. Since transactional analysis developed from more dynamically oriented roots, the rich potential for further development of Wyckoff's (and others') ideas through interaction with the family therapy schools was not fulfilled because at that early date there was simply too much myopic parochialism on all sides to permit cooperative cross-fertilization of ideas and techniques.

In the sexuality education literature, there is also little reference made to family therapy and its possible relationship to sexuality issues in families or the lives of individuals. A review of four commonly used college texts in human sexuality (Gagnon, 1977; Gagnon & Greenblatt, 1978; Victor, 1980; Doyle, 1985) reveals a total of three pages devoted to family therapy, does not describe it in the context of sexual problems, and references Framo, Minuchin, and Boszormenyi-Nagy and Spark only once.

Sexual problems and/or dysfunctions are also family-related issues, and not minor problems in the general population or in couples requesting therapy. Several studies have suggested that over 50% of couples have at least some complaints about their sex life or a specific sexual dysfunction. Yet, family therapists, including those who work primarily with couples, have been so uneasy with this topic, and/or so preoccupied with other issues, that an entire subspecialty, sex therapy, has been developed. Although practitioners of this subspecialty have done great service in integrating physiological information about sexuality with basic issues of education, learning theory, and dynamic psychiatry, a negative effect has been further fragmentation of the field. To some extent, simple sex therapy techniques have been rendered with an aura of mystery, which has made it even harder to incorporate them into usual family therapy approaches. Sex therapists, on the other hand, seldom use three-generation considerations in their work. Kaplan (1974, 1979, 1983), for example, makes extensive use of dynamic material, but utilizes few concepts from Bowen, Framo, etc.

The authors believe that family therapy theory has much to offer in the treatment of sexual issues and dysfunctions, and that sex therapy has much to offer to family therapy in terms of both theory and treatment. It is the thesis of this chapter that sexuality is best understood within the context of family theory, particularly those theories involved with family structure and three-generation transmission of loyalties and myths, as well as the more familiar dyadic issues of power, intimacy, and sex role learning. This chapter reviews salient issues in the field, as part of a beginning integration of sexuality into family theory. As an example of clinical integration, the authors offer a method of exploring a person's three-generation sexual history which links sexual issues to wider issues of family structure and loyalty. The specific technique described, the sexual genogram (Hof & Berman, 1986) and family journey, building on the work of Bowen, Framo, and others, has been found particularly useful in the treatment of a wide variety of sexual dysfunctions, as well as enabling a deeper understanding of the couple's issues of intimacy and gender.

THEORETICAL ISSUES IN SEX AND FAMILY

Sex and Family Structure

The need for appropriate boundaries and a functioning hierarchy has been a major concern of family therapists, especially those of the structural school (Minuchin, 1974). Well-functioning, intact families maintain relationships with previous generations with clear, appropriate, flexible boundaries and a clear hierarchy between grandparents, parents, and children. So-called single-parent families, where there may be a wide variety of part-time or alternate-generation caretakers, must establish their own system of maintaining boundaries and hierarchy. What is seldom mentioned is that sexuality plays a major part in the maintenance of such a hierarchy.

Parents' sexual behavior, a private activity that is known about (open secret) but is neither witnessed nor (mostly) discussed with the children, is proof of the parents' separateness and the inability of the children to take the place of an adult partner. The parents' closed door, a major symbol of the separation of generations in this culture, is most likely to be enforced not by a parental wish for privacy while reading, but for privacy while being intimate and especially sexual. The parents' ability to have a sexual relationship serves as a generational marker, proving their adulthood both to their own parents and to their children. The parents' willingness and ability to impart sexual information and values to their children, while helping them to delay expressions of some aspects of sexuality until developmentally appropriate, is a necessary part of parenting and is both an expression of and maintenance of appropriate family structure.

A lack of effective sexual expression or the presence of sexual dysfunction between the members of the dyad renders the couple more open to cross-generational coalition (as, indeed, cross-generational coalition and the forces that produce it may render a couple more vulnerable to sexual dysfunction). Cross-generational coalitions, traditionally between the parent who experiences his/herself as more helpless and a "helpless" child, may often have a strong sexual component which will strongly affect the internal life of the next generation.

> *Case 1*. A man in his 30s entered therapy for marital issues related to being "too close to his mother." He also reported lack of sexual desire, although not impotence. History revealed that his parents had been unhappily married, and that the mother had poured her energy into the child, who was breast-fed for four years and was permitted to sleep between the parents at will. The father had essentially "abandoned the field" and spent little time with his son. In therapy his fear of being disloyal to mother, and possibly contributing to a divorce if he abandoned her, emerged with great turmoil.

A family structure of cross-generational and cross-sex coalition, such as described above, encourages the development of internal conflicts in the child traditionally called Oedipal. The family model emphasizes the part of all three members in the development of these issues in the child. In addition, such structure will later produce severe loyalty conflicts in the child, which, as in the above, continue into adulthood.

Couples in the process of divorce may have major structural problems around intimacy and sexuality. During the extremely stressful period of separation and the early postdivorce period, a parent may lean inordinately on one or all of the children. It is common to find that, during a separation or divorce, one child begins to sleep with one of the parents. This behavior is stressful and confusing for both child and parent and, indeed, is doubly stressful since eventually the parent will choose to return to adult sexuality and attempt to remove the child from the bed.

> *Case 2.* When couple B divorced, Debbie, the nine-year-old eldest child, wanted to "sleep with Daddy, so he won't be so lonely; and besides, I'm afraid to be alone at night." The father was conflicted regarding the request, but nevertheless permitted the daughter to sleep with him for five months on weekend visits. When he started to date again, Debbie was enraged and refused to go with him on weekends. She expressed strong resentments toward "Daddy's girlfriend" and felt "more lonely than ever." With insight beyond her years, she mused, "I guess little girls can never win."

Following the divorce, both parents must negotiate issues around dating and forming other sexual relationships. Arguments over hierarchy may be remarkably worsened when a teen-age child just beginning to explore his own sexuality is living with a single parent who is just beginning to date again. These tremendous concerns about parent and child sexuality are often hidden beneath arguments over minor matters of dating such as curfews, avoiding the very real issue of what it means to both child and parent to be exploring their sexuality at different points in the life-cycle where one is still responsible for the other.

> *Case 3.* Two teen-aged children (ages 14 and 16), when confronted by both their divorced parents regarding their sexual activity, replied, "Why shouldn't we be allowed to have sex before we're married? You two are sleeping with your lovers, and you're not even married." The parents' reply was "We're adults and you are simply too young." Needless to say, the children were not satisfied with the reply, and the subsequent argument led to some much needed family therapy.

The most serious markers of dysfunction involving sex and family structure include cases of actual incest, which has been treated in the literature with considerable detail, and sexual intrusiveness, which has been less described. Sexual intrusiveness is here defined as a parent who becomes excessively involved in the child's sexual development to the point of, for example, bathing a 12-year-old child, giving frequent enemas, or demanding gynecological examinations in order to "find out the truth" about the child's sex life.

> *Case 4.* M, a 37-year-old woman, told of having to give her mother a "blow-by-blow" account of every date when she was a teen-ager, even being pushed to divulge details regarding "how far" they went. In her marriage, M felt sexually inhibited with her husband, and it was having a serious impact on their sexual enjoyment. In therapy, the lack of privacy when she was growing up and

her mother's intrusiveness were identified as the source of an ever-present "brake" on M's spontaneity in the sexual area. The brake enabled her to avoid embarrassment, punishment, or rejection, and to protect her own sense of self and power as a teen-ager. When she was helped to identify how her relationship with her mother was present in her mind in her current sex life, she was able to set more effective boundaries with her mother in other areas of her life, contributing greatly to the resolution of the sexual problem.

The therapist working with an adult couple must be able to reconstruct the structure in the family of origin, by history or interview of other family members. In this regard the genogram techniques described below are particularly helpful. The therapist working with cases where the therapy includes adolescents or children must focus primarily on the family's structure but within that, one must also consider the effects of sexual issues on the structure and consider the sex itself as a substantive content issue. A therapist's willingness to deal directly with the sexual issues, rather than with the peripheral issues of curfew, room cleaning, disobedience, etc., is extremely important since both parents and children tend to be reluctant to deal with sexual issues directly, even when these are uppermost in their thoughts. The therapist's ability to directly discuss sexuality opens the possibility for parents and child to have more appropriate communication.

Sex and the Family Life-Cycle

If sex within the dyad is a strong binding force, allowing a new family to develop out of the two families of origin, the developing sexuality of their children may be considered "subversive," albeit developmentally necessary. That is, the child's sexual urges move his life both in fantasy and in reality away from that of his parent's and into his own. The preschool child who learns to masturbate in private and who develops nonspecific but nevertheless sensually related feelings about other children is learning that it is possible for her to be a private and separate person with boundaries that her parents cannot breach. In the teen years, the crucial marker of adolescence and movement into adulthood is sex-hormone-related physical development, and the subsequent intense erotic/intimate attachments allow the person to move the emotional focus out of the home and begin to attach elsewhere. This normal developmental event can be impacted in many ways by parents, who may have their own unresolved sexual issues and be overly fascinated or frightened by the child's development. In the face of this tremendous concern in both the teen-ager and parents it is more remarkable how seldom these issues are discussed in therapy unless the child is specifically acting out sexually.

Obviously sexual issues can be hidden by other issues which appear to be unrelated power struggles. In addition, sexual developmental issues can mask or affect other problems.

> *Case 5.* C, a 39-year-old, single woman presented with a case of long-standing depression. Psychopharmacological intervention impacted greatly on the depression, but the client was still left with a sense of a vague, yet pervasive, cloud hanging over her that would not go away. A discussion of the nature of the cloud led to a sense that "it doesn't all belong to me," which led to an in-depth exploration of her mother's pervasive and untreated depression throughout C's life. Each of the five children in the family was expected to do nothing to "upset" mother, but C was specifically chosen to "make Mom happy." The criterion for her selection was her lack of physical development at puberty. The other children, one older and three younger, were all perceived to be appropriately developed, but C's lack of breast development led to protectiveness by her mother and father, which was expressed in statements such as, "Maybe you should wait before you date, because you might be embarrassed. After all, guys make fun of flat-chested girls, and the nice boys won't even look at you." The added comment "Besides, your mother will welcome the extra company" betrayed a hidden agenda designed to protect the mother and the marital dyad from having to deal with the consequences of her very real depression. C concluded that the onset of her own depression was at puberty, "or at least it became worse then," and she connected it with the heavy responsibility associated with "making Mom happy," with her sense of repressed and suppressed anger at being "the chosen one while the others got off the hook," and with her guilt at not being able to accomplish the assigned task.

The Transmissions of Sexual Loyalties, Values, and Concerns

Boszormenyi-Nagy and Spark (1973), Framo (1970), and others have eloquently discussed the transmission of family values from one generation to the next. Among the binding forces on each family member is the acceptance of at least some portion of the family's belief systems and traditions. This is part of "being loyal" as a family group member. Among the belief systems that are most central to family life are those of gender, intimacy, and sexuality. These are indeed matters of great interest to the culture at large, and each family interprets these in their own way. Beliefs about gender-based behavior in the family, e.g., men are powerful and women are passive, go hand in hand with beliefs and attitudes regarding intimacy and specific sexual behavior. It is not unusual, for example, to find that several generations of men in a given family (or only the youngest, oldest, or special child for several generations) have had a specific type of sexual dysfunction or a specific pattern of getting married and divorced. Sometimes a specific child in a single generation will be singled out to redress a long-standing family imbalance by becoming "Mom's child" or "the boy my mother never had" and may be programmed for a specific set of sexual attitudes and behaviors in this way. This information is seldom transmitted directly, especially about sexuality, but is usually conveyed through stories about other people whose behavior was acceptable to the family or stories about family members who have been cut off. These feelings and attitudes may be held very strongly and will certainly directly affect the sexual life of each generation.

> *Case 6.* A 21-year-old man entered therapy complaining of problems with his girlfriend which included a sense of personal passivity, inhibited desire, and frequent premature ejaculation. He was seen with his girlfriend, who was indeed the more extroverted and controlling of the two. He was then seen with his parents in a family session, in which his depressed and controlling mother complained about his passive and quiet father and hinted strongly at sexual problems. The father stated that his father (the patient's grandfather) had similar marital dynamics and to his knowledge his grandfather (the patient's great-grandfather) did too. The patient, who was overtly allied with his mother, was able to recognize that his behavior was, in part, a covert way of being loyal to father, as well as a set of well-learned behaviors.

Specific events in a family's life in one generation may dramatically alter the shape of the next. For example, a woman reported a family secret that her aunt had had a child out of wedlock. This had terrified her mother, who proceeded to raise the client with rigid strictures against sexual expression, which she was now passing down to her daughters. In families where strictures such as this become too binding, members of the next generation may rebel by acting out sexually and becoming pregnant. This will, of course, confirm the mother's worst fears.

It is not only patterns that are transferred. Older generations may directly intervene in the lives of the nuclear family, responding to their own concerns.

> *Case 7.* A three-year-old child was brought into the clinic a year after a minor episode of sexual touching by an adolescent stranger. This molestation was stopped in a couple of minutes, never repeated, and the child was not injured. Nevertheless, a year later the parents were still bringing the child into therapy (the clinic therapist was the third expert that the parents had consulted trying to find out if the child was all right). The parents had been treating the child somewhat like a wounded princess, interpreting any evidence of upset as related to her "trauma." The parents were having some conflicts, and it appeared that some of these conflicts were being detoured through the child. However, a brief review of the three-generation system revealed that the maternal grandmother had a sister who had been raped when she was 14. This had been extremely upsetting to the grandmother. It was she, in fact, who had been pushing the mother to take the child to therapy, repeating over and over that she was concerned about the child's mental health. A strong message was given to the

parents that the child was now "well" and that continued focus on the event would produce more problems. This enabled the mother, who had been feeling this way already, to reassure the grandmother with more conviction. She reported relief at all levels of the system.

It is probably fair to generalize that in the majority of American families, sexual "traditions" include insecurity about sexuality, inaccurate information, and silence within the family around sexual issues. A highly sexually focused culture combined with a ban on sharing information and feelings about sex produces great confusion in young people and leads to increased sex dysfunction. The specific ways a family copes with this cultural confusion are crucial to understanding sexual issues. Because sexual therapy has focused either on intrapsychic conflicts or on the dyad, less attention has been paid to multigeneration transmission of both sexual attitudes and handling of problematic sexual issues. However, as many of the above case studies have indicated, intergenerational messages, loyalty issues, and transmission processes are frequently core aspects of a sexual problem or dysfunction.

THE SEXUAL GENOGRAM AND FAMILY JOURNEY

Everything written to this point emphasizes that the sexual life of the adult client who arrives at the therapist's office is greatly impacted by family history and structure. The job of the therapist is to consider the effects of this on the client. For example, if the person is sexually ignorant, is he/she emotionally free to take in new information? If he becomes more directly sexual, will that be a betrayal of mother or father? If she becomes intimate, will she break a family tradition of distancing? Access to this material is best obtained by transforming some traditional tools of family therapy to gain some new information. The authors use the term sexual genogram (Hof & Berman, 1986) to describe a process designed to facilitate the gathering of that information.

THE SEXUAL GENOGRAM

The sexual genogram uses a traditional family therapy tool to explore issues of sexuality in the structure and belief system of the client's family of origin. The genogram itself, as developed by Murray Bowen (1978) and enlarged on by Guerin and Pendagast (1976) and Wachtel (1982), has traditionally been used to obtain an "aerial view" of the larger system.

The genogram is, basically, a three-generational diagram or map of the people who make up one's family. It can include whatever data the therapist wishes. At the minimum, births, deaths, marriages, and divorces should be included. However, feelings, myths, and stories about significant events can also be included. Its advantages over a standard narrative history is that it casts a wider net: by including everyone, not only those the clients see as important, it is more likely to reveal emotional cutoffs, secrets, and previously unnoticed alliances. The process of drawing the genogram gives a sense of organization and distance to the material, thus facilitating objectivity and rationality, and offers the possibility of increasing or decreasing affect as the history progresses. The family contacts which are usually initiated as a way of gathering history often contribute to basic shifts in family dynamics.

The authors have adapted it to pinpoint sexual issues, described in the section above. By providing a gentle, careful overview of sexual issues across generations, it enables the client to explore previously hidden affects and to study family patterns of interaction around sexual issues. This, in turn, provides information helpful in resolving immediate sexual problems and, often, shifts in the basic quality of the couple's relatedness.

THE SEXUAL GENOGRAM PROCESS

A sexual genogram is most appropriately utilized after the initial evaluation has been completed. The exploration of sexual issues is best done when a climate exists in which therapeutic trust and rapport have been established, there is no acute marital crisis, and the couple has agreed to explore their sexual issues and problems.

The process involves five component parts: introduction; creation and exploration of a genogram; creation and exploration of a sexual genogram; exploration and discussion of genogram material/issues with family members; and a review of the total process of integration with the treatment plan.

Introduction

The process is facilitated by a cognitively oriented explanation of the concepts and goals. The role of early learning, family structure, and intergenerational processes in the development of individual, couple, and family systems is explained. The concepts of "life script" and "family scripts," as utilized by transactional analysis therapists (James & Jongeward, 1971), and "family loyalties" (Boszormenyi-Nagy & Spark, 1973) have proven extremely helpful in presenting this idea to clients in a nonthreatening and interest-provoking way. Positive/facilitative and hurtful/destructive examples are drawn from the clients. Self-disclosure by the therapist may be used to model and emphasize the universal nature of these processes and normalize both positive and negative aspects for the clients. This can increase the likelihood of further exploration in sensitive areas by the clients which might be precluded if they believed that they were alone in their feelings, beliefs, or actions. As the concept is grasped and curiosity pricked, speculation as to how these concepts might relate to the presenting sexual problem is encouraged briefly. As the clients perceive the importance of considering the impact of their family of origin on their development, relationships, and the sexual problem, motivation usually increases to continue the process.

Creation and Exploration of a Genogram

A genogram is defined as a "diagram of extended family relationships including at least three generations" (Foley & Everett, 1984, p. 12). It graphically shows the names and ages of all family members; specific dates of significant life events — births, deaths, marriages, separations, divorces, etc.; and marginal notations regarding occupations, significant illnesses, and other important life events and transitions. We stress that although facts are important, we are also very interested in the client's perceptions regarding the identified facts or events. In other words, what was the impact on the client, other significant persons, and related systems?

Construction of the genogram can be done by the couple within the session, with the therapist and each partner in private sessions, or by the partners at home in private, with sharing done after the work has been completed. This is a matter of therapist preference, available time, and the clients' needs for either sharing or privacy.

Each client is instructed to use lines, symbols, and colors that might be personally relevant to show feelings, alliances, boundaries, coalitions, closeness, distance, emotional cutoffs, conflicts, connectedness, etc. Personal creativity is encouraged to make the process a lively one for the clients, tapping memories of things past and present. They are encouraged to look at family pictures and albums. Gaps, where information is missing, are noted, for these are often the domain of a living secret that still impacts on the system. Feelings, thoughts, and dreams experienced by the client as the genogram is being created are to be noted. If there is permission within the family system to talk openly regarding the "family tree," clients are free to do so, to gather information. However, if such a discussion would threaten the client or disrupt the broader family system, we advise waiting until later in the therapy process.

It is evident from all of the above that we are describing a graphic device that combines the data-gathering approaches of a variety of writers: the history-gathering aspects of Guerin and Pendagast (1976); the relationship/family "mapping" features of Minuchin (1974); the impact, internal images, and "story" aspects of Duhl (1981) and Hof and Miller (1981); and the projective emphasis of Wachtel (1982). Development, family structure, and family loyalties may all be highlighted.

If the genograms have been done separately, which usually takes one or two weeks, the couple is encouraged to discuss their findings with one another. Partners frequently hear the other's story from a new perspective and with increased sensitivity and empathy, as a result of adhering to this structured and reciprocal process. In addition, partners can frequently supply missing facts or remind the presenter of "forgotten" feelings, since they tend to be less emotionally involved in the family process of the presenter.

In the therapeutic setting, the therapist can facilitate the exploration of "what happened?" (identification of facts/events), "what was the impact on people and systems?" (analysis), and "what generalizations can be made?" (specific learnings), regarding the relationship of the "there-and-then" (one's living history) to the "here-and-now" issues that are the focus of therapy.

The therapist endeavors to help the client fill in gaps, make affective connections to nodal events, perceive overt and covert patterns, and remember positive images that may lie dormant, but which have been helpful in bonding this person with other persons in this unique family. Verbal and nonverbal clues are carefully observed and, where it is deemed appropriate, are explored to help create connections. The feelings, thoughts, and dreams experienced as the exercise was being completed are also examined.

Creation and Exploration of a Sexual Genogram

After the genogram has been created and explored, each partner is asked to reconsider it during the following week, with a specific focus on the following questions:

- What are the overt/covert messages in this family regarding sexuality/intimacy? Regarding masculinity/femininity?
- Who said/did what? Who was conspicuously silent/absent in the area of sexuality/intimacy?
- Who was the most open sexually? Intimately? In what ways?
- How was sexuality/intimacy encouraged? Discouraged? Controlled? Within a generation? Between generations?
- What questions have you had regarding sexuality/intimacy in your "family tree" that you have been reluctant to ask? Who might have the answers? How could you discover the answers?
- What were the "secrets" in your family regarding sexuality/intimacy (e.g., incest, unwanted pregnancies, extramarital affairs, etc.)?
- What do the other "players on the stage" have to say regarding the above questions? How did these issues, events, and experiences impact on him/her? Within a generation? Between generations? With whom have you talked about this? With whom would you like to talk about this? How could you do it?

- How does your partner perceive your family tree/genogram regarding the aforementioned issues? How do you perceive his/hers?
- How would you change this genogram (including who and what) to meet what you wish would have occurred regarding messages and experiences of sexuality/intimacy?

Answers to the questions are to be written in a free-flowing manner, with the assurance that what is to be shared with one's partner or the therapist is under the total control of the writer. Feelings, thoughts, and dreams which are triggered as these questions are considered are to be noted. Sometimes, lines, symbols, or colors on the original genogram are modified to express new realities discovered as these questions are considered. Partners are encouraged to share as much as possible and as much as they desire with each other prior to the next therapy session.

In the therapy session, meanings, insights, and ideas are explored using the process noted above with the genogram (i.e., identification, analysis, generalizations/learnings). When this has been shared between the therapist and both members of the couple, discussion is held to decide which issues could be, and/or need to be, explored directly and fruitfully with other family members. In some cases, this next step is not necessary, and we move directly to the fifth step in the process, "Review of total process and integration with treatment plan."

Exploration and Discussion of Genogram Material/Issues with Family Members

In most cases, the genogram is the first step in a family journey that leads to general goals of individuation and possible restructuring of family alliances in the present. Bowen (1978), Framo (1970, 1976), Paul and Grosser (1981), and Williamson (1981, 1982a, 1982b) have written extensively on various ways an individual can make contact with his/her family (with and without the therapist present), both for retrieving the past and for reconnecting and redefining family relationships in the here and now. Whatever the specifics of the approach, the goal is a slow, nonconfrontational connection, beginning with requests for information and clarification of family experiences. Respect for parents as well as children is crucial. Time for things to settle between contacts is always planned for. Confrontation or expression of painful feelings is done only when clients and family have been able to talk or share enough so that contact feels safe.

The client's fears and apprehensions are openly discussed, as is the potential impact on other family members who are to be approached, before any contact is made. The emphasis is placed on enabling persons to tell and hear each other's "story," to gather information (facts and feelings and impressions), to discover family scripts or legacies of an intergenerational nature, and to learn about one's family and use what is learned to facilitate understanding of current functioning and resolution of current problems.

With sexual material, this gradual and respectful attitude is even more critical. Clients are encouraged to make contact in a face-to-face manner if at all possible, by phone or letter if not. This is done without the partner present, since the goal is to deal with relationships within the original family. Most clients find it easier and more productive to deal with one parent or sibling at a time, in a private place. Sexual material is approached after other historical issues are covered. The easiest questions to ask are those about values (e.g., "What were you taught about sexuality as a child, what did you want me to know about it, to think about it?").

Parental ideas and feelings about sex are generally elicited far more easily than anxious adult children would believe. If the conversation becomes intimate, parents will often reveal sexual secrets—pregnancies, abuse, etc. It is seldom, if ever, necessary or desirable to obtain information about current sexual practices of parents, or for the client to share his/her own.

Clients are reminded that they should not expect, or even attempt, to cover everything in one meeting. If the client needs to discuss particularly painful material, such as sexual abuse by a parent, careful rehearsal and preparation is essential. Clients whose parents are dead, unavailable, or unwilling to talk should consider locating other family members. Siblings, aunts, uncles, and cousins usually are acutely aware of sexual feelings and attitudes of family members, and often repositories of secrets as well.

When the contacts are made, partners are encouraged to keep each other apprised of what has occurred and what feelings and thoughts have been experienced. Specific supportive responses are modeled and encouraged. Throughout the process, the therapist should be available for phone consultations as needed, and extended-family sessions where indicated.

After the contacts have been made, the conjoint therapy session is once again used to gather meanings, insights, and ideas from the exercise. The identification, analysis, and generalization/learnings process utilized above is once more used. This exploration leads naturally to the last component in the sexual genogram process.

Review of the Total Process
and Integration with the Treatment Plan

The therapist and clients do a reflective review of the total process, emphasizing questions such as "What have you learned?" and "How can we use what you have learned to help resolve the sexual problem?"

As the insights, feelings, and legacies are discussed, a new perspective frequently emerges, with greater appreciation, empathy, and objectivity regarding what occurred in one's family and how it impacted on all family members.

Insights regarding the etiology and maintenance of the sexual problem often lead to diminished blaming and a positive sense of reciprocity. These learnings and ideas of the clients and the therapist are then merged with the more traditional behavioral components of a sex therapy treatment plan to resolve the presenting sexual problem.

CASE ILLUSTRATIONS

The following two case illustrations will give the reader a sense of how a three-generational family model, and the sexual genogram process itself, can be of use in the treatment of specific sexual problems/dysfunctions.

Case 1

Betty and Bob, a well-bonded, married, middle-aged couple, presented with multiple sexual dysfunctions. She was preorgasmic (primary) and he experienced situational premature ejaculation. Both dysfunctions were rather tenacious, resisting prior treatment efforts with a trained sex and marital therapist. Traditional sex therapy approaches did not resolve the presenting problems, even when serious attention was paid to uncovering unresolved intrapsychic issues. It was evident to all involved that "something" was blocking the resolution of the problems.

The sexual genogram process was employed. The questions that were especially helpful to Bob were "What are the overt/covert messages in this family regarding sexuality/intimacy? Regarding masculinity/femininity?" He discovered, through his family genogram, that men were scripted to be less powerful than the women in the family and were not "allowed" to think "too highly" of themselves. Since he was a warm, personable, dynamic individual, and very successful in his own business, the premature ejaculation served as a way of "keeping him in his place." Discussions with other male family members gave him a clear sense that his dysfunction enabled him to remain faithful to a nonhelpful family script. An uncle, with whom he discussed some of the specific sexual questions, confirmed that the "successful" men in the family were frequently the object of "good-natured" teasing about their sexuality. In Bob's marriage, Betty played her part by teasing, and by occasionally blaming him and "his problem" for her inability to be orgasmic.

When Betty's standard genogram was discussed, she was struck by her drawing of thin, red, "angry" lines, showing a negative impact, underlying green "positive" lines, connecting her to her older brother, father, and grandfather (see Figure 1). The therapist was impressed by her frequent references to "how close we were as a family." In the subsequent week, as Betty wrote the answers to the sexual genogram questions, two had particular significance for her: "What were the 'secrets' in your family regarding sexuality/intimacy?" and "What do other 'players on the stage' have to say regarding the above questions?" What emerged was that she had kept hidden from her previous therapist and her husband a pattern of close sexual contact (fondling, but not intercourse) with her grandfather, father, and older brother.

At her own initiative, during the same week, but after she had written her answers, Betty approached her older brother, with whom she had a close and open relationship. She was seeking information from him regarding how he remembered those events and how the experiences impacted on him. When he responded, "Don't you remember how we both enjoyed it?" she was shocked, because she had "forgotten" the pleasurable aspects of the experiences.

As Betty, Bob, and the therapist discussed the sexual genogram, what emerged even more clearly to her than ever before was her resentment at the loss of control when she had been approached by her grandfather (a senile man) and her father, and her anger at her mother for not believing her when she told her as a young child of the abuse. She began to see how the in-

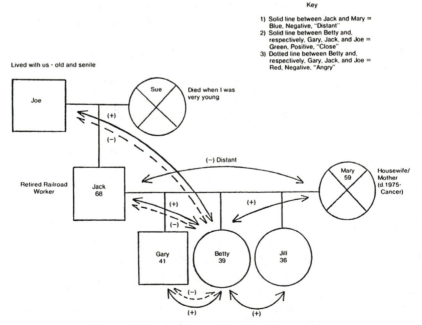

Key

1) Solid line between Jack and Mary =
   Blue, Negative, "Distant"
2) Solid line between Betty and,
   respectively, Gary, Jack, and Joe =
   Green, Positive, "Close"
3) Dotted line between Betty and,
   respectively, Gary, Jack, and Joe =
   Red, Negative, "Angry"

Figure 1. Selected elements of Betty's genogram.

orgasmia enabled her to maintain control and, at the same time, block the remembrance of sexual pleasure that was experienced in a self-labeled "sick" relationship with her brother.

Betty believed that the sexual genogram process had enabled her to approach her secret in a very gentle way, with her being able to maintain complete control. In the discussion with the therapist, the collusive elements of their relationship were also exposed—Bob helped protect her from remembrance of "sick" pleasure; Betty helped protect him from "thinking too highly of himself." When this material was explored, traditional sex therapy approaches to each of the sexual dysfunctions led to rapid resolution of the premature ejaculation, and to somewhat slower, but no less certain, resolution of the preorgasmic condition.

In addition, Betty had several discussions with her father during the course of therapy which helped her to put the past behind her and to understand in a new way his relationship with her long-dead mother. At first, she sought only information regarding several questions on the sexual genogram. She was instructed not to initiate a discussion of the overtly sexual aspects of their past relationship. Rather, she was to focus initially on her long-standing feelings at the "loss of control" in many aspects of her relationship with him. He surprised her by expressing remorse regarding several of the instances she noted, and by apologizing for his sexual intrusiveness and "taking advantage" of their close relationship. The genuine love between Betty and her parents was enabled to be experienced in a deeper way, and when he died some six months later, Betty had a sense that the unfinished business of the past was fairly well resolved.

Case 2

This second case illustration demonstrates how a family emotional legacy can be transmitted across the generations and impact on a later generation in a sexual dysfunction.

Janet and Dave, married for nine years, both aged 30 and college educated at the graduate level, presented with a case of long-standing inhibited sexual desire on Janet's part, both describing the marriage as being "in serious trouble." The sexual genogram process enabled both of them to see how the "abandonment" by their respective fathers (his at age eight via divorce and hers at age 12 via death) and the way it was handled (or not handled) in the family led to a significant amount of unresolved grief and a mutual-protection society between them, each endeavoring to help the other avoid pain of any sort. Contacts with their respective families enabled the grief work to be completed for each of them and allowed the extended family to address the long-avoided pain.

Janet and Dave were able to identify how they colluded in "not growing up," to avoid death and adult responsibilities. In addition, both were invested in not increasing sexual intimacy, so that love would not get too deep, so that the pain would not be so great when the "inevitable" loss would finally come again!

Janet also realized through this process that her maternal grandfather had literally abandoned her grandmother, mother, and her siblings, when Janet's mother was six years old. This fact had never been disclosed, the grandfather always being referred to as one who "died." Discussion of the genogram with a paternal uncle (the designated family historian) revealed this fact and led to a significant meeting with Janet's mother in which her long-denied grief was exposed in a helpful manner.

When Janet asked her mother how the abandonment experience had impacted on her, her mother replied that she "determined then and there never to get close to a man again — no one would do that to me!" In the therapy session, Janet's comment of "No wonder it's been so difficult, I've had to carry my grief and hers for over 20 years!" was significant in its truth as well as in its power to enable her to feel free to move closer to Dave sexually. In this case, specific sex therapy interventions were not needed to overcome the sexual dysfunction. As marital therapy continued, the inhibited sexual desire disappeared.

INDICATIONS AND CONTRAINDICATIONS

A brief and less detailed sexual genogram is appropriate as a part of any routine sexual history as a way of pinpointing potential problem areas. The length of time it takes to gather the information, and the amount of detail, vary with the therapist. A clinician who takes a primarily fact-oriented genogram in the office can accomplish a great deal in a short period of time. We see no contraindications to this type of information gathering, provided the couple is not in an acute crisis and is at an appropriate point to start discussing sexual issues. For therapists using a brief, behaviorally focused treatment model, the sexual genogram in its more detailed and elaborated form should probably be used only when an impasse has been reached.

The family journey is a more complex issue. Although there are probably no absolute contraindications other than active psychosis in one of the parents, timing and planning are critical. A person in the midst of a major, hostile struggle with parents needs to work through those issues with a therapist well trained in family-of-origin work before sexual themes are dealt with.

We have been using the sexual genogram method informally for several years, and in a formal manner for the last year, encompassing some 20 couples. In addition, students in the Marriage Council's family therapy and human development courses (35 students) have done family genograms and journeys in which some sexual material was elicited. We have not personally encountered serious problems, although some experiences were more helpful than others. This does not mean, however, that an unprepared client could not have a most unpleasant experience.

CONCLUSION

Family therapy theory adds much to the conceptualization of sexuality and its problems in dyads. Sexuality plays an integral part in organizing family structure along generational lines. Family-of-origin patterns, beliefs, and loyalties affect later sexual functioning in the family of procreation. The sexual genogram is a data-gathering and assessment process that enables people to explore multigenerational issues in a rapid, effective way. It may also represent the first stage of a treatment process which involves family exploration and family journey or may simply facilitate more traditional insight-oriented therapy. It may be used in combination with a variety of other therapy modalities and represents an addition to the usual sex and family therapy armamentarium.

REFERENCES

Boszormenyi-Nagy, I., & Spark, G. (1973). *Invisible loyalties.* New York: Harper and Row.

Bowen, M. (1978). *Family therapy in clinical practice.* New York: Jason Aronson.

Doyle, J. (1985). *Sex and gender.* Dubuque, IA: Brown Publishing.

Duhl, F. J. (1981). The use of the chronological chart in general systems family therapy. *Journal of Marital and Family Therapy, 7,* 361–373.

Foley, V. D., & Everett, C. A. (1984). *Family therapy glossary.* Washington, DC: American Association for Marriage and Family Therapy.

Framo, J. (1970). Symptoms from a family transactional viewpoint. In N. Ackerman, J. Lieb, and J. Pearce (Eds.), *Family therapy in transition.* Boston: Little, Brown and Co.

Framo, J. (1976). Family of origin as a therapeutic resource for adults in marital therapy: You can and should go home again. *Family Process, 15,* 193–210.

Framo, J. (1982). *Explorations in marital and family therapy.* New York: Springer.

Gagnon, J. (1977). *Human sexualities.* Glenview, IL: Scott, Foresman.

Gagnon, J., & Greenblatt, C. (1978). *Life designs.* Glenview, IL: Scott, Foresman.

Guerin, P. J., & Pendagast, M. A. (1976). Evaluation of family system and genogram. In P. J. Guerin, Jr. (Ed.), *Family therapy: Theory and practice.* New York: Gardner Press.

Hof, L., & Berman, E. M. (1986). The sexual genogram. *Journal of Marital and Family Therapy, 12,* 39–47.

Hof, L., & Miller, W. R. (1981). *Marriage enrichment: Philosophy, process and program.* Bowie, MD: Brady.

James, M., & Jongeward, D. (1971). *Born to win*. Reading, MA: Addison-Wesley.

Kaplan, H. (1974). *The new sex therapy*. New York: Brunner/Mazel.

Kaplan, H. (1979). *Disorders of sexual desire*. New York: Brunner/Mazel.

Kaplan, H. (1983). *The evaluation of sexual disorders*. New York: Brunner/Mazel.

Minuchin, S. (1974). *Families and family therapy*. Cambridge, MA: Harvard University Press.

Paul, N. L., & Grosser, G. H. (1981). Operational mourning and its role in conjoint family therapy. In R. J. Green and J. L. Framo (Eds.), *Family therapy*. New York: International Universities Press.

Steiner, C. M. (1974). *Scripts people live*. New York: Grove Press.

Victor, J. (1980). *Human sexuality: A social psychological approach*. Englewood Cliffs, NJ: Prentice-Hall.

Wachtel, E. F. (1982). The family psyche over three generations: The genogram revisited. *Journal of Marital and Family Therapy, 8*, 335–343.

Williamson, D. S. (1981). Personal authority via termination of the intergenerational hierarchical boundary: A "new" stage in the family life cycle. *Journal of Marital and Family Therapy, 7*, 441–452.

Williamson, D. S. (1982a). Personal authority via termination of the intergenerational hierarchical boundary: Part II — The consultation process and the therapeutic method. *Journal of Marital and Family Therapy, 8*, 23–37.

Williamson, D. S. (1982b). Personal authority in family experience via termination of the intergenerational hierarchical boundary: Part III — Personal authority defined, and the power of play in the change process. *Journal of Marital and Family Therapy, 8*, 309–322.

Wyckoff, H. (1974). Sex role scripting in men and women. In C. M. Steiner, *Scripts people live*. New York: Grove Press.

Chapter 4

Enhancing a Couple's Sexual Relationship

Stephen R. Treat

Educators and therapists concerned with sexual enhancement have traditionally focused on technique and performance. However, overemphasis on sexual positions and orgasms has too often overshadowed the more fundamental issues of intimacy, affection, and mutual respect. Likewise, many couples have failed to understand that sexual enhancement encompasses their entire intimate relationship. It deals with their ability to share conversation, be vulnerable to one another, touch and share affection, as well as experience sexual intercourse. Because of the many facets of sexual enhancement, traditional sex therapy, primarily emphasizing behavioral change in overtly sexual areas or dealing with a specific sexual dysfunction, is inadequate to address sexual enhancement. Working with a couple to facilitate sexual enhancement requires an examination of the entire dyadic relationship, with a major emphasis on issues of intimacy.

The purpose of this chapter is to offer the counseling professional information on how to enhance the sexual relationship of couples. Specific emphasis will be placed on couple interactions and how such interactions affect the couple's intimate relationship. A major focus will be on systemic interventions designed to increase the level of intimacy experienced by the couple. The systemic interventions will address what can be done *within the therapeutic hour*, not tasks assigned as homework.

Our use of therapeutic techniques to enhance a couple's sexual relationship has primarily emerged from the field of sex and marital therapy. Masters and Johnson (1970), LoPiccolo and LoPiccolo (1970), and Kaplan (1974) all espouse a combination of dynamic explorations and behavioral approaches for the resolution of specific sexual dysfunctions and the general improvement of sexual functioning. However, the enhancement of the sexual relationship needs to encompass far more than traditional sex therapy techniques. If growth beyond improved sexual performance into genuinely enhanced sexual intimacy is to be fostered, the couple must be enabled to explore their entire relationship. To facilitate this growth, the therapist must be able to demonstrate and utilize a solid background in marital and family theory and therapy. The clinician needs skills in working with the dyad as a separate subsystem of the entire family system, and in promoting change within the therapeutic hour. The fears and consequent resistance couples feel and experience in approaching their sexual relationship require the perspectives, attention, support, and confrontations of a marital therapist as well as those of the sex therapist. A traditional sex therapist, untrained in these other areas, will work with behaviors and confront resistance only as the couple is unable to accomplish the behavioral task. A marital therapist would work with the same behaviors and couple resistance but also the structure, communication, and family of origin of each partner throughout the therapy to facilitate truly integrated sexual enhancement.

FACTORS CONTRIBUTING TO
PROBLEMS WITH SEXUAL ENHANCEMENT

Although a great deal has been written on enhancing sexual performance (McCarthy, Ryan, & Johnson, 1975; Zilbergeld, 1978; Barbach, 1975), less is available on the broader topic of enhancing the total sexual relationship, including performance along with attitudes, expectations, myths, and general emotional closeness or intimacy. For many people, the early learnings in these latter areas were quite unsatisfactory. At a recent sexual enrichment program, the following question was asked: "What was taught about the sexual relationship in your early years?" Participant responses fell into three general areas. First, the secretiveness surrounding sexual material was shared. Sexuality was not necessarily presented as good or bad; it simply was not discussed. The nonverbal family message was "At the appropriate time, you will pick the right person and sexuality will be natural and wonderful." Second, the group described education on sexual relationships as being fraught with misinformation. Sexual ignorance was the current concern of those couples who felt that something was wrong but did not know exactly what. Third, sexual trauma in early relationships was noted. One participant shared a story of incest; however, the trauma for most individuals and couples concerned body image and social acceptance. Traumatized by being labeled by themselves or others as being too small, too fat, or too unpopular, individuals discovered that sexual relationships became an early source of fear and insecurity. However, the unspoken expectation was that even though sexual information was scarce, and often associated with ignorance or trauma, sexual relationships in later life would eventually be satisfying and fulfilling. Of course, for some couples this expectation goes unfulfilled, and at some point in their relationship they confront the fact that, with regard to sexuality, they are unfulfilled and dissatisfied (Frank, Anderson, & Rubinstein, 1978).

The lack of clearly expressed and agreed-upon norms and definitions of what constitutes a "healthy" sexual relationship has also been a block for many couples who are attempting to enhance their sexual relationship. What feels natural to one partner may be quite distressing to the other. They simply have not experienced sexual "health," which Maddock (1977) defines as:

> 1. The conviction that one's personal and social behaviors are congruent with one's gender identity, and a sense of comfort with one's sex-role behaviors;
> 2. The ability to carry on effective interpersonal relationships with members of both sexes, including the capacity for love and long term commitment;
> 3. The capacity to respond to erotic stimulation in such a way as to make sexual activity a positive and pleasurable aspect of one's experience;
> 4. The judgement necessary to make rewarding decisions about one's sexual behavior which are consistent with one's over-all value system and belief about life (p. 355).

What is often lacking are the relationship components needed to enhance sexual expression. Two of these components are particularly salient preconditions for effective sexual relations: differentiation and social development.

Adequate sexual functioning is in part determined by the level of differentiation attained by each partner. Differentiation is the intellectual and emotional separation of an individual from the family of origin as well as the society in general. It is the degree of individuality one has vis-à-vis others, defined by a continuum of, for example, "symbiosis, sameness, similarity, differentness, and oppositeness" (L'Abate & Frey, 1983, p. 125). Differentiation and identity formation happen concurrently. Differentiation determines the individual's ability to become committed to a loving partner while maintaining a sense of self at the same time. If identity formation is immature, the invasiveness of a visiting family, or the intimacy needs of a partner, can result in regression and defensiveness. Generally, the level of differentiation attained by an individual with parents will be enacted repetitively with a spouse (Bowen, 1974).

In many clients, the level of differentiation from the parents is quite poor. Indications of this are evident when a person describes one or both parents in superlatives, as being very powerful, all-consuming, all good, or all bad. If parents still hold such inordinate power over their 25-to-60-year-old "child," then differentiation is a difficulty. For instance, the "child" might have trouble with the right to make choices. This dynamic will then manifest itself directly in a committed sexual relationship. Partners will describe sexual power struggles, feelings of being controlled, and claustrophobic feelings as symptoms of a fear of loss of self. It is difficult for an undifferentiated partner to feel fully sexual toward a significant other who carries the perceived power or intrusive qualities of a parent.

For example, a wife asks her husband to change the color of his tie. Instead of responding "yes" or "no," the husband reacts resistantly, as would a teenager to a parent. He says, "Get off my back!" or "Mind your own business!" Similarly, the husband is unable to respond to his mother's "suggestions" and "advice" without some sort of regressive behavior. The poor level of differentiation that exists between the husband and his mother is acted out in parallel fashion with his wife, decreasing any real possibility for intimacy.

Effective sexual relationships are also strongly determined by the level of social development achieved by the couple, including communication skills and intimacy. Sexual closeness, as distinguished from other forms of intimacy, can be accomplished with little personal growth. That is, intercourse can be performed in a mechanical manner, with little feeling, meaning, or vulnerability. However, the process of sexual enhancement, as defined here, includes sexual intimacy as only one of a number of intimacies that need to be developed by the couple. Others include emotional intimacy, intellectual intimacy, aesthetic intimacy, creative intimacy, commitment intimacy, communication intimacy, and spiritual intimacy (Clinebell & Clinebell, 1970; Hof & Miller, 1981). Each form of intimacy is important to the healthy sexual relationship. In 1975 the World Health Organization described "sexual health" as "the integration of the somatic, emotional, intellectual, and social aspects of sexual being, in ways that are positively enriching and that enhance personality, communication and love. This concept requires sexual information and the right to consider sexuality for pleasure as well as for procreation" (D'Augelli & D'Augelli, 1981, p. 171). Effective differentiation and the development of a variety of intimacy skills contribute greatly to enhancement of the sexual relationship and the expression of sexual health.

PROMOTING SEXUAL HEALTH WITHIN THE THERAPEUTIC HOUR

In order for the clinician to work effectively with clients who want to enhance their sexual relationship, several criteria need to be met. First, the therapist must have integrated a wide variety of theoretical approaches and techniques. This is required because each of the schools of psychological and relational theory contributes to the understanding needed for couples to find enhanced sexual satisfaction. The individual schools provide a focus on identity issues, areas of repression, and early introjects which are likely to be projected onto a partner. Schools emphasizing family of origin stress differentiation and understanding of sexual legacies and loyalties. Structural schools emphasize the boundaries necessary for two individuals to be able to share their sexual selves in the midst of complex and complicated families. The communication and behavioral schools focus on practical skills needed by one person to share intimately with another. Without a thorough and broad eclectic base, the therapist lacks sufficient diversity to respond to the complex interactions and issues of couples presenting with concerns in the area of sexual enhancement.

Equally important as a multitheoretical approach is the skill of the therapist to think in terms of process as well as the content of a couple's conversations and relationship. Historically, treatment for sexual enhancement has strongly emphasized the content that a couple presents. This includes facts, dates, information, and stories related to the specific sexual problem(s) or dysfunction(s) that the couple or the therapist deems important. A process-oriented therapist, in addition to listening to and addressing content, needs to be extremely sensitive to the process issues, such as reciprocity, resistance, fear, collusion, and patterns of response, which may facilitate or hinder the couple in achieving their desired goals.

Many current process issues have roots in the couple's social learning (Bandura, 1969). Patterns that individuals learned, watched, modeled, rehearsed, and had reinforced in their formative years are often repeated in their adult relationships. Couples who have difficulty with intimacy will often report that they watched little intimate behavior between their parents. Lack of touching, outward signs of affection, and intimate conversation frequently characterized those relationships. In terms of the parent-child relationship, the general patterns were twofold: either one or both parents were too smothering of the child or were too distant and removed. Both processes affect and continue to affect the child's ability to be intimate with another person as an adult. Working to understand, modify, and resolve the negative impact of early learned patterns with the individual and his or her parent(s) is often very important in effecting change within the couple. Besides the work with the family of origin, addressing these patterns as they are reflected within the relationship of the couple, in the therapeutic hour, can yield significant insights for the couple and opportunities for intervention by the therapist, leading to the enhancement of the sexual relationship.

In-Session Process Considerations for the Therapist

The therapist must be keenly aware of certain specific process considerations as he or she works with the couple to achieve their objectives. These process considerations include the following: (1) the "intimacy dance"; (2) the general "balance" within the dyad; (3) the presence/absence of the "equal-partner" relationship; (4) the acceptance of personal responsibility for sexual happiness; (5) increasing responsivity, decreasing reactivity; (6) developing an appropriate level of affect between partners; and (7) attending to the nonverbal communications.

I. The "Intimacy Dance"

The "intimacy dance" is a metaphor for the means by which each member of a couple maintains a safe distance from the other, protecting his own and often his partner's vulnerabilities. Often, as one partner steps toward the other partner, the other partner collusively steps back. For example, a couple complained to a therapist that their sexual relationship had been unsatisfactory for nine years. During the first four years, the woman pursued her husband and he withdrew. During the last five years, the husband played the pursuer role and his wife rejected him. Dynamics of both rejection and intrusion (Napier, 1978) were manifested by the partners of the maintenance of a "safe" distance in the relationship. If the therapist does not comprehend this "intimacy dance," one partner will appear to be sexually dysfunctional and the other sexually adjusted, when, in actuality, both individuals of the dyad are exquisitely working together to maintain distance and protect each person.

The content of each session can be given far too much attention if the couple's "intimacy dance" is not understood. An example was when a couple who had been in therapy for several months came into a session feeling argumentative and hopeless. The session was particularly unsatisfactory for everyone. The therapist became exasperated and was confused, because during the previous session the couple demonstrated considerable warmth and intimacy. The therapist failed to realize that the couple's argument and hopelessness were "dance" steps to balance more vulnerable feelings of intimacy and emotional closeness that were felt during the previous week. The "intimacy dance" of this couple protected the relationship homeostasis, the tendency toward maintenance of balances within a dyad to keep a certain established equilibrium in the relationship (Jackson, 1957).

The intimacy dance is designed to avoid greater intimacy. Fear of intimacy can include fear of hurt, abandonment, rejection, intrusion, and loss of self. These fears can be increased or decreased based on the level of differentiation attained by each individual. A poorly differentiated person will often feel more susceptible to being overwhelmed. The "intimacy dance" can be comprised of sometimes obvious or, more often, subtle steps established for the maintenance of a protective shield for the individual and the couple, such as the following dances illustrate.

Dance 1. John and Susan have been married for seven years. John's mother is able to intrude into their married life in various ways and he cannot or will not stop the intrusion. In part, he fears confronting his mother because she will withdraw, as she has historically, and he will consequently feel guilty. John complains that Susan invades in the same way. Susan is secretly questioning her own femininity and helps to create an environment in which femininity or vulnerability never need to be addressed. She fears that if she were not in control, she would not be loved. Both partners have colluded in a "dance" to remain separate and to limit the threats of intimacy.

Step 1	John comes home from work and goes directly to the mail. Susan comes home from work and begins to make dinner.
Step 2	They begin to recount the day. If there is any sense that one might want to be close to the other, a fight starts. Susan says, "I am really glad you are home." John responds, "Why isn't dinner ready?"
Step 3	After dinner John does the dishes and Susan leaves the kitchen.
Step 4	Both watch TV in the evening but do not like the same shows. They watch in two separate rooms.
Step 5	John goes to bed earlier than Susan, and when she comes to bed, she undresses in the bathroom.
Step 6	They give each other an habitual kiss and go to sleep.

This dance is for the purpose of avoiding being close and vulnerable to each other. Sexual expression is limited and thus feelings of rejection and hurt are masked. The dance is designed with complex steps to limit intimacy. Sensitivity to this dance will allow the therapist to be balanced in approaching and supporting both, while confronting their fears. Each partner will need the help of the therapist to support the partner's movement, because homeostatic principles suggest neither individual will be able to initially support the other's growth and will often attempt to undermine it.

Dance 2. The Smiths are going on a week-long vacation. Their normal means of avoiding sexual expression, such as staying on the telephone, bringing office work home, doing individual chores around the house and yard, or concentrating on the children, will no longer be available.

Step 1	The vacation is planned, and romantic interludes and quiet time are fantasized by both partners.
Step 2	On the day they are to leave, one partner fuels a confrontation that leads into a severe argument.
Step 3	Both partners threaten not to go on the vacation, but they do.
Step 4	The argument lasts until Friday noon when the couple make up just in time to pack for the trip home.

Intimacy was frightening enough that both partners used anger and confrontation to maintain an adequate distance and safety zone. In this case, the parents of both partners provided little modeling for an intimate relationship. The parental dynamics were that each took turns dominating the other with little physical demonstration of caring. Because the vacation was ostensibly a time for physical and emotional intimacy, their fears of intimacy became predominant.

Dance 3. Alice and Mark are both very dissatisfied with their sexual relationship. Mark constantly pursues Alice, asking for holding, intimate conversation, and sexual intercourse. Alice resists all of Mark's advances. The consequence is that Mark consistently experiences feelings of rejection and Alice has feelings of being intruded upon.

Step 1   Mark chose Alice for his spouse unconsciously knowing that she was sexually inhibited and fearful.

Step 2   He then opened his arms to Alice, desiring intense intimacy at every turn.

Step 3   Because his wife was fearful of sexual intimacy in the first place, the invitations for intimate expression were/are threatening. His open arms cause hers to close.

Step 4   Mark solidifies the dance by continually having his arms open wide, enabling Alice to consistently withdraw and defend herself.

Step 5   Mark chooses a therapist who would be inducted into thinking that he was open and Alice had the sexual problems.

This dance fits Napier's (1978) classic description of a "rejection-intrusion" pattern. It appears that one partner is devoid of sexual interest and seeks to avoid engulfment and intimacy, while the other partner appears open to, desirous of, and actively pursuing sexual intimacy. In actuality, both partners are fearful of being close to the other and both fear rejection. Although their behaviors appear to be for different purposes, the outcome is the same, and the key dynamic for the therapist to watch is the avoidance of intimacy.

It is apparent from this perspective that the therapist working to enhance sexual relationships must be process-oriented and perceive these elaborate dances in which couples are involved. Most couples have perfected some dance that is uniquely their own, and it is the role of the therapist to learn the steps, anticipate the turns, and confront the process within the therapeutic hour. The couple's dance will have evolved out of a lack of personal differentiation and insufficient social skills, which in turn heighten fears of intimacy. This dance will serve to protect each person from the vulnerability needed in effective sexual expression. As noted above, if the therapist is unaware of the dance, the content of any given session can be allowed too much priority.

II. The General Balance Within the Dyad

Balance is a concept widely discussed in dyadic therapies. The construct generally refers to the amount of emphasis placed by the therapist on one partner in comparison with the other. This emphasis could be in the form of time, attention, or attribution of responsibility. Balance also refers to the dynamics between a couple. For instance, does each individual invest in the session, participate actively, and accept part of the responsibility for growth and change?

A major problem in sexual enhancement is the lack of, or loss of, balance. Intimacy can be threatened by one partner doing all of the initiating or all of the withdrawing. One partner could be significantly more committed to the relationship than the other, or more vulnerable. One person talking too much or too little can undermine effective communication. If any of these are the case, the effectiveness of the sexual relationship can be compromised, as can the therapeutic process. The role of the therapist is to pay strict attention to the issue of balance in the process of the therapeutic hour and facilitate the development of mutual responsibility, sharing, and initiation, which will enhance the development of an equitable, balanced relationship. For example, a woman dominated a session by explaining about her lack of desire for sexual intimacy. The therapist felt this to be valuable material to work with, and did so for several sessions while the husband passively watched. When the therapist was inducted into only listening to the wife, the lack of responsibility taken by the husband was overlooked. In actuality, the husband had been consistently angry and hostile toward his wife, greatly contributing to their overall sexual problems.

III. The Presence/Absence of an "Equal-Partner" Relationship

One assumption the author makes is that in an effective sexual relationship both partners need to approach "equal-partner" behavior. An equal partner is one who "tends towards independence; is cooperative and interdependent with mate; is more active than passive; is capable of close, sustained intimacy without clinging; has no great fear of abandonment; and, has a well developed and defined style but also respects mate's" (Sager & Hunt, 1979, p. 13). If one individual plays the role of parental partner, as a mother or a father or a superior person, and the other a child or inferior person, sexual desire can be negatively affected (Kaplan, 1979). The therapist needs to be sensitized to the language used by one partner to position himself or herself above, below, or apart from the other. Consider the following statements, which represent an unequal balance of power in the relationship:

Parental statements	Childlike statements
• "I've been trying to tell you this." (critical tone)	• "I'm not sure this is right, but . . ." (meekly)
• "How many times do I have to tell you this?"	• "I promise to try harder next time."
• "Should I spell it out for you?"	• "I know you know better than I, but . . . "

The sexual relationship could be affected quite negatively by such superior or inferior positioning.

In a similar manner, the relational intimacy possible in a therapeutic session is in part governed by the language of the therapist. If the therapist needs to talk down to a client or react in an inferior or defensive manner, the relationship and change possibilities will be limited.

IV. The Acceptance of Personal Responsibility for Sexual Happiness

Unfortunately, many people believe that the sexual problems being experienced in their relationship are caused totally by their partner. This belies the fact that responsibility for sexual happiness needs to rest on each individual. The use of personal power, defined here as the ability to change one's own behavior not dependent on the behavior of anyone else, is a core aspect of this issue of personal responsibility. A person has power to effect change within himself but little power to force another to grow. Many couples feel quite powerless for this reason, seeing themselves as being unable to influence the other person to change. Such people often come to therapy after months of trying in powerless ways to get their partners to change or grow. The therapist needs to encourage the belief in, and effective use of, each person's power.

Sexual enhancement requires effective use of personal power, which necessitates a balance between self-understanding and feedback to one's partner. Some reflection and objectivity are necessary for a couple to be in a posture to grow. One role of the therapist is to monitor where each partner's energy is directed. For instance, is a man attempting to change his partner's mind and convince her why she is wrong, or point out where she is to blame? Such blaming and judgment are defined here as powerless and can only lead to feelings of defensiveness and anger within the partner, or to coerced change which is not really the basis for continuing and shared intimacy. Sexually skilled couples working toward intimacy are able, perhaps with the help of a therapist, to reflect on their own functioning and responsibility as individuals and then to communicate "powerfully" wants, needs, and desires to the partner. Dialogue between such a couple would start with phrases such as "I realize that . . . " or "I know that I have contributed to the problem by . . . ."

V. Increasing Responsivity, Decreasing Reactivity

The act of being responsive means maintaining a balance between one's intellect and emotion for the purpose of building a more productive and satisfying relationship (see Hof, Chapter 1, this volume; Egan, 1970; L'Abate & Frey, 1983). Dynamically, such balance gives one's partner permission to express fears, hurts, needs, etc. A person who responds will inquire, share feelings nonjudgmentally, and encourage elaboration. A reaction, a defensive posture designed to protect the self by attacking the other, limits the freedom of a partner to express feelings and needs. Reactions contribute greatly to the loss of the balance of intellect and emotion, contributing to exchanges becoming mostly emotional and defensive posturing. In intimate communication a speaker must share both intellect and emotion directly, using "I" statements, followed by a feeling or a thought, sensitively and empathetically demonstrating a desire to be understood and to understand. A responder needs to demonstrate the ability to listen accurately and empathetically by reflecting back what was heard, asking appropriate questions, and not contradicting or giving an opinion prematurely. The responder being too emotional, with either hysterical crying or anger bordering on rage, or too intellectual, with no sign of affect or empathy, is often the reason that the person sharing a feeling will feel misunderstood.

The following are examples of reacting and responding between partners:

1. Person A: "I really felt hurt by what you did."
   Person B: "You hurt me worse." (reaction)
   "How did I hurt you?" (response)
2. Person A: "I really hate you sometimes."
   Person B: "I really dislike you also." (reaction)
   "What do you hate about me?" (response)
3. Person A: "I would like to be hugged this way."
   Person B: "You never hug me." (reaction)
   "You mean like this?" (response)

Sexuality will rarely be enhanced if a couple is reacting too frequently to each other. Reaction, for the most part, blocks the ability to listen. Neither partner, therefore, feels understood or appreciated. A reactive couple is enmeshed, undifferentiated, and diffuse. The therapist's task is to confront reactivity, encourage support, and teach responsivity.

VI. Developing an Appropriate Level of Affect Between Partners

Sexual enhancement will be negatively affected with both too little or too much emotional intensity. The verbal intensity needs to be perceived as demonstrating both genuine interest and respect for a person's integrity. In general, anger and aggressive tones of voice show neither. If sexual intimacy is requested aggressively, a partner will most likely withdraw, feeling attacked or vulnerable. If the affect is too emotional, as in "I can't live without you!" or "Why can't you just love me!!" the listener will similarly be repelled. The therapist needs to teach clients how to communicate with a level of affective intensity that can be advantageous to building intimacy.

Some couples show so little affect that emotional bonding is very difficult. However, this type of disengaged dyad, a "rational partner with a rational partner" (Sager & Hunt, 1979), is less likely to enter therapy. A more likely type of couple to enter therapy is one that communicates with such intensity that each partner constantly feels either rejected or invaded, as is often the case with "childlike and childlike" partnerships (Sager & Hunt, 1979).

Communication training can be an important intervention in this situation. When a client asks angrily, "Where have you been?" the therapist can help the client restate and reframe the question into an "I" statement such as "I worry when you are gone." The latter "I" statement communicates the actual feeling of the client, one that perhaps he or she felt too vulnerable to say. Needless to say, the working through of family-of-origin issues, which frequently block the learning and use of more effective communication skills in the present, frequently must precede such communication skills training. On the other hand, the learning of communication skills and receiving the here-and-now benefits may highlight prior deficits in social learning and make it more possible for the couple to do the needed family-of-origin work.

VII. Attending to the Nonverbal Communication

The therapist needs to address many of the nonverbal communications that can affect sexual relations. Often these communications are symbolic representations of each partner's intrapersonal process. Folded arms and legs, facial expressions, and positions of the body are obvious considerations. Less obvious ones might be subtle movement of the chairs (e.g., forward or backward) or types of clothing worn (e.g., inhibiting, seductive, etc.). In one sexually dysfunctional couple, the wife expressed that she felt she had no space or personal integrity in the relationship. During each session, her partner would move the chair four or five inches closer to her as he sat down; she would then move back. This was a metaphor for their entire relationship. Nonverbal communication that is made conscious can often release some of the blocks to sexual feeling.

Awareness of the role of touch is also important. Does the couple touch each other during, before, or after the session, and with what sensitivity? How sensual is each individual? Does the client's clothing suggest an openness and vulnerability, or the opposite? Equally important as the therapist's assessment of the nonverbal behavior is the manner in which each partner interprets the communication of the other. The therapist's role is to ascertain what meanings each individual draws from the nonverbal messages. This is done by asking each client, for example, "What does this behavior mean to you?" "What do you think that your partner is trying to say?" "How do you interpret this message?"

In-Session Techniques for Sexual Enhancement

Therapists utilize a number of techniques to enhance a couple's sexual expression and improve the overall relationship. Social learning approaches can contribute greatly to breaking negative patterns of reciprocity, which tend to become more fixed over time. The major premise is that most behaviors in a sexual relationship have been learned socially and can therefore be unlearned and replaced with new ways of relating. The "caring days" (Stuart, 1980) ritual, for instance, requires that a couple spend time thinking positively about their partners and demonstrating affection and respect through small, nonthreatening, specific, positive behavioral expressions. Such an experience can often interrupt a negative reaction cycle and begin, in its place, a more positive and responsive interaction.

Although much has been written about homework assignments (e.g., Zilbergeld, 1978; Stuart, 1980; Barbach, 1975) to alleviate sexual problems, much less emphasis has been placed on in-session techniques. Yet, a great deal of the therapist's power to influence change can be directly expressed within the therapy session, where a couple's vulnerabilities and resistances, collusion and homeostatic balance can be monitored, supported, and confronted as needed. Relying on a couple's reporting on the process and effects of doing a homework task can be highly inaccurate and misleading for the therapist. Asking couples to demonstrate their skills and share their needs, concerns, and feelings within the therapeutic hour is far more revealing of the couple and may provide more reliable data for the therapist. This enables the therapist and couple to then make much more efficient use of time, data, and resources in treatment planning and facilitating change.

Several in-session techniques that the author has found to be extremely helpful in working with couples to enhance their sexual relationship are described under the following four major headings: (1) the use of language to lower anxiety; (2) modifying cognitions to increase sexual enhancement; (3) sharing emotion to build intimacy; and (4) the use of touch and eye contact in building intimacy.

I. The Use of Language to Lower Anxiety and Increase Intimacy

Anxiety is a major etiological factor in sexual dysfunctions as well as in blocks to sexual and relational intimacy. The sexual secretiveness, ignorance, and trauma that many individuals and couples have experienced throughout their lives make communicating about sex without anxiety extremely difficult. This lack of open, comfortable, and anxiety-free communication leaves room for exaggerations, misinterpretations, and generalized fear. The following language tasks are used for the purpose of lowering anxiety and increasing comfort levels with discussion/communication of sexual material.

The Greek chorus. One of the difficulties in communicating on sexual topics is that many sexual words are rarely used or found acceptable for use in the course of everyday conversation. Consequently, sexual words are often charged with undue emotional energy and can produce awkwardness and anxiety. In Greek drama, a chorus often echoed the words of an actor on stage. In a similar manner, clients might repeat after the therapist, saying words such as intercourse, penis, vagina, masturbation, etc. The Greek chorus can have the effect of lowering the emotional charge often given to sexual words by clients and diminish their anxiety.

After the clients repeat the sexual words out loud, the therapist should ask them to process the feelings and thoughts that rose out of the experience. Besides the benefit of lowering anxiety for the couple, the repeating of the sexual words often lowers the anxiety between the clients and the therapist, affording the couple increased permission to present sexual concerns in the session.

Creating a sexual language. One of the difficulties in communicating about sex and sexual intimacy is the lack of a widely agreed-upon language to use. The therapist can discuss with the clients the difficulty in finding an appropriate language for sex. Sexual language generally falls into three categories:

1. Clinical language includes words such as clitoris, scrotum, sexual intercourse, fellatio, etc. Clinical words are often difficult to use in relationships because of the lack of emotional warmth they convey. A partner saying "I want to have sexual intercourse with you" can lose some emotional

depth in conveying the desire for sexual intimacy, especially if the partner views such expressions as "cold" or "clinical."

2. Street language includes all of the words mostly seen in graffiti. Fuck, screw, balls, tits, etc., are examples. It is clear that street language is inadequate to describe the breadth of sexual expression, especially since the same words are so frequently used to express hostility, berate another person, or are part of a "dirty" or "obscene" joke. "I want to screw/fuck you" is a statement/request that may lack the sincerity and emotional connection of a mature sexual relationship desired by the partner. Such language, however, although degrading to some, is exciting to others.

3. Colloquial language is the closest accommodation to the sensitivities of a wide range of people. "Sleep with," "make love to," "be with," and "caress" are phrases that are widely used. The difficulty is that this language is highly inaccurate and ambiguous.

After explaining each category to the couple, the therapist can encourage the clients to discuss words in each of these categories, the process of which can, in itself, have a calming effect. In so doing, the therapist can develop with clients the language they would be most comfortable using within the session and to be generalized for use between the couple at home.

The written word. Besides the verbalization of sexual words by the couple, writing the words down, especially in front of the therapist, can be helpful in surfacing emotions and lowering anxiety. This exercise would be a natural conclusion to the first two. After the therapist lists clinical words such as penis, vagina, intercourse, breasts, heterosexuality, homosexuality, oral-genital sex, masturbation, etc., as headings on separate sheets of paper, he or she can ask the clients to list all of the clinical, street, and colloquial terms they can imagine and have the clients print them under each heading.

Through the implosion of the written word, and its subsequent discussion, anxiety will often rise and then fall, allowing for more humor and more natural affect to preside. Hopefully, the clients will begin to realize that sexual words should not be credited with the kind of anxiety and power often attributed to them. Having clients process their feelings after the exercise with the therapist is especially important to increase comfort within the session and integration of the sexual material.

II. Modifying Cognitions to Increase Sexual Enhancement

The next three interventions deal with the thought processes of the clients. Because thoughts can be the precursors to feelings (Ellis & Harper, 1975; Burns, 1985), it is important that they be able to be articulated and discussed. Cognitive distortions and conceptual misunderstandings are often considerable factors in the breakdown of sexual enhancement (see Chapter 1 for a more detailed discussion of cognitive distortions).

Cognitive distortions. There is perhaps no area in human relationships fraught with more cognitive distortions than the area of human sexuality. Some of the distortions are individual. "I'm not attractive," "He doesn't love me," and "She will reject me" are examples of cognitive distortions that elicit feelings of rejection and may limit sexual expression.

1. A helpful exercise would involve the therapist explaining the concept of cognitive distortions to the couple and then encouraging and enabling them to be aware of the distortions they each apply to themselves. As each person identifies and shares his/her distortions with the partner, the opportunity for cognitive correction, empathetic support, and encouragement between partners usually increases dramatically.

Other cognitive distortions are more interpersonal in nature. Because of the tendency to utilize cognitive distortions, and a general lack of communication skills, many partners misinterpret remarks made by their spouses. They are unable to discover what each actually hoped and intended to communicate, and thus frequently respond defensively. For example, John asks Mary, "Would you like to make love?" The therapist thinks that this is a thoughtful and reasonable request, but holds this thought and asks Mary, "How do you interpret this request?" Mary says, "It means that if I don't make love, he will withdraw and abandon me." She feels hurt and defensive.

2. The therapist can intervene in this process by requiring each partner to discover exactly what the other means by asking for further clarification and explanation. Instead of following through with an initial reaction to a statement by the partner, the hearer is encouraged to *respond* by inquiring about the genuine, and hopefully positive, *intention* in the partner's communication. This structured process can help reduce and limit defensive reactions and increase positive communication processes, a necessary prerequisite to integrated sexual enhancement. In the former example, Mary became able to hear John's request as a positive statement, and John realized the extent of Mary's fears of abandonment.

Another couple found out that on many nights they both wanted to make love, but never quite connected. When the interpretations were traced, the following is what each privately had concluded, unbeknown to the other:

- If dinner was not ready when he came home, he concluded that she did not want to make love.
- If he wore pajamas, she concluded that he was not interested in sex.

- If she brushed her teeth in the morning, he concluded that she wanted to make love.
- If at 6:00 P.M. she said, "I'm tired from a long day," he concluded that she did not want to make love at 11:00 P.M.!

Clarification of these distortions led to more frequent and direct expressions of sexual intimacy between them.

In summary, the therapist needs to ask every couple to explore interpretations of their daily behaviors that might be significantly affecting their sexual intimacy. As these interpretations are expressed within the session, the therapist's role is to first question whether there are possible distortions present. Second, the couple needs to be taught to clarify intentions and meanings. Third, each partner may need help discovering where the interpretation originated. The cognitive distortions that will be revealed often have roots in the family of origin.

Demythologizing. Couples with poor sexual skills often relate out of myths, both individual and societal, about what the partner enjoys and what constitutes really "good" sex. Many such myths can be destructive to the relationships. One role of the therapist is to ask the couple to make these myths explicit in the session. Requesting each partner to respond to open-ended statements such as the following can help the couple to demythologize aspects of their sexual relationship: Really good sex is . . . I am especially satisfied when . . . A good sex partner would . . . In finishing these sentences, clients can begin to work with their inner mythology and expectations. Differentiation between what society portrays as "reality" and what each individual actually enjoys and desires is almost always helpful.

Limiting the negative/focusing on the positive. One difficulty for many people in intimate relationships is the inability to focus on positive sexual thoughts or the positive attributes of one's partner, or to block out negative thoughts. In order for feelings of love and caring to be expressed and received openly, positive thoughts and feelings must be able to be focused on and negative thoughts and feelings must be able to be put into perspective. If a husband says, "I love you and respect you, but hate the way you make love," the negative cognition will tend to be weighted more heavily than the positive expressions in many couples. In relationships, one negative thought can easily be given more power than all the positive thoughts and expressions. The following exercise in focusing can help clients focus on the positive aspects of their relationship and gain some control over negative thoughts which may become reasons or excuses for distancing.

The therapist asks the couple to shut their eyes for a moment and sit back in their chairs. Then he or she says: "Become aware of your breathing. Breathe in slowly and deeply; hold it, and now exhale. Think for a moment about your partner, about a wonderful time you spent together. Put yourself in that time and at that place. Remember the positive feelings. Nod your head when you have placed yourself in that memory. Remember what you were thinking and say those things to yourself now. [Wait for both to nod.] Now think of a time when you were angry at your partner. Put yourself in that time and place. Remember the negative thoughts and feelings. Nod your head when you have placed yourself in that memory. [Wait for both to nod.] Now return to the pleasant experience. Nod when you have recaptured it." The couple repeats this experience, going from positive to negative to positive, etc. The exercise is then processed, with an emphasis on the importance of limiting the negative thoughts and focusing on the positives.

III. Sharing Emotion to Build Intimacy

Emotions such as love, hate, joy, fear, hope, and anxiety, to name just a few, bind people together. Although at the surface it seems contradictory, negative emotions such as hate bring people closer together, albeit in a destructive way. If you hate someone, you will spend considerable energy thinking about or staying away from that person, as in the case of emotional cutoff in families. The effective use of emotion is a *sine qua non* of intimacy and enhanced sexual expression. The following exercises are designed to help each individual of a dyad develop emotional expression. Again, the emphasis is on the therapeutic hour, not on homework assignments.

An emotional list. Have the clients list 30 or more feelings. They often are able to identify the secondary feeling of anger, but do not address the primary feelings of abandonment and hurt. Once the clients list these feelings, having them refer to the list often saying, "I feel . . . ," followed by one of the words on the list, will increase the intimacy of the session. Practice in sharing feelings can serve to strengthen emotional bonding and sexual intimacy.

Emotional levels. Most couples, as one aspect of their intimacy dance, have learned to speak to one another on a rather superficial emotional level. Although this idea is abstract, clients can readily understand the meaning of an emotional level if examples are given. Varying affect, voice tone, and word choice can connote differing levels of emotional depth. In order to do this exercise, a couple needs the ability to first recognize and label their feelings. Second, a couple needs to give each other permission to express these feelings. Permission is usually granted by the type of response given by the partner who is listening to the feeling. If the partner is attentive and empathetic, deeper emotional levels can be communicated. If the partner withdraws, changes the subject, criticizes the feeling, or gets angry, deeper emotional levels will be difficult to attain.

Each couple is encouraged to develop and share a verbal hierarchy, moving from superficial to deeper, more intense communication with his/her partner. For example, the wife might make the following five statements as her hierarchy:

1. "Hi."
2. "How are you?"
3. "It is very nice to see you."
4. "I was hoping we could get together."
5. "I've missed you."

Her partner might then share a very different hierarchy. For example,

1. "You are late."
2. "Where have you been?"
3. "I was getting nervous; where have you been?"
4. "I worry when you are late."
5. "I missed you; I'm glad you're okay."

Examples such as these, with appropriate affect, suggest a hierarchy of emotional levels that a couple can become aware of and utilize. The more a capacity is developed to speak at the deeper levels, the more depth of emotion can be part of the relationship. Often, a person feels at a deep level but fears of intimacy or rejection contribute to the person talking on a more intellectual plane. "I missed you" becomes "Where have you been?" The therapist needs to be able to recognize the possibilities for deeper levels of emotional speech, teach couples how to communicate at the varying levels, and encourage clients to risk using them, especially the deeper levels.

The use of the present tense. In the therapeutic hour, as well as at home, a couple with intimacy difficulties will try to avoid talking in the present tense. If permitted, couples will spend hours talking to the therapist about events of the week, instead of sharing the present thoughts and feelings about those events. If the therapist is content oriented, he or she will get inducted into recalling past events as part of a dance that avoids the potential intimacy of the moment. It is more difficult for a client to learn to share "I feel hurt now" than to say, "Three weeks ago you hurt me." The first statement is vulnerable and the second is safer and more distant from the feeling. Sexual enhancement within a therapeutic session is best done in the present tense!

The role of the therapist in this exercise is to stop the couple's communication every time they attempt to relate present emotions in the past tense, as if they don't feel them anymore. It is often helpful to the couple for the therapist to ask, "Do you feel these feelings now?" If the answer is "yes," the therapist should ask them to use the present tense, "I feel . . . ." If the answer is "no," the therapist should ask the couple to pick another topic in which the feelings are more presently available.

Pronouns and feelings. Fears of intimacy affecting sexual skills can manifest themselves in pronoun usage. The words "I feel" followed by a feeling are likely to be self-revealing and sexually enhancing. For example, "I feel close to you" and "I feel hurt" are relatively vulnerable things to say. However, the phrase "I feel that you . . ." is going to be followed by a statement, thought, or judgment and will probably serve to distance the partner, as, for example, "I feel that you don't care for me." In reality this statement is a judgment, not a direct statement of the individual's feelings. As in all communication, the use of "I" messages is a key for developing and maintaining intimate relationships. The therapist should be especially aware of the client's use of the pronouns him, her, he, she, we, and us. These pronouns are often used unconsciously to create distance and decrease vulnerability. Asking the clients to change these pronouns to "I" messages, followed by a feeling, will deepen the emotional tone of the session.

Balance of emotion and intellect. The differentiated individual in a marriage has a balance of emotional and intellectual expression. On the surface, it might seem that the emotional person has a greater capacity for intimacy than the intellectual partner. This is rarely the case. Unboundaried emotion functions in a similar manner to exclusively intellectual expression in that it can create distance with a partner. The therapist needs to monitor the cognitive and emotional styles of both clients and work toward increased expression of the more undeveloped part and decreased expression of the overdeveloped part.

Role reversal can be a helpful technique. The therapist asks the polarized couple, one more emotional and one more intellectual, to express their needs in the style of the partner. The more intellectual partner would be asked to speak with more emotion and the more emotional partner in a more controlled and rational manner. The therapist then needs to help the couple process their feelings and further broaden their personal styles. The level of intimacy within a session can be greatly enhanced if a balance can be taught, modeled, and learned. Emotion in more hysterical form and intellect in more obsessive form both have the power to undermine all aspects of intimacy.

Congruence of emotion. Sexual intimacy can be lost if there is not some congruence of emotion with facial expression and general nonverbal communication. The words "I want to be near you" can be simply words if they are not matched with a congruent affect and facial expression. "I'm afraid of you" and "I want to understand what you are saying" are all intimate expressions which, if not paired with a sensitive and emotional tone of voice and body position, can be misunderstood, not believed, or not even heard.

For example, a male client in a monotoned voice, with folded arms and legs, said, "I need you and want you close to me." He was never heard. A female client said to her partner in an angry tone and defiant body position, "I want you to be with me!" Upon hearing the demand, the partner became more distant. Furthermore, the therapist noted in a controlled and intellectual manner that more emotion would help; consequently, the intervention was not heard.

The therapist can offer feedback to each partner regarding the congruence/incongruence of his emotional expression. Partners can also be encouraged to give each other such feedback, assuming the intention is to increase effective expression and subsequent closeness. Alternative ways of expressing emotion, so that they are perceived as being more congruent, can be discussed and practiced.

IV. The Use of Touch and Eye Contact in Building Intimacy

The concluding interventions are designed to encourage and clarify the role of touch and eye contact between partners and the possible positive and negative effects on sexual intimacy.

Touching and dialogue. The use of touch between two individuals in a therapeutic hour can be very helpful. It is common within the session, as at home, for an individual who feels threatened or frustrated to withdraw physically. In order to prevent such flight from intimacy, a therapist can suggest some form of touch. Mutual agreement by both partners is crucial so that issues of invasiveness or smothering are not overriding factors possibly creating an increased desire to withdraw. With mutual agreement, touch, combined with discussion, can be very powerful. Through touching and discussion, couples become increasingly aware of when they want to pull back and what topics or behaviors by their partners specifically threaten them.

One helpful intervention is to suggest that a couple sit close enough so that they can touch hands while having a discussion. Judgment, blame, and defensive postures are more difficult during physical contact and tend to decrease. By pointing out when each individual wants to withdraw, the therapist can help the couple be aware of areas of vulnerability and fear and hopefully help them to resolve the issues in more productive, intimacy-enhancing ways.

Eye contact. Couple eye contact can increase and decrease based on the level of comfort the couple feels with issues of intimacy. A therapist can suggest that the clients look at one another. Most clients will find this difficult and will ask questions that they know will interest the therapist or simply look at the therapist instead in order to avoid such intimacy. The therapist can look down in a way that does not diminish the level of presence felt, thus forcing the couple to become engaged in eye contact with each other again. With increased ability of the couple to maintain eye contact, there is more potential for an intimate conversation. As with touch, if the eye contact is too threatening, it is important for the therapist to discuss the feelings and issues involved with the clients.

SOME CONSIDERATIONS
REGARDING THERAPEUTIC STYLE

Many different therapeutic styles have been effective in working with couples desiring to enhance their sexual relationship. However, there are some common denominators for the therapist and therapy which are needed if more than the act of sexual performance is going to be addressed. These common denominators concern the following: (1) the anxiety level of the therapist; (2) the use of affect by the therapist; (3) the importance of a multitheoretical approach; and (4) the importance of sexual knowledge.

Anxiety Level of the Therapist

A therapist who is overanxious about sexual issues is unlikely to be able to work with a couple's sexual relationship. Most partners are already anxiety laden upon entering therapy, and the therapist's anxiety can greatly compound and heighten these feelings. Sexual language must be spoken naturally and matter of factly. Words such as penis, vagina, intercourse, masturbation, etc., should be said without an emotional charge.

If a therapist does experience such anxiety, increased supervision or his own therapy may be considered. Possibly more helpful would be enrolling in a week-end long sexual enrichment program (SEP). The SEP uses implosion, combined with group process. In this process, the anxiety of participants is raised by showing some explicit films on differing themes and discussing feelings and thoughts in small groups. After hours of being imploded with such films and participating in discussion groups, a person is often desensitized to the sexual material, and anxiety drops. The time at which the anxiety lowers is called the "point of educability." At this point, a participant often discovers a new-found ability to talk about sexual material with diminished anxiety.

Use of Affect by the Therapist

A therapist needs to relate both cognitively and affectively with clients working on sexual intimacy. Without the affective component, a therapist will intellectualize and stress ideas and the discovery of cognitive distortions, missing the affective dimensions. The feelings of the clients are what will bind them together. The emotions of the therapist can help elicit these feelings. Caring, hurt, joy, sadness, and even anger are but a few of the feelings a therapist needs to be able to communicate. Often, a therapist's caring or sadness for a couple can break negative reaction patterns. A statement such as "It saddens me the way you both hurt each other" can sometimes undermine some of the clients' anger and bring therapy to a different and more productive emotional level. A therapist who is seeking to enhance emotional intimacy for couples needs to appropriately model such intimacy for each client during each session. Understanding and confrontation need to be paired with empathy and caring for the most creative interventions.

Importance of a Multitheoretical Approach

As mentioned earlier, and stressed once again, because there are many types of intimacy, and defenses against being intimate, included in work in sexual enhancement, a therapist needs to approach sexual enhancement from a multitheoretical standpoint. A therapist who assigns a behavioral task needs to understand the underlying dynamics of the couple. If he or she does not, a behavioral task could be more harmful than productive. For example, a therapist could behaviorally encourage a husband to be more sexually assertive toward his wife without realizing the terror the wife feels owing to an incident of sexual abuse in her past. The more he reaches out to her as per the instructions of the therapist, the more she withdraws and feels threatened. Equally sensitive or ineffective approaches can be made by therapists who look only at family of origin, structure, or levels of differentiation. An integration of approaches is needed. This does not mean a scattering of superficial ideas and techniques, but a genuine eclectic approach, an integration of marital and sexual schools of thought into a style that suits the therapist's personality and the multifaceted needs of presenting couples.

Importance of Sexual Knowledge

Some therapists who attempt to work with couples in sexual enhancement are less effective because they lack basic knowledge concerning human sexuality and the sexual response cycle. Sometimes issues presented in therapy as complicated dynamics between partners have roots in lack of understanding and general ignorance on topics of human sexuality. If the therapist cannot educate the couple when necessary, the roots of these issues may never be properly addressed. In one case, a woman avoided having sexual intercourse because it simply hurt. This avoidance was interpreted by the partner as rejection, and dysfunctional dynamics ensued between the partners. Although it was important to discuss the relational dynamics, the key issue was that the woman was not lubricating sufficiently before intercourse. The use of a common lubricant, along with a lengthier time spent in foreplay, alleviated the problem. The dysfunctional dynamics were resoved quickly as sexual satisfaction increased. Many therapists can be too quick to assume that all sexual problems have intrapsychic or relationship foundations. The sexually knowledgeable therapist is less likely to make errors in this area, and more likely to be able to help couples sooner.

CONCLUSION

The therapist working with couples to enhance their sexual relationship needs to understand the many factors that can contribute to sexual devitalization. Secretiveness in nuclear families and society, misinformation, childhood or adult trauma, and a general lack of norms and definitions are part of the problem. Two relationship components are specifically important for the therapist to examine: the couple's level of differentiation and their level of social development and social skills.

In promoting sexual health, a multitheoretical approach, a process orientation, and knowledge of the relationship of social learning to current behavior are important. These three components are applied through an attention to the process considerations of the therapeutic hour, and through the application of in-session techniques for sexual enhancement. Process issues of importance are "the intimacy dance"; general balance of the dyad; presence/absence of an "equal-partner" relationship; acceptance of personal responsibility for sexual happiness; increasing responsivity, decreasing reactivity; developing an appropriate level of affect between partners; and attending to the nonverbal communication. In-session techniques for sexual enhancement emphasize language tasks to lower anxiety, understanding the role of effective and distorted cognitions, examining the role of emotion and intimacy, and the use of touch and eye contact to enhance the intimacy within the therapeutic hour.

The therapist working to enable a couple to enhance their sexual relationship will have to work as hard in the therapeutic session as he/she would with any other issue. However, the reward of seeing a couple increase their capacity for, and experience of, sexual and other intimacy is well worth the effort.

REFERENCES

Bandura, A. (1969). *Principles of behavior modification*. New York: Holt, Rinehart, and Levinson.

Barbach, L. (1975). *For yourself: The fulfillment of female sexuality*. New York: Doubleday.

Bowen, M. (1974). Toward the differentiation of self in one's family of origin. In F. Andres, & J. Lorio (Eds.), *Georgetown Family Symposia* (1971–1972). Washington, DC: Georgetown University.

Burns, D. (1985). *Intimate connections*. New York: Signet.

Clinebell, H., & Clinebell, C. (1970). *The intimate marriage*. New York: Harper & Row.

D'Augelli, A., & D'Augelli, F. (1981). The enhancement of sexual skills and competence. In L. L'Abate & G. Rupp (Eds.), *Enrichment: Skills training for family life*. Washington, DC: University Press of America.

Egan, G. (1970). *Encounter: Group process for individual growth*. Belmont, CA: Brooks/Cole.

Ellis, A., & Harper, R. (1975). *A new guide to rational living*. Englewood Cliffs, NJ: Prentice-Hall.

Frank, E., Anderson, G., & Rubinstein, D. (1978). Frequency of sexual dysfunctions in normal couples. *New England Journal of Medicine, 3*, 111–115.

Hof, L., & Miller, W. (1981). *Marriage enrichment: Philosophy, process and program*. Bowie, MD: Prentice-Hall.

Jackson, D. (1957). The question of family homeostasis. *Psychiatric Quarterly Supplement, 31*, 79–90.

Kaplan, H. (1974). *The new sex therapy*. New York: Brunner/Mazel.

Kaplan, H. (1979). *Disorders of sexual desire*. New York: Simon & Schuster.

L'Abate, L., & Frey, J. (1983). The E-R-A model: The role of feeling in family therapy reconsidered. In L. L'Abate (Ed.), *Family psychology: Theory, therapy, and training*. Washington, DC: University Press of America.

LoPiccolo, J., & LoPiccolo, L. (1970). *Handbook of sex therapy*. New York: Plenum.

Maddock, J. (1977). Sexual health: An enrichment and treatment program. In D. H. Olson (Ed.), *Treating Relationships*. Lake Mills, IO: Graphic.

Masters, W., & Johnson, V. (1970). *Human sexual inadequacy*. Boston: Little Brown.

McCarthy, B., Ryan, M., & Johnson, F. (1975). *Sexual awareness: A practical approach*. San Francisco: Scrimshaw.

Napier, A. (1978). The rejection-intrusion pattern: A central family dynamic. *Journal of Marriage and Family Counseling, 4*(1), 5–12.

Sager, C., & Hunt, B. (1979). *Intimate partners: Hidden patterns in love relationships*. New York: McGraw-Hill.

Stuart, R. (1980). *Helping couples change: A social learning approach to marital therapy*. New York: Guilford.

Zilbergeld, B. (1978). *Male sexuality*. Boston: Little Brown.

Chapter 5

Counseling Couples to Deal with the Sexual Concerns of Their Children

Maggi Ruth P. Boyer

In the aftermath of the so-called sexual revolution, it may seem strange that parents would have difficulty in dealing with the sexuality education of their children, but the data show that they do (Roberts, Kline, & Gagnon, 1978). Although our society has changed greatly in the past 25 years, sexuality education for children, sadly, has not. In this culture, we have discovered that sex sells, and we have used it vigorously in advertising, television, movies, and music. There is no shortage of sexual innuendo and implication (Alan Guttmacher Institute, 1985). Unfortunately, there is a critical shortage of sound, effective sexuality education for children and teens, particularly if, by sexuality education, we mean not just providing factual information, but also the following: (1) nonjudgmental dialogue between young people and adults in which values and opinions are explored, exchanged, and encouraged to develop; (2) dialogue in which decision-making skills are taught and nurtured to foster a clearly accepted sense of the consequential nature of sexual behavior; and (3) dialogue in which each person is encouraged to develop a happy acceptance of her/his own body and a positive sense of self-esteem.

Children in our society are growing up no less curious than generations before them, but also no more knowledgeable. For example, in a study by Kantner and Zelnick (1973) only about two-fifths of the adolescent girls surveyed had a generally correct idea of the time during the menstrual cycle during which there was the greatest risk of conception. These same teens are, however, more sexually active than those of previous generations, and they become biologically mature at a younger age. The average age of menarche is now twelve and a half years, and more than half of all high-school students will have had sexual intercourse before graduation. Each year, over one million adolescent girls in this country become pregnant; of those girls, approximately 600,000 give birth each year. In addition, there are two million new cases of sexually transmitted diseases annually among persons under 25.

A recent exhaustive study by the Alan Guttmacher Institute (1985) reports that the United States is the only country among the seven Western countries most closely studied in which the teen-age pregnancy rate has been increasing. The U.S. rate for 15–19-year-olds is currently 96 per 1000. It is also significant to note that the maximum difference in adolescent pregnancy rates between the United States and the other countries studied occurs in the most vulnerable age group, girls under 15 years old.

Clearly, parents have reason to be concerned about sexuality education for their children because of a desire to prevent unplanned pregnancy and sexually transmitted diseases as well as possible emotional distress. But, parents have begun to recognize that there is more to the sexuality education process than punitive, negative sex messages and value pronouncements. They have shared with the author and with other professionals that there are some things they want their children to know about sexuality in a more positive light, and that they want to be the ones to teach their children. These parents have expressed that they want their children to "take care of their bodies, recognize their own feelings, but know that feelings don't necessarily lead to actions, respect other people, avoid activities that would hurt them or others, and be 'one of the kids' but think for themselves" (Benesch & Cook, 1985, p. 1). In a group conducted by the author, parents indicated that they want to know the following, among many others:

1. "How can we incorporate the aspect of responsibility in a sexual relationship without taking all the fun out of it?"
2. "How honest should you be with your kids? Are you entitled to privacy or must you answer all questions, i.e., were you a virgin when you were married?"
3. "If you are beyond the bathing-the-baby age, do you wait for the kids to ask or bring up the discussion yourself?"
4. "How do we handle a situation when husband and wife have very firm but very different opinions about birth control, abortion, premarital sex?"

However strongly parents want to be the primary sexuality educators of their children, at the same time, there is ample evidence that they are not actually doing so. The findings of the study *Family Life and Sexual Learning* (Roberts et al., 1978) support what many professionals suspect: parents seem to be repeating a pattern they experienced with their own parents, i.e., little — if any — verbal communication about sexuality. The study points out that although the behavior of parents in regard to sexuality education mimics that of their own parents, there are some subtle changes in the attitudes and values of many parents. For the fathers, much of the change has to do with questioning values they have been taught, particularly those concerning marriage and relationship roles as well as sex role behaviors. For instance, the study found that less than half the fathers participating felt it necessary for their own children to marry. In addition, many fathers do not cry themselves, but believe it is acceptable for a man to cry and, even further, wish they could model this behavior for their sons.

The study further found that in most families, the mother is still seen as the person responsible for what verbal sexuality education does occur. When such conversation does happen, it is most likely to be a discussion of reproduction. Very few parents discuss erotic behavior with their children.

Finally, the study hypothesized that this exclusion of men from sexual discussions in the family may imply to sons and daughters that "sex" itself may be a concern for men, but men are not interested in the process of sexual decision making and are not at all interested in their children's social and sexual growth. On the contrary, exactly the opposite appears to be true: fathers are interested, they have strong opinions about their children's development, but they remain unavailable to their children.

This appears to create a dilemma for many women. Although many of them want to be relieved of the total responsibility for sexuality discussions and for representing their husband's or partner's views about sexuality, they have also learned that nurturing the children is primarily their responsibility. Thus, many women find it difficult to help their husbands find ways to be more actively involved.

The results of this study pointed out a few of the reasons for parents' hesitations or confusions about being the primary sexuality educators of their children. They also help us understand why many parents figuratively throw up their hands in despair and retreat into silence. Yet, even in their silence, parents are the primary sexuality educators of their children, because such education is only partly comprised of verbally conveyed information. As Mary Calderone and Eric Johnson (1982) pointed out,

> As children grow up, some of the most important things they learn have to do with their sense of a sexual self. Children are constantly learning, by observation, by being taught, or by experiencing, what their culture considers desirable for males or females to be or do. . . . Your sexual self is your whole self as girl or boy or woman or man; your sexual feelings are feelings that have to do not just with the physical but also with your own male or female role in life, or the relationships you may be having with people of the opposite sex, at whatever age. Very often these may have nothing to do with physical actions. (p. 2)

Thus, children learn a great deal about being male or female, with its genital, affectional, and role components, by observing and participating in family interactions. Even if parents never say a word to their children about sexuality, the children still observe and learn from what roles are accepted in the family: who mows the grass, does the dishes, cleans, and changes the oil in the car. Children watch parents hug, or not hug, and absorb understandings of the appropriate quantities and methods of expressing affection, such as, who initiates touching, what parts of the body may be touched, how long the touch is held, and whether the touch is reciprocated.

A strongly negative message is conveyed if parents are silent about sex. Regardless of how positive a behavioral role model the parents may provide, silence teaches children that sexuality is not a subject that can be talked about. The silence may even imply a negative value or taboo to the subject, suggesting there is something secretive or mysterious about sexuality, often contributing to guilt and confusion.

Since all children are naturally curious about their bodies and reproduction, this implied taboo can prevent them from acquiring the factual information they want and need. Children typically want to know answers to questions such as the following: How does my body work? Who am I? What is okay to do and what is not? Am I normal? How do I relate to the other sex? How do I express loving feelings? What does sexuality all mean? (Benesch & Cook, 1985). In one group conducted by the author in 1984, young teens in seventh through ninth grade developed this list of questions they would like to feel able to ask their parents:

1. How old were you when you first had sex?
2. What is masturbation?
3. What do parents think about it, really?
4. How does a person catch V.D.?
5. How do you feel about sex before marriage?
6. What is homosexuality?
7. What do parents think kids our age think about sexuality?
8. Why does the girl most of the time get the blame for teen-age pregnancies?
9. Why is sex bad in the teen-age years?
10. How old should I be the first time I have sex?
11. What do you feel about abortion?

In the more difficult area of values and beliefs about sexuality, silence only heightens confusion. In a culture as pluralistic as ours, children are exposed to a stunning variety of values regarding sexuality. One of the major functions of the family is to transmit values from one generation to the next. In a family context in which there is no discussion of sexual values and attitudes, the child is not assisted in grounding sexual behavior in a value context and is surely bewildered by the spectrum of choices.

In short, by active involvement or by default, parents *are* the primary sexuality educators of their children and many parents find this a confusing role, one they may be hesitant to accept.

PARENTAL CONCERNS ABOUT
PROVIDING SEXUALITY EDUCATION

When parents are asked what their hesitations are in teaching their children about sexuality, they cite several reasons. One frequently mentioned is their own embarrassment about sexuality. Having been raised themselves to feel at least private, if not secretive or guilty, about sexuality, parents often feel too embarrassed to talk openly with each other about their sexual concerns. Furthermore, they are not eager to manage their own discomfort with their children, because many parents believe they should present only an assured, confident face to their children.

Intrinsic in the embarrassment-hesitation is parents' fear of "not knowing." They worry that their children will ask a question for which they do not have an answer. Initially, when parents talk about this concern, they refer to factual information. Many adults simply have not had access to good sexuality education themselves. Many do not understand even the basic facts of human reproduction. In addition, as research about human sexual behavior becomes more disseminated, parents feel they are even more ignorant. In and through the popular media, parents read or hear about sexual subjects of a highly technical nature (transsexual surgery; AIDS; infertility research; contraceptive advancement), and they may begin to feel even more unsure of what they really know about sexuality. Facts they thought they understood are changing and new facts emerge rapidly.

When parents begin to talk about their fear of not knowing factual information about sexuality, another concern frequently surfaces. Parents are concerned about not being sure about what they truly believe about a number of value issues, such as the following: premarital sex; sexual orientation; contraception; contraception for adolescents; pregnancy options such as adoption, unmarried parenthood, and abortion; and sexual expression issues such as oral or anal sex, and the use of vibrators and other sexual aids.

Not only do many parents feel unsure about their own values and beliefs, but there are also parents who disagree with each other about sexual values. In such a situation, when parents have actually been able to talk with one another with enough depth to discover the values disagreement, they may not know what to say to their children, because they assume they should present a "united front." Therefore, they frequently say nothing at all, or they convey the attitude of the more verbal or powerful parent. Uncertainty about their own values is, thus, a concern for many parents.

Another concern for parents is the lack of appropriate, comfortable language for sexual communication. Many parents are uncomfortable with the proper terminology for the reproductive parts of the human body and for other sexual subjects. They are uncomfortable because they do not actually know the words, they have seldom heard them used, or they have infrequently or never used appropriate language themselves; i.e., they have had few opportunities to master the language. Yet, many parents are also not comfortable talking with their children using sexual slang. Language itself, then, can create anxiety.

Parents also lack a positive role model for the task of providing sexuality education for children. In their own families, in their own childhood, many of today's adults did not receive sexuality information from their own parents. For most other parenting tasks, from planning meals to maintaining the house, from caring for children to helping with schoolwork, most adults learned at least one way of accomplishing these tasks by observing and remembering their own parents. If no sexuality education occurred at home, a role model is not available to serve as a guide. It is, of course, possible that today's parents did receive a sexuality education in their childhoods, but it may have occurred in a way recalled as negative, punitive, or simply "not enough." As a result of their own experience, combined with so few other models available, these parents may know they do not want their children to have the same experience, but not know what else they could do.

Another significant possibility is that one or both parents may have had a seriously traumatized childhood with regard to sexuality. They may have been the victims of molestation, sexual abuse, or incest. We have no way of knowing how many parents have been affected in this way, since we are only beginning to comprehend the extent of the problem. It does seem likely, however, that for parents who have been traumatized in this way, attempts to provide sexuality education for their own children may be truncated or distorted. Such trauma may result in inability to talk about sexuality, inability to distinguish appropriate from inappropriate touch behavior with children, overprotectiveness, and generalized fear of dealing with sexuality issues and children at all. It is also possible, however, that parents who have been victimized or exploited as children, and who have successfully processed the experience and integrated its occurrence into their lives, will not necessarily have any more difficulty in their role as sexuality educators than other parents. Certainly, more research in this area is needed.

In speaking further of their concerns about providing sexuality education for their children, many parents mention a rather vague, yet persistent concern that by providing information about sexuality to children they will inadvertently "overstimulate" children, heighten curiosity unnaturally, or contribute to precocious experimentation. Such a concern does not appear to be well founded. In fact, many children who are not as verbal as others can suffer as a result of this concern, because they will not begin to ask questions they want answered until parents initiate a discussion. In addition, in a study by sociologist Brent Miller (Elias, 1984), it was reported that teen-agers are least likely to be involved in sexual intercourse if parents talk openly about sex and enforce fairly strict discipline. Parental silence about sex, teamed with either very strict rules or permissiveness, leads to more sexually active teens (Elias, 1984). Although a recent study by Newcomer and Udry (1985) questions this assumption, the study does point out that what parents perceive to be communication about sexuality is generally so vague or limited that it has no impact.

Finally, and in a more global sense, the author has noted two additional underlying causes of parental hesitation to provide sexuality education for their children. The first is our cultural discomfort and confusion about nonprocreational sexual expression. With the technological ability to separate conception from the experience of intercourse, an entire set of morals and values has been called into question. It has only been in the last 30 years that people have had the reasonable capability to choose when and whether to have children. That development, coupled with even more recent ones, such as *in vitro* fertilization, surrogate mothers, and frozen embryos, has created an entirely new ethical scenario. At least a part of that scenario concerns the meaning and significance of sexual pleasure in people's lives. Many parents raised with a Judeo-Christian ethical (if not religious) background are at least ambivalent about sexual expression as pleasure alone. This fact makes it difficult for them to talk effectively with their children about these new value-centered questions.

The second, more general cause of parental hesitation is a basic lack of knowledge, understanding, practice, and skill in communication itself. If parents are not able to talk with their children authentically and nonjudgmentally about less emotionally charged issues, it will be difficult to do so about sexuality. Even with the plethora of parenting classes and workshops in the last decade, the most basic need for some parents may be the need to acquire effective communication skills such as the use of "I" messages and reflective and active listening.

COUNSELING APPROACHES

In view of the numerous hesitations and concerns of parents about being the sexuality educators of their children, it is almost amazing that couples or parents *do* want to be able to talk with their children about sexuality. It is certainly not surprising that therapy can be helpful to parents and that some couples will seek assistance. What, then, is the role of the therapist who is dealing with parents who want to be more effective and caring with their children in providing sexuality education? The therapist will be most effective in working in the following four areas: (1) increasing knowledge and practice of communication skills; (2) increasing client level of knowledge about sexuality; (3) facilitating value exploration and clarification; and (4) increasing skill in communication with each other and children specifically about sexual subjects.

Increasing Knowledge and Practice of Communication Skills

Initially, it is important that the therapist conduct an assessment of the couple's relationship. For some couples, the inability to talk with their children about sexuality can be a mask for a couple's dissatisfaction with their own sexual relationship, a more significant and specific sexual dysfunction, or inclusion, control, or affection disparities within the relationship. (See Chapter 1 for a detailed discussion of assessment issues.)

Conversely, a couple may not recognize the need for communication with children or teens about sexuality. Occasionally, parents will send their son or daughter to the therapist for a behavioral problem such as school truancy, the discovery of the teen's use of a contraceptive method, or general control problems. During sessions with the young client, the therapist may discover that one of the issues needing attention is the lack of clear communication within the family about sexual behaviors, expectations, and values. In such a situation, the therapist has a responsibility to work with the parents as well as the identified client, to help the parents perceive and accept the need for such communication. In therapy in which the parents are not willing to confront sexuality education issues, the therapist can simply continue to affirm that sexuality education is, indeed, an issue and that the therapist is willing and available to help parents.

If, however, the therapist finds the couple is ready to authentically talk with their children about sexuality, the next step is to evaluate the couple's level of communication skill. Most couples need at least reminders of skills previously acquired. Many other couples will need to be taught these skills for the first time. Standard communication skills are important here: "I" messages; reflective listening; active listening; sending congruent messages, etc. Whatever approaches the clinician normally uses to teach such skills can be used in situations such as this as well.

Increasing Client Level of Knowledge about Sexuality

It is important to continue to weave communication skill development, practice, support, and encouragement throughout specific skill acquisition in sexuality education. Questions such as "How else can you say that?" "What are some other ways to say that?" "What specific words could you use to talk about that?" can be helpful.

At the outset, it can be useful for therapists to set the tone for the work to be done by sharing with the client couple the therapist's "basic assumptions" about sexuality education. These assumptions generally include statements such as the following:

1. Parents have the right and responsibility to share what sexual values are important to them with their children.
2. It does not really matter whether those values are liberal or conservative; it only matters that they are shared effectively and caringly.
3. Parents do not have to have all the answers to be successful (McCormick & Boyer, 1981).

It is possible to reinforce these assumptions by having them visually available, perhaps on a poster, during counseling sessions, or by giving the couple a copy of them. In one sense, this provides an informal, initial contracting with the client couple. The therapist can also use the discussion of the basic assumptions to assess the parents' perception of sexuality education and their role in it.

Since we know that many parents feel uncertain of their own level of knowledge about sexuality, one of the significant ways to increase their comfort in talking with their children is to build their knowledge base. Activities and structured interactions which accomplish that task can contribute to practice and increase skill in communication with each other about sexuality.

For instance, the therapist may begin work on sexuality education issues by administering either a formal or informal knowledge inventory. One useful informal instrument is presented in *Sexuality Education: A Curriculum for Parent/Child Programs* (Brown, 1984). After the couple has completed the inventory, there are a number of ways to proceed. The therapist may want to use the knowledge inventory to begin a dialogue for the couple. The therapist might have the couple read items from the inventory aloud, perhaps reading a few initially to "model" the reading. The couple can be encouraged to say what they know as fact about the items and to add to each other's knowledge. The therapist can clarify information, give new information, and monitor the interaction to be sure both persons participate. It may be helpful to frame the therapist's intervention in what can be referred to as "the language of possibility." For example, the therapist might say, "That's quite a common understanding of . . . yet current research seems to indicate. . . . " The therapist can also encourage the couple by using inviting questions such as: "What else have you heard about . . . ?" or "What other questions do you have about . . . ?"

If the therapist perceives that either member of the couple has anxiety about this testlike situation or would like an alternate way of increasing the couple's knowledge level, the therapist can conduct the knowledge survey more like an "open-book" activity. This can be accomplished by providing the couple with a number of texts or other books and letting them research the answers together. The activity can then be processed in much the same way already described. This "research activity" can be done during a therapy session or may be given as a "homework assignment." The therapist may want to provide the couple with several texts to use as resources or may suggest the couple use a library. Parents have found *Raising a Child Conservatively in a Sexually Permissive World* by Sol and Judith Gordon (1983) and *The Family Book about Sexuality* by Mary Calderone and Eric Johnson (1982) to be helpful. A small, but very practical book, *Straight Talk* by Ratner and Chamlin (1985), is also an excellent resource. Pamphlets may be more financially available and less imposing. "Parents: Yes You Can!" by McCormick and Boyer (1981), "Starting Early Experience" by RAJ Publications (1981), and "Sex Education at Home" by Syracuse Planned Parenthood (1974) are frequently used. When the task is given as homework, it is also possible to have the couple complete their research individually. If individual research is done, the couple can either compare their research at home and return to therapy with a list of prepared questions they would like more information about, or they may be instructed *not* to compare research until the following session when their interaction can be more easily monitored.

It is important to process these reading assignments when the couple comes for the next session. Processing can be highly structured or informal. The therapist might ask the parents to bring an index card to the session on which they have written at least two concerns or questions the reading has raised or two questions or issues about which the parent has gained new information. Another possibility is for the therapist to process the reading with parents by asking a set of questions that the author has labeled the "significance series." These are a series of questions that help the client focus on what was important or significant about the reading or other learning. Since there are many ways in which a particular reading or task may be important, the series of questions emphasizes the significance to that particular client. Questions in the "significance series" include: What did you learn from this? What was the most important part of this reading for you? How was this reading important to you? What did you discover in this reading? What questions or concerns did this reading raise for you?

Another new option to increase the couple's knowledge is the use of videotapes. We know that many people have reading difficulties, and that people do not all learn with the same learning style or from the same stimuli. Videotapes may be a better teaching tool. Two videotapes are readily available about puberty: *Am I Normal?* and *Dear Diary* by New Day Films, Wayne, New

Jersey. In addition, many other educational films about sexuality are now available for professionals in both Beta and VHS format. The processing procedures for viewing an assigned videotape can be the same as those used with the reading assignment.

Facilitating Value Explorations

In addition to helping parents become better informed, the therapist must help parents clarify and articulate their values (opinions, beliefs) about sexuality. This can be accomplished by using an open-ended questionnaire containing relatively few items. Therapists can develop their own list quite easily and might consider using items such as: One sexual topic I would feel quite comfortable talking with my children about is . . . One sexual topic I would have difficulty talking with my children about is . . . The sexual topic I feel most confused about is . . . I would like my partner to know that I feel most strongly about . . . I would like to know what my partner believes about . . . This activity may be either conducted during a session or assigned outside the session and, again, careful processing of the activity using questions such as those contained in the "significance series" is critical to optimum learning.

The Family Life and Sexual Learning Study (Roberts et al., 1978) identified a lack of clarity about own or partner values as a major inhibitor of family communication about sexuality, particularly with reference to erotic behavior or controversial topics such as premarital sex, abortion, sexual orientation, and contraception. Therefore, to help parents become better communicators with their children in this area of sexuality, they must be enabled to clarify their own values.

For some couples, significant anxiety may be experienced as they begin, perhaps for the first time, to talk about sexual values with each other. The therapist may need to normalize the anxiety and to prompt responses by asking the couple to create a list of sexual topics they believe are perceived by themselves, their friends, or the culture as difficult or controversial. Having created such a list, perhaps even having jotted down the list during the session, the couple can then be invited to complete the informal attitude survey mentioned above.

During any value exploration that occurs, it will be the responsibility of the therapist to reinforce the assumption that consensus about values is not the task, clarity is; and to help the couple view their values on a cultural continuum. In other words, the couple learns the range of values that are extant in our society about sexual issues and can place their values within that range, appropriately.

Value exploration can also be facilitated by giving each parent a list of sexual topics and asking them to rank-order them from those about which they have the strongest feelings or values to those about which they have the weakest feelings or values. The therapist then clarifies factual information disparities between the parents and uses the "significance series," including suggestions such as the following: "What would you like to tell your partner about your values regarding . . . ? How can you help your partner understand your values about . . . ? What is it about what you have just heard that you can support? What is it about what you have just heard that concerns you?

Increasing Skill in Communication with Each Other
and Children Specifically about Sexual Issues

The transition from gaining knowledge and exploring values and attitudes to developing skill in talking with children about sexuality often arises spontaneously from activities such as those suggested above. Parents will begin to wonder how to use the information they are gaining with their children. They will wonder how to begin a conversation or venture a question about how to deal specifically with their children. One experience that can foster the transition from learning to application is to have parents participate in a "remembering journey." The therapist can invite the couple to relax and become comfortable by using some brief relaxation techniques. The therapist may suggest that the client couple close their eyes to create a greater sense of privacy about their thoughts. The clients are then told that they are to think back over their own learning experiences about sexuality, using a series of questions and directions the therapist will give as guides for their thoughts. The couple is not to respond verbally, only to remember what they can. The therapist then poses a series of questions designed to focus their thinking on childhood, adolescence, and young-adult sexual learning. For example, the therapist might suggest that the parents imagine being in the house where they lived when they were four years old. They might be asked: Who lived with them? What was their room like? Did they share it? With whom? What were their family patterns about nudity? Who taught them about puberty? How did they learn to kiss and hug? With whom did they feel most special? With whom did they have the first date they can remember? When did they first feel sexually aroused? How did they find out about intercourse? Who taught them? How did they find out about contraception? Where did they get the first contraceptive they ever used? What was their first intercourse like? What questions did they have when they were teens about homosexuality? About sexual limit setting?

At the conclusion of the therapist's queries, which should move in a logical progression from childhood issues to adolescent issues and then adult issues, the couple can be invited to explore the content of their memories briefly. However, the major focus should be on the question: "If you could go back and live your childhood and adolescence again, what would you change about the way you learned about sexuality to make the experience better?" The therapist can then assist the parents in identifying which of those changes they can apply to their interactions with their own children. The therapist next helps plan how they can actually put their thoughts into action.

For some parents, another helpful bridge toward building practical skills is to write two lists: one list contains the reasons they may find it difficult to talk with their children about sexuality, and the other is a list of things they want to tell their children about sexuality. Frequently, the result of this activity is that parents realize that no other institution or societal system, with the possible exception of religious institutions, can give their children a family-centered, value-centered approach to sexuality and relationship issues. The lists also help the therapist understand what particular hesitations or concerns the couple has about talking with their children about sexuality.

The "teachable moment" concept is an approach to providing sexuality education that is reassuring for parents who may be somewhat overwhelmed by the seeming enormity of the task of being the primary sexuality educators of their children. The therapist can assist the parents to understand that in the normal routines of living, there are literally hundreds of opportunities daily for conversation with children about sexuality. Examples of teachable moments include: television shows or advertising, the pregnancy of a neighbor, new kittens, newspaper or magazine articles, jokes, and cartoons. Parents can be helped to understand that a teachable moment can be used successfully as an opportunity for sexuality education in a very brief conversation, and these conversations, accumulated over the years, can alleviate the need for the mutually embarrassing "birds and bees" lecture. The use of the teachable moment concept helps parents realize that sexuality education happens daily.

Having explained what a teachable moment actually is, the therapist can facilitate parents using those moments in a three-step process. First, the therapist can have parents identify teachable moments as they occur, perhaps bringing a list to the next session. The next step is to have parents use the teachable moment they have listed as a stimulus to talk with one another: "What could we do with this? What do we want to say about this? What words might we use? What might happen if we do or say this?" Next, the parents are encouraged to respond to teachable moments when they occur between sessions, using the acronym V.I.F. as a guide (McCormick & Boyer, 1981). V.I.F. stands for values, information, and feelings and reminds parents of the three important elements of the teachable moment. Since, at this point in the process, the therapist is encouraging conversation with the couple's children, as well as with each other, it can be helpful to talk over with the parents some general guidelines for talking with children about sexuality (see Appendix). These guidelines can be shared verbally and then given to the parents to take home with them as reminders.

When the parents come to the next counseling session, the therapist can review their experiences using the teachable moments and suggest alternative approaches. The "significance series" can be helpful for the experience: What did you learn from this experience? What would you change about it? What was important about this to you? What did you do well? How else can you deal with this situation or question? etc.

A helpful technique for parental skill development is to have the couple actually practice, rehearse, or role-play their responses to particular questions or situations. In this activity, the therapist may have prepared a set of index cards, each with a typical question or concern that children have. The couple can read through the cards, initially, selecting the ones with which they feel most comfortable to practice. Rather than theorizing how they might respond, the therapist can ask the questions in the role of a child so the parents can respond with the actual words they might use. Processing consists of exploring how else they might answer, identifying what other words they might use, and discussing important values, information, and feelings they want to convey. This activity continues, as the couple's confidence and skill increases, by asking them to address the more difficult issues presented on the cards. It is also possible to have them identify what situation or question they imagine their child might ask that would be the most difficult for them. The parents can then practice the skill they will need to adequately handle that difficult situation. During this activity it is important to stress that parents should not intellectualize and that there are many different, appropriate answers. Although most parents are anxious about this activity, they also report that it is, in retrospect, one of the most genuinely useful activities.

For clients with poor reading skills, the therapist might also prepare an audiotape with typical questions or situations, leaving adequate time following each for a parent to respond. In their home, the parents can either tape their responses for review or simply use the tape for additional skill practice. For parents with particularly busy schedules, even the commute to and from work could be used as practice time. Significant progress has been made once parents have gotten to the point of actual conversation with children, are feeling more comfortable doing so, and can express that comfort to the therapist.

Once the therapist believes that no further sessions are necessary, those perceptions should be verified with the couple. If they feel more comfortable, more skilled, and more knowledgeable about their role as sexuality educators of their children and have demonstrated that skill, termination is appropriate. In addition to using the "significance series," the therapist can invite the couple to share with each other, as well as with the therapist, what they have learned and what has been important to them about this experience. The therapist may also assist the couple in projecting how they perceive the entire process may change, intensify, or recede as their children grow. To facilitate the continuing process, the couple may want to write a contract with one another, setting specific goals, specifying areas of responsibility, including dates for reevaluation.

CONSIDERATIONS FOR THE THERAPIST

It is imperative for therapists who want to be effective in helping couples with concerns about sexuality, including being the primary sex educators of their children, to recognize that therapeutic expertise and previous training alone may not have adequately prepared the therapist for this work. Therapists have grown up in the same culture, for the most part, that client couples have. This culture is generally negative about sexuality or sexually silent. Thus, therapists may experience some of the same hesitations and concerns about talking with clients about sexual issues as the clients have about talking with one another or with their children. It seems essential, then, for therapists to avail themselves of training opportunities in sexuality to accomplish three tasks: (1) increased knowledge about sexuality; (2) increased awareness of their own values and attitudes about sexuality and about the range of such values and attitudes in our society; and (3) increased skill in effective communication about sexuality.

One of the most critical elements of such training is the therapist's awareness of her or his own "red-flag issues" — sexual issues that have been or are anxiety provoking or traumatic or are in critical transition for the therapist. Since therapists are decidedly human, there generally will be such issues in their lives. The existence of such issues need not interfere with the therapist's effectiveness with clients, particularly when the therapist is aware that those issues are current and emotionally powerful. It may be wise, however, for the therapist to strategize methods for handling therapy situations in which couples raise issues for therapy attention that the therapist is aware are red-flag issues. One example of a red-flag issue for a therapist might be that of a couple who raise their concern about the sexual activity of their 15-year-old daughter at the same time the therapist is confronted at home with a request from his or her own teen-ager for permission to get and use birth control. Red-flag issues, of course, change as time and life situations change; so a therapist dealing with sexuality issues professionally has a responsibility to constantly be aware of those shifts.

In much of the interaction with parents about sexuality education with children, therapists need to recognize the importance of themselves and the therapy process as role models for parents. Therefore, the therapist's use of appropriate language, attention to communication dynamics, and the use of the same basic guidelines about sexuality communication that they hope to foster in parents are important areas of focus.

In addition, the setting for therapy can do much to foster more comfortable growth and learning. Therapists might want to examine their physical setting and consider such questions as, "How is furniture arranged and what is that arrangement saying about power or communication dynamics?" It may also be possible to consider how visuals in a therapy session might contribute to the therapy process. Something as simple as a photograph or poster of parents walking with their arms around their children could trigger questions or concerns about touch or about settings for sexual conversations. In the waiting room, samples of sexuality education pamphlets or a bulletin board with articles from popular magazines about sexuality subjects, cartoons, or book reviews can begin the entry into the therapy process for couples even before they encounter the therapist. Such attention to detail can also do much to create a general atmosphere of acceptance of sexuality concerns and can effectively "give permission" to couples to verbalize their own concerns and issues. They also can model some of the techniques and approaches that parents may be encouraged to use as teachable moments, and, as such, add reinforcement to that process.

The therapist accustomed to working with couples with tenacious dysfunctions and deep-rooted issues may find that working with a couple who genuinely want to become more effective and caring, more skilled and comfortable in talking with their children about sexuality can be a particularly gratifying experience. If there are no hidden agendas or complex childhood traumas discovered, progress toward comfort and competence can be remarkably quick. When such a learning experience occurs, the progress and results can be richly rewarding for clients and therapist alike.

REFERENCES

Benesch, J., & Cook, A. (1985). *Tips for parents.* Washington, DC: Sex Education Coalition of Washington, DC.

Brown, J. (1984). *Sexuality education: A curriculum for parent/child programs.* Santa Cruz, CA: Network Publications.

Calderone, M., & Johnson, E. (1982). *The family book about sexuality.* New York: Harper and Row.

Elias, M. (October 18, 1984). Less teen sex if parents talk frankly. *USA Today.*

Gordon, S., & Gordon J. (1983). *Raising a child conservatively in a sexually permissive world.* New York: Simon and Schuster.

Alan Guttmacher Institute. (1985). *New study of teenage pregnancy in 36 other developed countries suggest reasons why U.S. teenage pregnancy rates are highest in the western world.* New York: Alan Guttmacher Institute.

Kantner, J., & Zelnick, M. (1973). Contraception and pregnancy: Experience of young unmarried women in the United States. *Family Planning Perspectives, 5*(1), 21–35.

McCormick, S., & Boyer, M. (1981). *Parents: Yes You Can!* Bristol, PA: Planned Parenthood of Bucks County.

Newcomer, S. F., & Udry, J. R. (1985). Parent-child communication and adolescent
    sexual behavior. *Family Planning Perspectives, 17*(4), 169–174.
RAJ Publications (1981). *Starting early experience*. Denver: Author.
Ratner, M., & Chamlin, S. (1985). *Straight talk*. White Plains, NY: Planned Parent-
    hood of Westchester.
Roberts, E., Kline, D., & Gagnon, J. (1978). *Family life and sexual learning*. Cam-
    bridge, MA: Population Education, Inc.
Syracuse Planned Parenthood (1974). *Sex education at home*. Syracuse: Author.

APPENDIX:
GUIDELINES FOR TALKING ABOUT SEXUALITY

1. BE HONEST! Be honest about your feelings, your values, your knowledge,
   your ignorance.
2. USE TEACHABLE MOMENTS. There are many opportunities for talking about sexuality with children, which occur throughout the normal day's
   activities. A one- or two-sentence comment about a neighbor's pregnancy,
   the adoption of a child, seeing a woman in a nontraditional occupation
   can provide a lot of information for your child about what values are
   important to your family. Using teachable moments often says to your
   child that talking about sexuality is okay. It also helps avoid the necessity
   for the "big talk."
3. KEEP V.I.F. IN MIND. "V.I.F." stands for values, information, and
   feelings. These are three key elements in discussions about sexuality. Communicating information is important, but communicating values and feelings is equally (if not more) important.
4. CHILDREN LEARN BY OBSERVATION TOO. Even if you don't say
   a word to your child about sexuality, your child will learn by observing
   family patterns about touching, sex roles, nudity, affection, discipline, etc.
   If you don't "say a word" about sexuality, your children will also learn that
   there is something off-limit, mysterious, secretive, or bad about the sexual
   parts of our lives.
5. BE PATIENT. Your children hear and learn about sexuality from lots of
   different sources. You will need to clarify, repeat, and build on your child's
   knowledge as s/he grows and matures. You can expect the same questions
   to occur lots of times.
6. LANGUAGE IS IMPORTANT. Give your children the vocabulary they
   will need to continue to ask questions. Whenever it is possible, use the
   proper terms for the reproductive parts of the body and for sexual functions.
7. LISTEN TOO! When talking with your children about sexuality, it is
   important to listen too. It helps you know what they are thinking and what
   further information or discussion might be helpful. You can help your

children talk about sexuality with you by asking open-ended questions such as: How do you feel about that? What else do you think she or he should do? What else would you like to know? How do you think we would solve that problem? What have you heard about that?

8. MAKE A COMMITMENT. Make a commitment to see that sexuality education happens for your children. If you feel nervous or anxious about talking with your children about sexuality, share that with them and then say what you believe is important. If you are very uncomfortable about sexual topics and sense it would be harmful for you to try to talk with your children, see to it that your children get the information from someone else. Other resources could be relatives, your doctor, your minister, or a professional counselor or therapist.

9. SEXUAL LEARNING IS A LIFELONG PROCESS. Sex education never stops, just as we never stop being sexual during our life-span. Read factual information about sexuality. Talk seriously about it with your partner, your close friends. Find out if your church or synagogue will sponsor a discussion group on sexuality and faith. Explore your own values.

Chapter 6

Sex Hypnotherapy with Couples

Daniel L. Araoz and Ellen Kalinsky

This chapter will present the basic concepts underlying sex *hypno*therapy, a discussion of the most common interactional sexual problems, and several specific clinical conclusions.

The rationale for using hypnosis with couples having sexual difficulties has been given elsewhere (Araoz, 1982). Briefly, when a person who is in a stable relationship has a sexual problem, *the couple* has a sexual problem whether they perceive it as such or not. Not to involve the two people in therapy delays the process by ignoring valuable aspects of their interaction (Masters & Johnson, 1970). Regarding the hypnotic work, to isolate one member of the couple system denies the nonconscious elements shared by a couple: hopes, fears, frustrations, and other nonspoken messages about feelings which hypnosis can bring to awareness. By involving the couple, rather than merely the person "who has the problem," the therapist gains understanding of how each partner influences the other. For example, a husband called asking to be helped for his "impotence." In the first session, when the couple was invited to imagine vividly a good sexual experience and to get in touch with the feelings elicited by it, she was able to become imaginatively involved in a loving, happy, and satisfying mental scene. He, on the contrary, kept placing performance demands on himself: "I must last longer; I must satisfy her; she'll be angry at me," he found himself saying to himself. The therapy focused not so much on his sexual dysfunction but on his exaggerated expectations, sexual myths, and self-concept. Because the couple were seen together, it was easier to challenge his irrational beliefs and self-imposed demands.

What must be emphasized is the need to deal with both sexual partners whenever possible. There are no individual sexual problems in people who are in a relationship of commitment and stability. Whatever is one partner's problem becomes the other person's trouble. This fact serves as the basis for the interactional approach to sex therapy. Only when a person is not involved in a relationship is there some justification for dealing individually with a sexual difficulty from an individual perspective. A case in point may be a man who dates many different women and with all or most of them has recurrent sexual difficulties. In such a case, regular psychotherapy might be indicated rather than sex therapy as such.

In our hypnotherapeutic approach, as described in this chapter, we assume that there is a good relationship. By this we mean a relationship in which both people find stability and, at least, some degree of mutual commitment; a relationship based on trust, mutual respect of each other as individuals, and sharing. Another assumption we make in this chapter is that we are dealing with psychogenic sexual difficulties, not with medical problems. In all cases in which there is a presenting sexual dysfunction, a preliminary medical examination is strongly advised in order to eliminate the possibility of neurological, endocrinological, or other medical problems underlying the sexual dysfunction. Once these two conditions have been ruled out, namely, the lack of a relationship and the presence of causative medical problems, sex hypnotherapy can be used most effectively.

BASIC CONCEPTS

Two main general concepts need to be clarified in order to effectively apply hypnotic procedures in sex therapy. The first is that of the new hypnosis; the second is negative self-hypnosis (NSH), which is part of what can be called the *hidden symptom* in psychogenic sexual problems.

Traditionally, when hypnosis was applied to clinical work, many principles were carried over from the experimental laboratory, principles such as hypnotizability, hypnotic depth, and ritualized induction procedures. The new hypnosis (Araoz, 1985) discussed here is a relatively new approach to clinical hypnosis. It started with research done since the 1950s and became commonly accepted in the 1970s. The research owes much to scientists such as Barber (1969), Hilgard (1970), Diamond (1977a, 1977b) and Katz (1979), among many others. Proponents of the direct clinical applications of the new hypnosis consider Erickson (see Rossi, 1980) and his disciples as the primary exponents.

The new hypnosis begins from the premise that every normal person is able to use hypnosis; that hypnosis is a natural modality of "thinking" or employing one's mind; that people can benefit from this mental activity if they learn to take advantage of definite clues leading to nonconscious processes; that ritualized inductions are unnecessary; and that the depth of one's involvement increases with practice. Hypnosis is seen as a skill that can be learned rather than as a personality trait. The focus is not on the hypnotist, as in traditional hypnosis, but on the patient, who has to practice this skill in order to master it. In short, the new hypnosis stresses self-hypnosis. The "hypnotist" simply teaches, guides, and supervises the patient's practice of self-hypnosis.

Patients requesting help for their sexual problems have been practicing negative self-hypnosis for some time without realizing it. Negative self-hypnosis (NSH) appears in most emotional and behavioral difficulties (Araoz, 1981) and especially in sexual dysfunctions. It can be called *the hidden symptom* and consists of the self-defeating affirmations and mental imagery patients engage in based on the differential symptom they experience. For example, a man who starts having erectile problems — the differential symptom — often engages in negative self-talk, which, accompanied by mental images of repeated failures, reinforces the outward symptom. This cycle is known as NSH. He may say to himself, "This will happen again," "It's going to get worse," "She must be laughing at me," etc., while at the same time imagining himself in bed with his partner and failing again. The consequence of this follows the same dynamics of posthypnotic suggestions: the next time he is in a sexual situation, he is expecting the worst, feeling tense and apprehensive, unable to enjoy the situation in a relaxed manner. Repetition of this pattern aggravates the erectile problem, always assuming, as we said earlier, that it is psychogenic in nature.

Therefore, the first step in sex hypnotherapy with couples is to uncover the hidden symptom. Questions and exploratory directives such as "What comes to mind when you think of your sexual difficulty?" or "Become aware of the mental images that come to your mind when you think of your next sexual encounter" or "What do you say to yourself about your sexual problem?" are helpful in introducing the concept of NSH and facilitating the discovery of the hidden symptom.

The next step is to enable the couple to become aware of other, more positive and constructive aspects of their sexual reality. In other words, it is true that they have been experiencing difficulties, but there are also other true aspects of their whole sexual picture. For instance, they may be so attentive to the problem that they are missing other pleasurable sensations. We try to shift their attention from the dysfunctional aspects to other pleasurable realities that take place during their sexual encounters. Most couples realize that they can pay attention to enjoyable sensations in nonsexual parts of their bodies and can, for instance, make their fingertips more sensitive and alive — or, for that matter, any other area of their skin, like nipples, back, feet, etc.

Once they have understood the concept and have agreed that a pleasurable event occurred during sex, we start the hypnotic work by using what they have agreed on. For example, if the couple has admitted that lately they are less aware of sensations in other parts of their bodies, we help them to construct enjoyable mental pictures which emphasize the positive realities they have been missing. These are used to take the place of the NSH affirmations. We invite the couple to relax, close their eyes, and slowly repeat to themselves the new affirmations they have agreed on. Gradually, we introduce the mental images of enjoying sex while concentrating on the "new" realities (not on the problem as before). This activation of the couple's imagination acts as a rehearsal of what their sexual enjoyment can be. We further recommend that they spend some time every day in this form of mental rehearsal.

This preliminary hypnotic approach is used with all couples before we focus more specifically on their particular problem or on the area of their differential diagnosis. One of the reasons is that this mental exercise acts as a diagnostic tool. If they are unable to imagine themselves enjoying sex together, without worries, it may point to other difficulties, either in the relationship (e.g., unacknowledged resentments or anger, expectations, faulty communication, etc.) or within one of the individuals (e.g., fear of closeness, fear of "romantic success," etc.). One couple that was unable to engage in this mental activity was separated so that each partner could be seen individually. In his session, the husband explained that in the last year the thought of sex triggered homosexual fantasies with which he was very uncomfortable and which made him tense and anxious. He had not told his wife about it for fear that she might reject him. The decision was made to concentrate on the relationship as such rather than on the sexual problem. They were advised not to have sex during the next couple of weeks and to concentrate on mutual trust and honest communication. We worked to facilitate this in the conjoint sessions, while in the individual sessions we focused on building ego strength with each of the spouses. Over a period of four weeks, there were four individual sessions for each partner and two conjoint sessions. The use of the initial hypnotic exercise described above gave us the opportunity to look beyond the presenting symptom and to help the husband resolve a personal problem (i.e., homophobic and rejection fears) that was interfering with their sexual expression but which, on a more positive note, became the opportunity for greater closeness and trust between the two spouses as they learned to communicate their fears to each other and respond empathically and supportively.

Clinical Paradigm

The application of new hypnosis principles to sexual problems always follows a simple sequence of steps. The first and most important one is to start with the patients, focusing on what they say, the expressions and figures of speech they use, gestures they produce nonconsciously, changes in emphasis or tone of voice, and other spontaneous aspects of their style and process of communication, rather than focusing on the content and intellectual meaning of their communications.

Thus, the first step is to uncover their NSH. However, instead of asking for detailed explanations centering more sharply on the NSH, we request immediately that they expand their perception and acknowledge other aspects of the total picture of their sexuality. This leads "naturalistically," as Erickson (Erickson & Rossi, 1979) described it, into the hypnotic work. The couple can be led into right-hemispheric activation without formal inductions, leaving behind for a while the surrounding reality and getting involved in their inner images and feelings more fully than ever before.

To summarize thus far, uncovering the NSH leads to discovering other, more positive and true aspects of the total picture. This process leads into self-hypnosis with the assistance of the therapists, which, in turn, leads to resolution of the problem. However, if there are blocks in this process, other directions must be taken temporarily, as in the case just mentioned. Two basic techniques are used to deal with these blocks in a hypnotic way: personality parts activation and age progression.

The first technique, personality parts activation, involves establishment of a healthy personality split. Whoever in the couple is unable to imagine him/herself enjoying sex without the difficulty that brings them into therapy is asked to check different parts in the personality. One wants help—that is the reason they are in the therapist's office—but there seems to be another "person" inside, one who is sabotaging change or at least not believing that change can take place. Slowly, we lead the persons to hypnosis through relaxation, focusing first on their breathing. Once they are relaxed, we ask them to "think" of the part in them that wants to change. How does this part look? What does this part say? Why does this part want to change? Then, we may say: "However, it seems that there is another part of you that disagrees with the first part. Try to focus on this other part. How does he (she) look? Is this part of the same age you are now? Take your time and look inside yourself. This other part is there. It seems to me that this part is not in agreement with the first part in you. Maybe it does not want to change. Maybe this part is afraid of changing. Go slowly and listen to this part's voice. Does it sound like the voice of someone else? Is it your voice? Imagine the two parts facing each other, talking to each other. What do you hear? What's happening now?" This manner of speech is continued for a while, very slowly, in a relaxed tone of voice. In most cases, the individual recognizes "another part." As a matter of fact, patients often "invite" the therapist to use this technique by using expressions like "One part of me wants to do such and such but another part seems to stop it." (For a comprehensive understanding of this technique see Watkins and Watkins, 1979, and Edelstien, 1981, under "Ego State Therapy".)

Gestalt therapists may use the same technique, though many prefer to add the prop of an empty chair. In calling these techniques "hypnotic" we refer to right-hemispheric activation, away from intellectualization and logical analysis. It is not our intention to take credit for any of the techniques listed here. Our operating rule is that any psychological intervention that helps the client to experience him/herself differently though truthfully is hypnotic, right-hemispheric. To avoid controversy with traditional hypnotists, we call it new hypnosis (Araoz, 1985).

The other basic technique used to deal with blocks or resistance is age progression. This means that the person is encouraged to imagine in a very vivid manner how he/she will be in the future when the problem is gone. We insist on proposing this hypnotic exercise to the couple because we have found that often the one who is unable to see the future without sexual difficulties is the partner presenting without the overt sexual problem. The inability of the nonsymptomatic partner to project him/herself into the future without the sexual problem points to secondary gains obtained from the spouse's "sexual problem." At this point, psychotherapy for personality development is necessary. The "healthy" partner has such investment in the sexual problem of the identified patient that no cure will be possible until the neurotic need of the "healthy partner" is resolved in an effective and constructive way.

Age progression is attempted by providing the scenario of a joyful sexual interaction between the two spouses "in the not too distant future." Statements such as the following may be used: "You may imagine yourselves in the not too distant future, enjoying your sexual encounter without the old problem. You are now in the future. You are able to make love with great satisfaction, with peace of mind, relaxation, enjoyment. It's so good to have left the old problem behind. It seems to be so long ago, so far away. It's in the past, never to come back again. You are now enjoying sex like never before, much more than in the past. Put yourselves in slow motion now and go very slowly through every movement, every sensation, getting a lot of pleasure from it. Enjoy everything you are aware of: the slightest sound, the faintest smell, the softest sensation in you, in your spouse. Experience an environment of joy, together, loving each other physically like never before."

We also suggest the use of a variation of the age progression technique when some couples find it difficult to stop thinking of their problem. In this case, a progressive approach is expeditious. The couple is asked to consider another person whom they, or one of them, regard as a very sexual individual. This may be someone they actually know or a movie star, a "sex symbol," one or both of the couple believe to be a very sexual person. Once agreed, they are invited to imagine that person making love, enjoying sex, and very involved in that activity. This is done hypnotically again, and when the couple is greatly involved in this right-hemispheric activity, the therapist starts to suggest that as *that* couple can enjoy sex, so can they. Slowly the model couple is deemphasized and the patients become more and more the focus of attention until they can see themselves in their mind's eye as fully engaged in joyful sex. During this last process the level of relaxation should be carefully monitored by the therapists so that the moment some tension is noticed, the couple return in their mind to the model couple making love instead of focusing on themselves.

These two techniques, activation of personality parts and age progression, can therefore be used in cases of unconscious resistance on the part of the couple working on a sexual problem.

MOST COMMON PROBLEMS

In this section, we concentrate on what Walen (1980) called "the core ingredients in all of the diagnostic (sexual) categories" (p. 96), and what Kaplan (1974) has previously referred to as sexual anxiety stemming from fears (of performance, of not satisfying the partner, etc.) and leading to perceptual and intellectual defenses against erotic pleasure.

We have found five main problems of this nature, always greatly overlapping in couples requesting sex therapy: (1) false beliefs; (2) boredom; (3) lack of spontaneous arousal; (4) false expectations; and (5) faulty communication leading to suppression of images, curiosity, and desires. Hypnotic techniques for each of these problems will be presented. A brief comment will also be added on premenstrual syndrome. The reader is referred to Araoz (1982) for hypnotic techniques and approaches that are especially useful with specific sexual dysfunctions such as vaginismus and erectile problems.

False Beliefs

The most common myths we find in our practice are that sex always has to end in intercourse, that intercourse is the end of sexual activity, and that age and time together weaken romance, sexual arousal, and performance. Kassorla (1980) addressed herself to the first myth and proposed helpful techniques for the couple to go beyond intercourse.

In her chapter on "the romance of the soft-on," she suggests that the couple do not view lack of erection (due to psychological causes) as the enemy but as a challenge to discover new dimensions in their lovemaking. She insists on telling couples to stop the negativism that comes from the belief that sex equals coitus and reminds them that the penis, erect or soft, is sensual. She compares erection to the tide of the sea which inevitably returns in order to help the couple counteract early and erroneous messages received from the penis-centered Western culture. Her "pleasure process" helps the couple become aware of these damaging messages they have accepted blindly.

We use the therapy session to mentally rehearse variations in their lovemaking, always within the parameters of their values and general style. In order to teach the couple mental rehearsal, we ask them to relax with their eyes closed and to visualize as vividly as possible a good sexual encounter, paying attention to what goes on in their mind and focusing on their enjoyment and general feelings of well-being. In other words, we encourage them to go mentally past intercourse, based on Kassorla's (1980) suggestions. We discuss with them the nature of their experience, to understand the extent to which they are accepting of the new possibilities. We go back to the hypnotic mental rehearsal again and again, until they actually become curious about trying to make love without being overly concerned with intercourse.

The belief that age and time together weaken romance, sexual desire, and performance is handled by activating their imaginations, often activating that personality part in them that still wishes exciting sex. Examples of older people actively enjoying sex or couples married for many years and still keeping a romantic relationship are used to correct their erroneous belief. We do not provide the couple with these examples ourselves; rather, we ask them to think of them or to look for such instances in popular magazines and novels. We then discuss how they can apply these images to themselves.

We may also use hypnotic relaxation to help the couple connect their belief to the past. We may say, "Perhaps memories of people you knew in the past start to form in your mind. Perhaps stories you heard or read. Listen carefully. You may hear the voice of a parent or older relative, that of a preacher or teacher, and you want to hear it clearly." All this is done to get to the origins of their belief. It is encouraging for the patients as well as for the therapists when the former have a sudden awareness of where these beliefs come from. This often produces amusement and a sense of relief. One such couple, both aged 27, presented with multiple sexual dysfunctions (erectile dysfunction and inhibited sexual desire). They had been raised in a small New England town, where much of the social activity centered around the church. They realized the impact on them of the constant insistence on procreation and the not so subtle condemnation of sexual pleasure for its own sake they had repeatedly heard as children and adolescents. By connecting with their past messages in hypnosis, they were able to make their own decisions in a mature and free way. In this case it meant to recognize the unique circumstances in which they lived, to enjoy sexual pleasure for its own sake in the present, and to plan to have the children they wanted a few years later. The presenting problem of this couple was his inability to maintain an erection in order to have coitus and her lack of sexual desire. By the time they came to sex therapy they had been married three and a half years and had never had full intercourse after the marriage.

Many other myths are found in couples with sexual difficulties, some related to the children finding out about their sexual intimacy, others related to what is healthy from a physical or emotional point of view. In all these cases the best way to appeal to their rational self is by helping them get in touch with the origins of their false beliefs. If it is a matter of physical health, for instance, the hypnotic approach aids in separating neurotic fear from reasonable precautions that might be necessary. A man, aged 53, who had had a heart attack eight months previously and was now "in better shape than I was for the last 15 years," as he put it, was still afraid of "getting too excited during sex," even though his cardiologist had reassured him repeatedly that there was no danger to his health. By using the technique described above, he "connected" with a story he had heard from his mother when he was perhaps 10 years old, the story of a friend of the family who had died of a heart attack in the arms of a prostitute. Once he uncovered this negative message from his past, he was able to engage his rational mind in order to realize the difference between that past event and his present situation. This "connection" alone produced great progress toward this couple's full sexual enjoyment.

Boredom

"The honeymoon is over," "Marriage ruins a good relationship," and similar sayings of a rather light nature seem to contribute to the conviction in many couples that sex must become routinized after X number of years in the marriage: First they do it triweekly, later, it is try weekly, and finally it is try weakly. In situations where such beliefs are operative, hypnosis can help the couple to get in touch with their NSH, as we explained before. When boredom is the problem, we ask the couple to, first, think of something romantic they would like to do with each other, encouraging them to freely think of their preferences. Then we ask them to guess what the other spouse thought about. If their guessing is correct, we shift into mental rehearsal and allow them to check how it feels to do what they would like to do in order to add romance to their relationship. If their guess is incorrect, we simply let them negotiate some new behavior they believe may enrich their relationship. Then we use self-hypnosis to rehearse it until they feel completely comfortable "doing" it in their mind. During this hypnotic exercise we emphasize sex appeal, sexual desire, and other aspects of their sexuality.

Boredom with each other, as sex therapists know, is inevitably connected with lack of sexual desire, which will be treated in the next section. In order to avoid sexual boredom, the couple has to be willing to enrich their relationship *as a couple* in several areas of their life. Many couples, for instance, avoid being alone by doing many things together but always with friends or relatives. This aspect cannot be ignored by the sex therapist either in the initial appraisal of the situation or in the therapeutic plan. In the initial evaluation it is essential to find out in detail how they spend their free time: often television absorbs all their leisure time, and the couple's commitment to modify this aspect of their lives is a prerequisite to enhancing their sexual enjoyment of each other.

Once they have agreed on a few of the changes to be made, we enable them to hypnotically use a double mental screen. On one, they see themselves very vividly as they were once before, perhaps many years ago, enjoying sex with each other. On the other, they see themselves now as it can happen again. They are asked to compare and to realize the advantages they have now based on their years together and their sharing of many things other than sex. Ultimately, the "now screen" predominates, and they are, once more, mentally rehearsing what can happen in their lives now, what they want to happen from now on, what will happen as long as they keep this picture in mind.

A couple who had been married 16 years presented sexual boredom as their problem. They had been experiencing this problem for the last two years and had tried different "methods" to solve it: group sex, sex with separate partners away from the other spouse, mild forms of sadomasochism, and the introduction of their dog in their sexual play, but all to no avail. They were still unexcited about each other, feeling more of an obligation to have sex than a real desire. They also told us that they spent practically no time talking about their feelings, dreams, fears, etc. In fact both seemed to be quite removed from their inner lives. As part of treatment, they were taught how to communicate, how to become sensitive to each other, and how to spend time doing silly little things with each other. When we asked them what they would want the other to do with them outside the bedroom, neither could think of anything. We then suggested possibilities such as taking a walk together, going to a concert or a museum, visiting different quaint places, etc. When they could not agree with any of our suggestions, we asked them to go back in time and try to remember pleasant things from the time before marriage. We asked them to keep quiet for a while and let the images flow without any order or sense, assuring them that we would have plenty of time later for discussion and analysis. This procedure, incidentally, is a naturalistic way to lead patients into hypnotic activity without making any announcements: the more involved they are in this imaginative activity, the more "hypnotized" they are. The images themselves act as suggestions: without saying it, the message they are giving themselves is that sex can again become satisfying and exciting as it was before between them.

They spent about five minutes reviewing mentally their personal connections, associations, and pairings. After this time they had a lot to exchange and discuss. They were told to avoid sexual involvement for a week and to spend time doing this type of mental exercise. They were assigned specific times—which they agreed on in front of us—to talk about these images without interruptions or distractions. Not only did they "disobey" us and have sex "in a very different mood" during the following week, but they also found their manner of talking very rewarding and had prolonged their assigned time in several instances.

Lack of Spontaneous Arousal

Many couples have seriously argued with us about the "problem" of not experiencing *spontaneous* sexual arousal, believing that it must always be so without their conscious, voluntary control. First, we briefly explain that they should be able to *voluntarily* trigger sexual desire. Then we teach the couple to talk "sexy" by asking them to bring to mind a good sexual situation they have recently experienced with each other. They may either discuss between themselves which sexual encounter they are referring to or each may simply go inside him/herself and recall a good sexual situation with the other. Next they are encouraged to close their eyes, relax, and concentrate on this scene as intensely as they can, involving as many inner senses as possible, activating them so they can enjoy to the fullest every sensation in each bodily receptor. They spend several minutes in this activity, guided by our directions, which are never specific enough to make either feel uncomfortable or self-conscious. We might say, "Enjoy touching her in the most intimate way" rather than "Feel your fingers gently touching her anus or labia." Since we are working in a state of relaxation where resistance is minimized, we want to preserve this bodily and mental relaxation by using words they can accept readily and comfortably.

When this hypnotic exercise is ended, we request that they exchange impressions with each other, paying attention to anything that might have surprised them while they were doing it. The therapist may need to be persistent, because the couple often claims that, yes, they went over some scene but nothing happened. Once they start exchanging the inner experiences they just had, we give them a little time to get used to it and then label this talk "sexy." We strongly encourage them to do this once in a while when they are alone, to exchange sexual memories, to become aware of what is often triggered in one's mind by one simple sexual thought. We use Kassorla's (1980) explanation of the "beautiful hidden room" (Chapter 2) full of personal erotica and recommend that they try her method of eliciting beautiful erotic images from one's past. Kassorla, without mentioning hypnosis, proposes a method that is hypnotic in nature.

The main point is that couples who complain of lack of spontaneous sexual arousal must learn to arouse themselves by employing imagination and using the erotic wealth of material that lies dormant in their inner minds. This technique assumes that the two people involved have a basically good relationship, as explained at the beginning of this chapter. In addition, the couple must recognize the Hollywood image of romance as a myth and accept the need to intentionally tend to the sexual aspects of their relationship.

False Expectations

When we recommend Kassorla's book, we also give couples two other very helpful publications, Zilbergeld's (1978) and Barbach's (1983). The reading of these three books can contribute greatly to the reduction or elimination of many of the false and destructive expectations couples have. Our emphasis here is more on the anxiety these expectations create than on the myths themselves. Kaplan (1974) identified anxiety arising from fear of failure and overconcern about pleasing one's partner as the main factor creating sexual anxiety in a relationship. In our clinical experience, these factors are quite common complaints of couples. One or both become anxious about performance and, without realizing it, create a demand for performance for either one or both partners.

For example, a couple in their midforties complained that since the children had left for college they were having sex more often but that she was unable to reach orgasm. In the preliminary evaluation, it became clear that he was constantly monitoring her sexual reactions, as if she had to perform. He also implied that she was supposed to reach orgasm in a predetermined period of time. Without fully realizing that her husband, who otherwise was very loving and attentive to her, was producing expectations that led to unnecessary anxiety in her, she continued to blame herself. She thought she was "past her prime," "that perhaps the gynecologist missed something," or that she "was never that sensual when I was younger." Our treatment strategy was to help both get in touch with their anxiety. Asking them to sit comfortably and to pay attention to their breathing, we suggested that they concentrate on the anxiety and give it some picture or image. She became aware of a dark, dirty, thick rope around her sexual areas. He had first a difficult time visualizing anything, but then imagined a very heavy fog connecting his mind with his penis and scrotum. We invited them to stay with these images and to allow them to develop in any form they might. Both images intensified, and both spouses reported increased discomfort and anxiety. Our next step was to suggest that they could imagine something removing that rope or at least loosening it and something blowing away the fog. As each of them did this, the anxiety diminished, and we asked them to allow their inner mind to bring forth the causes of the anxiety. She discovered that his "supervision," as she called it, made her tense to the point of losing all of her sexual excitement. He became aware of his fear of getting old, and he "heard" voices from the past (his parents and a teacher) stating something to the effect that after 40 years of age sex was unnatural. They stayed with this new awareness for a while and later, when out of hypnosis, they discussed their experience and made plans to avoid what was causing the anxiety and her self-misdiagnosed "frigidity." Further sessions taught them how to use hypnotic rehearsal of relaxed and enjoyable sex as well as to use the erotica found in nonconscious levels of their memories. For the first time in her life, the wife started to enjoy multiple orgasms regularly.

By uncovering NSH the therapist is able to sense the degree of anxiety in the couple. At that preliminary state of sex therapy it is already important to mention to the couple that they are producing anxiety with their own thoughts and that they can learn to diminish that anxiety through hypno-relaxation. We recommend that they practice relaxation plus pleasant (nonsexual) imagery as a new skill they are trying to learn, so that when anxiety arises in a sexual situation, they are better able to ward it off or overcome it. The pleasant imagery can be as uncomplicated as being in the woods, enjoying the quiet, feeling very safe and at peace. The 25 standard structured images proposed by Kroger and Fezler (1976) are quite convenient for use by the therapist who is not yet fully familiar with hypnosis, as long as they are not memorized and repeated by rote. In our experience, patients who learn hypnorelaxation early to overcome and prevent anxiety resolve their psychogenic sexual problems quicker than those who do not recognize and attend to the importance of sexual anxiety.

Suppression of Images, Curiosity, and Desire

Many couples frequently engage in satisfying sexual behavior but never talk seriously about their own sexuality. Any conversation about sex is either in jest or impersonal. When spouses start to feel less happy with their sexual relationship, it is worthwhile to inquire how much they talk about their own sexuality, their fantasies, their wishes, what they might be curious about in terms of sexual behavior, etc. This idea is related to Kassorla's (1980) suggestion that couples verbalize any nonrelated images, memories, or fantasies that may arise spontaneously during sex. We extend her method to encourage couples to verbally share any thoughts, fantasies, memories, curiosities, or fears each might have about sexual matters. Couples who learn to talk freely about their own sexuality invariably report an increase in playfulness and experimentation—a renaissance in their sexual interaction. Conversely, sex seems to become stale, routine, and boring without verbal sharing of each partner's inner thoughts about it.

Kassorla's (1980) theory is that "distracting" thoughts during sex can be traced back to associations made earlier in life and, without awareness, connect sexual pleasure with other items or circumstances. She gives the example of a child, who at the age of three or four might be touching himself sexually while looking out of the window and seeing beautiful flowers. A nonconscious association is thus formed and later, as an adult, in the middle of lovemaking, the image of flowers may flash through his mind. To avoid distraction, he may then try to reject and do away with that image, and he may even start to worry about this occurrence. The opposite may also be true, that the sight of flowers might bring about some sexual feelings, causing him to be concerned about a "fetish." The effort to suppress this association can produce tension and anxiety, while the gentle acceptance of it can have rewarding results in terms of inner peace and a sense of freedom.

We hypnotically encourage patients to follow whatever images come to mind in connection with sexual matters. In the peaceful state of hypnosis the mind is slowed down so that the person is able to enjoy each aspect of his/her image, allowing it to unfold spontaneously in any way it might go. The therapist guides the patients, not as in the case of guided imagery where preplanned images are suggested, but simply accepting fully and without judgment any new detail into which the images develop. This exercise, practiced as a couple, ends with a conversation between them about the experience they have just had. It is not difficult to understand that this exchange teaches them to talk about their sexuality in a way they have not been able to do previously.

A couple in their midforties was in marital therapy for problems related to trust and commitment when, in passing, the husband mentioned that he was worried about this "damned thought of a bicycle that I have every time we have relations." He had not mentioned it to his wife before, but he had become quite concerned about it, starting to fear that there was something mentally wrong with him. We asked him to expound on his "thought," but he was not too clear: he saw an old-fashioned bicycle with big, wide wheels in an open place, with a full tree on the back. The outdoor place seemed to have a gentle hill to the right. With this scenario in mind, we asked the husband to relax for a moment and to try to visualize the complete picture as clearly and sharply as he could. A few moments of verbal encouragement on our part made it easier for him to see himself in this picture. In merely a few minutes he understood what the bicycle was all about. As a 12-year-old, he used to spend time with an older boy who was his "teacher" in sexual matters. They used to take bicycle rides in the country, where his family used to live, and away from the sight of grown ups and strangers they would spend much time talking about sex. On one of those occasions, his friend had taught him the "right way to masturbate." The husband remembered that on that occasion he had experienced his first "superclimax," as he called it. The association between his distracting scene and sexual pleasure was obvious. The couple learned how to talk about sex and how to take seriously any mental productions that appear in connection with sex.

In general, then, we encourage couples to talk about sex, no matter how bizarre, embarrassing, or frightening the thoughts might be. We explain and model through hypnotic practice the amorality of these thoughts: having them is unavoidable, talking about them often leads, as in the case outlined above, to a new understanding and to closer communication between the spouses.

Premenstrual Syndrome

Many couples have sexual difficulties around "that time of the month," either because of her change of mood or her unwillingness to have intercourse, or because of his complaints about her periods or his wanting other types of sexual activity, such as anal intercourse. Although this chapter does not lend itself to deal with all the tangential issues of the premenstrual syndrome (PMS), we want to mention an important psychological aspect of it. When women have severe behavioral and emotional changes before their period, we recommend that they see their physician for medication to alleviate some of the distress caused while hormonal changes are affecting their bodies.

But the psychological aspect of PMS (Hopson & Rosenfeld, 1984) deserve careful attention since in many cases we believe the PMS has become a self-fulfilling prophesy. Self-hypnosis can prepare them for these days of past misery so they become more tolerable and even enjoyable. In the office, we guide the couple through a form of fantasy in which the wife imagines herself just before her menstruation completely symptom-free. The fantasy or "pretend" aspect of this exercise is stressed in order to override the objections of some women who have felt "out of sorts" during the days preceding menstruation for many years. We ask them to involve themselves in the fantasy and to imagine their own forces of health making good use of the medication so their bodies can function even better than without the remedy; to notice that they feel energetic, with a new sense of inner peace and well-being, cheerful and in control of their thoughts, moods, and feelings.

We may say something like this: "Sit back and think only of relaxing. Feel your breathing, gently, slowly, and with every breath imagine your body becoming more relaxed. Every part of your body, calm, untense. Relax now. Check if you still sense any tension anywhere. Allow your breathing to take the tension away. Like a gentle breeze, blowing away the tension, giving room to comfortable relaxation. Image the word R E L A X written in the sky. Follow each letter slowly, while breathing naturally. When you come to the "X," ex-out any remaining tension. Feel good and listen to my voice, even if distracting thoughts come your way. The distractions can simply move over while you continue to relax. And while you are relaxing, imagine the forces of health in your body. The health forces may appear to your mind like a beautiful light circulating through every part of your body, strengthening your body. Your forces of health and life, your energy actively at work this very moment, in every part of your body. Take your time. Don't rush. Become aware of your vital energy, your forces of health. Allow yourself to connect with the miracle of life in you, feeling a greater sense of peace and confidence in your inner vitality. Your health forces are at work, using the medication you have been given. Imagine the health forces using the medication, changing your body chemistry for your benefit. You can feel yourself well and comfortable during your period. The days of your period become good days too, comfortable and cheerful and happy and full of energy. Project yourself there. Be in your new future. Watch the movie in your own mind: See yourself during the premenstrual days, full of energy, cheerful, feeling so good. Put the movie in slow motion and savor every detail of your next premenstrual days. Take your time. Enjoy what you know can be your experience. Say to yourself: Yes! I believe I will have good days during my period and before my period."

Another hypnotic technique for this condition is to ask the woman to relax and to help her through her breathing and pleasant imagery and then to suggest that perhaps voices from the past will come back to her, giving her different messages about menstruation, the way her body functions, her sexuality, etc. We have been amazed at how rapidly this simple method elicits old memories and even facilitates spontaneous age regression. One 37-year-old woman who had tried different types of medication for her PMS, to no avail, found herself in her inner mind as a little girl of six or seven years listening to the conversation two of her aunts were having one hot summer afternoon over iced tea. She heard them talking about the "curse," the "sickness," and snickering with disgust while referring to the "bloody mess" that makes you sick one week out of every month. As a little girl, our patient had realized they were talking about something that would also happen to her, and at that point she started to "program" herself to be miserable around menstruation days. It is interesting to underline that, according to this patient, she had not remembered this incident before. As she explained after the hypnotic experience, while she was thinking of this she had felt again like that little girl, confused and fascinated, fearful but eager to be old enough to go through this misery which, supposedly, made her a grown-up woman. It is helpful to make it possible for the woman suffering from PMS to find out whether something in her past has predisposed her to expect discomfort during menstruation and around that time, so that now, as an adult, she can evaluate those early messages and free herself from their negative implications.

CLINICAL CONCLUSIONS

Hammond (1984), in an important chapter on the use of hypnosis in sex therapy with couples, proposes more than 10 different techniques, as "powerful addition(s) to more standard methods" (p. 128). He reminds us that in many difficult cases failures in treatment come from the clinician having exhausted his/her therapeutic repertoire. By adding hypnosis to our armamentarium of sex therapy, we increase our potential for effectiveness, especially if we follow the clinical paradigm mentioned in this chapter. The new-hypnosis approach assumes that the patients we are dealing with can benefit from right-hemispheric activation and can find new choices and options if they tap their imagination with the therapist's guidance and help. Because of this fact, we always start with the patient, where he/she is at this point in time in the inner mind activity. We guide the patient to enable him/her to fully take responsibility for whatever is going on in the inner mind and to follow that through until a new perspective, awareness, understanding, or interpretation emerges. The suggestions we offer are not arbitrary and do not stem from our own values and preferences. Our suggestions are always based on what the patients have discussed with us before using hypnosis. When we offer suggestions, we are merely voicing what they — at least a healthy part of their personality — want to accomplish and believe can accomplish, as they have explained it to us initially.

This naturalistic way of introducing hypnosis acquaints clients with the procedure first and lets them understand it after they have experienced it. Often, after the couple has gone through a hypnotic exercise, one of them asks whether this has anything to do with hypnosis. Our answer is affirmative, but we explain that many experts would not consider this type of mental activity hypnosis as such. The important point is the benefit they can derive from learning to use their minds in this way, not the theoretical disputation. As part of the effectiveness of this method we recommend daily practice at home. In order to facilitate it, we often make an audio recording of the hypnosis portion of our therapy session so that they can use it repeatedly at home.

As we said at the outset of the chapter, the couple has to be seen together whenever possible in order to redefine the sexual problem as a systemic phenomenon, with both contributing to it without realizing the complexity of the interaction. This does not mean that we imply fault or that we blame one or both spouses. As a matter of fact we insist that the couple not use blame words.

The complexity of the couple's interaction lies in the fact that each of them has much in their mind that they are not aware of: what they would want the other to be or do or not do, what they wanted in a serious relationship long ago, insecurities about themselves and their mate that all normal people have, etc. Since it is assumed that the couple love each other, we request that both enter into the adventure of finding out how many elements from their complex personalities and interactions contribute to the problem. When one spouse claims that the other person's problem does not bother him/her ("She wants to come a few times each time we do it" or "He would like to stay longer, you know what I mean?"), we readily agree but add that we are sure it bothers them since it bothers the other. No one has denied this statement in many years of practice. From that point, we proceed to request the non-symptomatic spouse to help us (the therapists) by attending the sessions with the "problematic" spouse in order to move quicker and more efficiently. In situations where the nonsymptomatic spouse has refused to cooperate, we conclude that we misdiagnosed the relationship as basically healthy when, in truth, it was one that was deteriorating at the time they sought sex therapy.

We also find that couples often express sexual concerns as a smoke screen for relationship issues such as love, commitment, trust, and the like. In those cases the focus should be on the relationship. Resolving relationship problems frequently resolves the initial sexual problem. In our contemporary society, when sexual matters are so much in the open, many couples find it easier to talk about sex than about intimacy. Kaplan (1974) has also mentioned problems with intimacy as one of the underlying causes of sexual dysfunctions, and we are ever on the lookout, at the earliest stages of sex therapy, for the possible intimacy problems that a couple may be having.

Finally, we want to emphasize the enrichment aspect of all sex therapy. The pleasure process proposed by Kassorla (1980) has as its goal a constant growth of intimacy through the celebration of the body in sex. Emphasis must be placed on playfulness, enjoyment, and free sexual expression as a symbol of a spiritual communion between the two people involved. Technique and sexual prowess, so popular in sex manuals, must be deemphasized. We can help couples find the joy of sex in an atmosphere of loving and mutual giving without forcing them to go through the job of sex.

REFERENCES

Araoz, D. L. (1981). Negative self-hypnosis. *Journal of Contemporary Psychotherapy, 12*(1), 45–51.

Araoz, D. L. (1982). *Hypnosis and sex therapy*. New York: Brunner/Mazel.

Araoz, D. L. (1985). *The new hypnosis*. New York: Brunner/Mazel.

Barbach, L. (1983). *For each other*. Garden City, NY: Doubleday.

Barber, T. X. (1969). *Hypnosis: A scientific approach*. New York: Van Nostrand Reinhold.

Diamond, M. J. (1977a). Hypnotizability is modifiable: An alternative approach. *International Journal of Clinical and Experimental Hypnosis, 25*, 147–166.

Diamond, M. J. (1977b). Issues and methods for modifying responsivity to hypnosis. *Annals of the New York Academy of Sciences, 296*, 199–228.

Edelstien, G. (1981). *Trauma, trance, and transformation*. New York: Brunner/Mazel.

Erickson, M. H., & Rossi, E. L. (1979). *Hypnotherapy: An exploratory casebook*. New York: Irvington.

Hammond, D. C. (1984). Hypnosis in marital and sexual therapy. In R. F. Stahman

& W. J. Hiebert (Eds.), *Counseling in marital and sexual problems*. Lexington, MA: Lexington Books.

Hilgard, J. (1970). *Personality and hypnosis: A study of imaginative involvement*. Chicago: The University of Chicago Press.

Hopson, J., & Rosenfeld, A. (1984). PMS: Puzzling monthly symptom. *Psychology Today*, August, pp. 30–35.

Kaplan, H. S. (1974). *The new sex therapy*. New York: Brunner/Mazel.

Kassorla, I. (1980). *Nice girls do*. New York: Playboy Paperbacks.

Katz, N. W. (1979). Increasing hypnotic responsiveness: Behavioral training vs. trance induction. *Journal of Consulting and Clinical Psychology, 47*(1), 119–127.

Kroger, W. S., & Fezler, W. D. (1976). *Hypnosis and behavior modification: Imagery conditioning*. Philadelphia: Lippincott.

Masters, W., & Johnson, V. (1970). *Human sexual inadequacy*. Boston: Little, Brown.

Rossi, E. L. (Eds.). (1980) *The collected papers of Milton H. Erickson on hypnosis* (4 vols.). New York: Irvington.

Walen, S. R. (1980). Cognitive factors in sexual behavior. *Journal of Sex and Marital Therapy, 6*, 87–101.

Watkins, J., & Watkins, H. (1979). The theory and practice of ego state therapy. In H. Grayson (Ed.), *Short-term approaches to psychotherapy*. New York: National Institute for the Psychotherapies and Human Sciences Press.

Zilbergeld, B. (1978). *Male sexuality*. Boston: Little, Brown.

Part II

Special Problems

Chapter 7

The Crisis of Infertility:
An Opportunity for Growth

Patricia P. Mahlstedt

For most couples the decision to have children marks the beginning of a period characterized by excitement, confidence, intimacy, and reward. After several months of anticipation, they conceive, joyfully announce their accomplishment to friends, anxiously shop for maternity clothes and baby things, and conscientiously begin to prepare emotionally for the changes that pregnancy and children will bring to their lives. For these couples, conceiving is a natural process which culminates in the fulfillment of their lifelong dreams of becoming parents.

For the other couples, the approximately 17% who have an infertility problem, the decision to start a family heralds the beginning of a very difficult life experience. Usually unanticipated, both the diagnosis and the treatment critically affect every facet of a couple's life. Paradoxically, these couples commit their lives to a stressful medical regime of daily temperature charting, regular doctor appointments, multiple medications, painful surgeries, and scheduled intercourse in order to achieve the "natural" act of conception.

Because of the overwhelming pressures of the medical treatment, they delay vacations and career changes, postpone visits with friends and family, and avoid social and religious gatherings. If and when pregnancy occurs, the couple is often reserved in their excitement, reluctant to tell others, and more concerned about maintaining the pregnancy than preparing for a baby—all reserved, difficult responses.

Infertility extracts a heavy toll on the quality of life and affects in some way the emotional, social, physical, occupational, intellectual, and even spiritual well-being of those it touches. Though normally not visible to others, its impact is profound, leaving couples in a crisis which threatens the major needs and goals of the individual and the couple.

Infertility is a major life crisis that blocks the way to the life goal of parenthood. It poses a problem that often is insolvable because it is beyond traditional problem-solving methods (Menning, 1977). Prolonged and open-ended, like a chronic illness, infertility overtaxes the existing resources of the persons involved. Similar to other crises, infertility brings to the forefront and magnifies unfinished business from within the marriage and from each partner's family. Moreover, it creates a psychological disequilibrium that elicits common emotional reactions and proceeds to either an adaptive or maladaptive resolution (Frank, 1984).

The goal of this chapter is to describe the medical and psychological components of infertility in order to enable therapists who work with infertile couples to facilitate a positive resolution of the crisis of infertility. The Chinese symbol for crisis is composed of two words: danger and opportunity. Infertility is a crisis that involves a multitude of personal risks and yet can become an opportunity for growth.

THE MEDICAL COMPONENT OF INFERTILITY

Infertility is defined in medical terms as the inability to conceive a pregnancy after at least one year of regular unprotected sexual intercourse or the inability to carry a pregnancy to live birth. At a time when most couples believe that conception and birth are a matter of planned and timed choice, infertility comes as a brutal and unanticipated shock. The numbers are increasing, and it is estimated that 3.5 million (17%) of the American population of childbearing age have an infertility problem. According to the American Fertility Society, the increased incidence of infertility can be attributed to a variety of factors: the pressures of work, family, money, and other personal problems; the trend among women to delay having children until after the easiest years for conception; the use of contraception which may later impair a woman's ability to conceive; an increased incidence of the venereal disease gonorrhea and its relationship to pelvic inflammatory disease (PID), which may damage the fallopian tubes; and, more recently, *Chlamydia* infection, which may produce pelvic adhesions (American Fertility Society, 1980).

A common myth identifies infertility as primarily a female problem. On the contrary, approximately 40% of infertility problems can be attributed to the male partner, 40% to the female partner, and 20% to the couple. In about 10% of all couples studied, no cause for infertility can be determined. However, over 70% of infertile couples can conceive with proper treatment.

The process of conception is complex and involves the intricate interrelationship of various organs and hormones. Female fertility relies on the proper functioning of the cervix, vagina, uterus, fallopian tubes, and ovaries while the brain simultaneously releases hormones from the pituitary gland. Male fertility relies primarily on the production of large numbers of sperm with proper motility and morphology.

Numerous factors contribute to male infertility. Generally poor health can be one cause of male infertility. For example, an obese man or one with poor nutrition may not produce adequate numbers of motile sperm or may lose interest in sex altogether. Sperm production can also be decreased by chronic fatigue; excessive use of tobacco, caffeine, or marijuana; too frequent intercourse; nervous stress; fear of impotence; hormone abnormalities; chronic illness; and certain medications and treatments such as radiation to the testes. Moreover, an undescended testicle or underdeveloped testes will fail to produce adequate numbers of sperm. Sperm number and motility can be affected by varicocele, a condition that causes dilation of veins near the testicles. This is the most common cause of male infertility. To make a diagnosis and to decide on the proper treatment, the physician will gather an accurate case history, complete a thorough examination, and perform a semen analysis.

The complexity of the female reproductive system can create more problem sources. First, infertility can be caused by the failure of the cervix at midcycle to secrete mucus, a necessity for sperm survival. Ovulatory defects can also cause infertility through the inability of an ovary to develop or to release an egg or of the hypothalamus, pituitary, or ovaries to produce their hormones in proper amounts or sequence. Ovarian dysfunction can result from stress or from dysfunction of any aspect of the entire hormonal system, from the hypothalamus, pituitary, or ovary. A third major reason for infertility is the inability of the fallopian tube to retrieve an egg, resulting from blockage or from adhesions caused by inflammation or from other disease in the reproductive system. The mechanism by which endometriosis decreases fertility is not known, but it is also a significant problem.

Other causes related to the physical factors involved with infertility include sexual dysfunction, inappropriate timing of intercourse, and immunological factors. The mind/body connection cannot be overlooked in infertility. Personal problems, stressful life-styles, career pressures, and general mental health may have physical effects on a man or woman. In some cases, no physical reasons can be detected as an explanation for infertility.

In general, the treatment of infertility is directed at diagnosing and treating the physiological condition that interferes with a couple's ability to conceive. Since each couple is a unique physiological pair, they may have more than one problem that contributes to failure to conceive.

The specific treatments of infertility vary widely depending on the patients and the physician. Generally, male fertility is tested with a semen analysis to identify the number, motility, and morphology of sperm. Problems are solved primarily through surgery and drugs.

The causes of female infertility are often more difficult to detect than those of male infertility, but treatments are more effective. First, there is a history and physical examination. Then the physician will instruct the woman to chart her basal body temperature. Each morning before rising, she must anchor a thermometer under her tongue for five minutes and record her temperature.

The physician will then use this chart to determine whether she has ovulated. Ovulation can also be detected by blood tests and endometrial biopsy.

Although no test designates all tubal functions, about 24% of infertility in women is caused by a tubal problem. A procedure for studying patency is the Rubin test, in which carbon dioxide is passed through the tubes. Because this is sometimes insufficient, a physician will x-ray the reproductive tract or perform a hysterosalpingogram. For this procedure a dye is injected through the cervix into the uterus and fallopian tubes, allowing an outline of those parts to be seen on an x ray. This procedure will detect any abnormality of the uterus and any tubal blockage that may be present. Two additional common procedures to evaluate infertility are blood and urine studies to determine estrogen, gonadotropin, and progesterone levels, and cervical mucus tests to determine whether the sperm can actually penetrate and survive in the cervix.

If any of the preceding tests do not clearly define the nature of the problem, the physician may recommend a laparoscopy. This is the best diagnostic procedure. Through a small incision adjacent to the navel, the physician inserts a tubelike scope with which to see the anatomy of the reproductive system and any disease or blockage. Depending on the diagnosis, the physician may recommend major surgery to correct certain conditions, a course of drug therapy to help correct a hormonal imbalance, or both courses of treatment.

Finally, if it is determined that there is little chance of the sperm and egg uniting in the fallopian tube, a couple might consider artificial insemination or *in vitro* fertilization. In artificial insemination, sperm from either the husband (AIH) or a donor (AID) are collected and then injected into the woman's cervix. In *in vitro* fertilization, several eggs are removed via a laparoscopy and placed in a special dish with the sperm. If they unite and begin to divide, the fertilized eggs are transferred to the uterus where they can attach (or implant) and continue to develop.

Even after the patient becomes pregnant, the impact of infertility does not end. Some women may be required to take drugs, have minor surgical procedures, limit their physical activity, or remain bedridden in order to maintain their pregnancy. For those and many others, there is often the ever-present fear of miscarriage that is a part of the nine-month journey. As one woman said:

> If I had a miscarriage, that would kill me. To finally get pregnant and have it taken away — I would rather not get pregnant at all.

And finally, the worst of all scenarios, the treatment for infertility can be prolonged for years. It can involve multiple medical problems, numerous and expensive bills, disruption of life plans, and still treatment may not work.

THE PSYCHOLOGICAL COMPONENT OF INFERTILITY

The process of diagnosing and treating infertility has a pervasive impact on the lives of those couples who encounter it, creating conflict in the most stable marriage or exacerbating existing problems between the partners. Even though this impact is usually greater when the treatment process is prolonged and/or unsuccessful, the psychological component begins to develop when a couple realizes they are not conceiving as planned. They begin to worry, have doubts, become frustrated, and wonder why they can't do something as natural as conceiving.

Life changes dramatically for the couple after medical treatment begins. A large measure of their independence is lost as their lives now revolve around the physician's plan for conception. Their attention becomes focused on this singular lack of accomplishment, and other goals and needs are neglected. Most often, this focus negatively impacts their confidence, self-esteem, health, relationships, security, and even their ambitions. Each month there is hope for two weeks and grief for the next two weeks. A cyclical roller coaster is created, with hope on the upturn and depression, anger, and guilt on the downside.

Physical losses are also prevalent. Many couples experience loss of potency and/or interest in intercourse. This not only puts additional stress on their marriages, but also interferes with their treatment.

Recent research categorized losses in adulthood which are of greatest importance as etiological factors in depression (White, Davis, & Cantrell, 1977). They include losses of relationships, health, status or prestige, self-esteem, self-confidence, security, a fantasy or the hope of fulfilling an important fantasy, and something or someone of great symbolic value. Any *one* of these losses could precipitate a depressive reaction in an adult. In varying degrees, the experience of infertility involves them *all*, thus creating a crisis of major proportions to many couples.

The Losses of Infertility

The loss of a relationship with an emotionally important person because of death, divorce, the waning of affection, or separation. Whether perceived or not, infertility can become a wall that separates individuals with infertility problems from fertile spouses, parents, siblings, in-laws, and friends. The wall serves to protect the infertile from the well-intentioned, but often thoughtless remarks of others and from the pain each feels, as well as to protect family, friends, and spouse from the sadness. As one woman shared:

> My husband was so frustrated because I was down. I didn't want to upset him so I kept a lot to myself. He said he wanted to crawl inside my wall and find out what was going on inside me.

Both parties know that the wall exists. Though yearning for its downfall, they often feel safer by its presence. As the sister of an infertility patient explained:

> I am avoiding my sister, and I think she is staying away from me and my children. When we are together, she tries to enjoy my family and I try to support her, but our attempts are awkward and painful. We used to be so close, and now we can hardly talk.

It is as if each is at a loss for how to relate to the other, all because one of them cannot conceive a child. Why does the process of infertility create this tension in relationships? Why is it so difficult to maintain friendships throughout the treatment process?

Infertility comes as a tremendous shock to most people. Concerned about unexpected conceptions, individuals become authorities on how to prevent pregnancies, never imagining that conceiving might be a problem. They know what causes unwanted pregnancies and what they would do if one occurred; they know nothing about infertility or what to do about it. Not knowing what to do is one element that makes infertility a crisis. A couple's usual coping mechanisms are inadequate for handling the impact of infertility, and others do not know how to help. Soon they resort to coping strategies that do more harm than good. These include isolation, denial, withholding, fighting, and obsessing.

Lack of information about infertility is a contributing factor to the tension between men and women and their family and friends. There is a confusion among some about the meaning and causes of infertility. Some believe the myth that infertility is a psychological problem that can be solved by a change in attitude or mood. Well-meaning advice and attempts to comfort from other people can be a source of great frustration when they are based on myths or erroneous information about infertility.

Those who believe that infertility is a psychological problem encourage couples "to relax" or "to adopt a child" to facilitate conception. Others say these things to avoid discussion of the pain. Such attempts to help frequently leave couples feeling frustrated and guilty as they question their responsibility for their infertility. Even though they have been told that their problem is a medical or physiological one, infertile couples have doubts and are vulnerable to self-blame. So they pull away.

Infertile couples often keep their failure to conceive a secret. Fearing that others will not understand, they isolate themselves so that they do not have to admit their "inadequacy" and their jealousy of others. Rather than helping, pulling away increases the curiosity of family and friends, cuts off possible sources of support, and intensifies fears of the couple that they are losing control.

Infertility bombards the life of a couple in so many ways that helping is very difficult. After two years of treatment, one woman's mother tried to comfort her by saying:

> You've been so successful and are so devoted to your career. I can't imagine your putting so much emphasis on children. Lots of people would trade places with you.

Within families, there are unspoken expectations of young couples. There are deep fears, for example, that parents will withdraw their affection if a couple does not produce a child by a certain time.

Prospective grandparents also feel the loss caused by their child's infertility. They feel powerless to help and in their own sadness may pull away at a time when the child needs to be loved and reassured of his/her value. The infertile couple needs and expects help from others—sometimes hoping that others, if supportive and loving, can take away the pain. These types of unspoken expectations lead to conflicts within families when they are not met.

Within the marriage, unspoken expectations and unresolved past issues are exacerbated during the infertility crisis. The unspoken expectations refer to subtle agreements that individuals make with each other early in their relationship. The agreement may be that each will help the other to resolve past pain and to alleviate present pain. When this cannot be accomplished, the resulting failure leads to feelings of deprivation, inadequacy, and blame. Fighting can become a way to cope and sometimes enables a couple to survive for a time. They can release pain without looking too closely at the real issues.

Unresolved past issues also are brought to the surface by this crisis. Old family themes can interfere with understanding in a relationship. A husband's reluctance to talk may remind a woman of her own father's quiet nature which had made her feel unimportant to him as a child. Her anger and frustration at her husband may then be exaggerated and misunderstood.

Guilt can also place a wedge in the marital relationship. There is guilt for being infertile, for having such intense feelings, for depleting savings to pay for treatment, and for disrupting so many aspects of their lives. Guilt is often felt by the infertile partner, who may search deeply to identify reasons for their inability to conceive. The infertility is perceived as a punishment for some mistake. Such self-blame is often aggravated when the infertile partner is revealing his/her medical and sexual history (Frank, 1984). Guilt is also felt by the fertile spouse, who worries that his/her disappointment may intensify the spouses's existing guilt. The guilt experienced by the couple often causes serious marital problems. Guilt is also a futile attempt to answer the unresolved question "why" (Mahlstedt, 1985). If there were an understandable reason, many would feel less frustrated, less angry, less depressed.

Because infertility can affect each partner differently, couples can sometimes move apart from one another. Men and women often cope differently. Some men, for example, deal with their pain by keeping it within while focusing attention on their wives. Some women, on the other hand, cope by talking continually about their pain. Eventually their husbands, feeling powerless to eliminate the pain, stop listening.

The cycle continues as the woman, in order to get her husband involved, increases her complaints while he becomes more distant, frequently stopping participation in the treatment process altogether. At a time when she needs him most, she feels abandoned. Conversely, he feels overwhelmed because of her needs. They eventually begin to resent and even to stop helping each other.

Feeling inadequate, both partners sometimes fear being abandoned. The infertile spouse is afraid the fertile partner either wants to or will leave. Conversely, some infertile partners entertain the possibility that they will divorce their spouse so that the other partner can marry a person who is fertile.

Although divorce is infrequently a consequence of infertility, individuals in treatment are hurting, tired, and depleted of physical and emotional energy. They may become less able to fulfill each other's needs and become depressed, not only by their failure to conceive, but also by their loss of closeness and ability to understand. Marriages, friendships, and extended family relationships suffer during this crisis. Most survive the ordeal, but some are lost.

The loss of important body functions, or physical attractiveness, due to disease, injury, aging — in short, some loss of an acceptable self- or body image. The body image reflects feelings about physical well-being, fantasies about what can be physically endured, as well as physical intactness or defectiveness. Formed from experiences in early childhood, body image is the nucleus around which personal identity begins to be shaped (Kraft, Palombo, Mitchell, Dean, Meyers, & Schmidt, 1980). People with positive body images feel attractive, normal, and acceptable to others both inwardly and outwardly. The discovery of a physical defect, such as infertility, threatens the stability of that image. Regardless of the causes of infertility, men and women believe their bodies are damaged or defective. Some believe they have a "closet disease" and are terribly ashamed.

> My body has betrayed me. It won't do what it's supposed to. At 33, I feel like an old woman. It is quite a blow.

Women become angry at their bodies, which they are unable to control. The physical defect, though often invisible to others, is experienced as if it were obvious to all.

A physically and emotionally healthy person who is unable to conceive enters the treatment process and, in no time, finds that medication, surgery, and depression become a way of life. Though sometimes successful, the medical treatment can be humiliating, painful, invasive, and interminable. Men and women may enter the hospital feeling good and leave the hospital physically debilitated—and all for an illness they do not understand.

> With all the medications and surgeries, I began to think of myself as a "sick" person. I came to depend on the doctor to make me "well" and when nothing seemed to be working, those feelings of being unhealthy or ill were intensified. I even have a scar as a reminder of my "illness." (Mahlstedt, 1985, p. 338)

Medications and treatments have effects on how patients feel physically. Women may experience cramps, nausea, headaches, and other negative side effects. Then there is the physical and emotional trauma of surgery from which men and women must recover: the fear, anesthesia, pain, recovery time, physical scars, weight gain, and sexual consequences.

Physical aspects of various problems are also responsible for decreasing sexual satisfaction. Women who receive progesterone for endometriosis may experience decreased libido (Keye, 1984). Moreover, the pain incurred during surgery and subsequent recovery interferes with sexual activity and enjoyment.

Because having a baby is often seen as a normal fulfillment and expression of one's sexuality, infertile couples often transfer the failure to conceive to their entire sexual identities. Sexual competence is measured in terms of one's ability to produce a child and not in terms of pleasure (Keye, 1984). Therefore, another aspect of this loss is that of being a fully functioning sexual person. An interaction that usually brings pleasure becomes associated with their failure to conceive.

Since the course of treatment requires scheduled sexual intercourse, sex becomes regimented, perfunctory, and mechanical. The medical workup probes the couple's sex life, a highly private area, and demands performance. To have such an intimate part of one's life examined by an outsider is intrusive and controlling and creates rage, sadness, and emotional distance in the relationship. Men are often required to produce semen specimens, which, for some men, is embarrassing and degrading. For many, it is as if the totality of their masculinity and femininity is being examined and evaluated.

One or both partners are likely to feel inadequate, self-conscious, and apprehensive about sex in response to the pressures and demands of a programmed and evaluated sex life. Most couples report lower levels of satisfaction in their sexual relationship, probably caused by having intercourse without emotion or closeness or by one person's excessive demands for intercourse. When having sex, whether at fertile times or not, thoughts of infertility intrude on lovemaking. It is difficult for sex to be enjoyable or satisfying when it becomes a job with one purpose: to make a baby. The stress of infertility sometimes leads to more serious sexual problems including decreased levels of sexual activity, ejaculatory problems, and impotence in men, and inability to achieve orgasm, diminished libido, and vaginismus in women (Berger, 1977). Some couples avoid sex altogether in order to protect themselves from the disappointment of not conceiving.

After the diagnosis of male infertility, a pattern of impotence and depressed mood in the husband and hostility and guilt in the wife often develops (Berger, 1980). Men are often afraid to voice their fears and anxieties surrounding sexual performance imposed by treatment demands. Anxiety and fear of failure may result in performance failure and lessen the man's sense of sexual adequacy. One man responded:

> My wife was scheduled to have a postcoital test late one afternoon. Because of our work schedules, we met at a motel close to the doctor's office to have intercourse. At first, I could not maintain an erection, and when I finally achieved that, I could not ejaculate. We tried everything we knew, and after no success, we dressed, checked out, and went home . . . where we tried unsuccessfully again. This whole charade was so humiliating and painful for me that I could not imagine attempting such a thing again. (Mahlstedt, 1985, p. 337)

Both may resent each other when sexual experiences are disappointing. For men who see fertility and virility as being intertwined, infertility can devastate their sexual image:

> When I went through infertility treatment with my ex-husband, he was threatened by the virility issue. He was so intimidated by the programmed sex that he ended up having an affair.

Frustration and the inability to perform during ovulation make a woman feel inadequate, too. How does one get out of such a situation? What can anyone say? Far removed from the earlier sexual relationships, these humiliating encounters result in lovemaking as a mechanical chore and a painful reminder of the failure to conceive. The healthy bodies of men and women, once the source of personal pride, become the source of embarrassment, frustration, and rage.

The loss of self-esteem (or pride in oneself). For some couples, making the decision to consult an infertility specialist is similar to making the decision to see a psychologist or psychiatrist. Before making that decision, a person must acknowledge that there is a problem—that something is *wrong*. One woman said:

> I can't emphasize how devastating infertility is to one who has spent a lifetime basing her sense of self-esteem on "what I can do." When you can't have

children—the most natural and important aspect of life—none of your previous accomplishments seem important. They are overshadowed by this *supreme* failure.

Being infertile was an insult to her self-esteem.

Since the treatment assumes center stage in the lives of infertile couples and because their performance in this process is judged inadequate month after month after month, pride in themselves plummets to an all-time low. One man explained that every month when their attempts to conceive failed, he and his wife would examine everything they did to determine *why* they had been unable to succeed. They believed that *they* were responsible for this failure.

For adults, self-esteem is enhanced by basic personal, academic, and professional accomplishments as well as by the perceptions of how others see them (Mahlstedt, 1985). As previously mentioned, infertile couples feel abnormal and unacceptable to many others in their lives. They suffer intense pain and rejection when they find that validation from family and friends occurs infrequently. The wound created by the feelings and attitudes of others hurts deeply and creates doubt about personal self-worth. At a deeper level, pregnancy means one has "grown up." Failure to complete such an important personal life task as procreation may diminish pride in themselves both as a unit and as individuals.

Another reminder of failure is brought on monthly by menstruation. Patients collect temperatures and consume medication, experience surgery, have sex around fertile times, and then fail again. Having committed so much to the goal of conception, couples are devastated when failure is evident. While wondering why they go through all the pain and sadness, couples are reluctant to stop, thus creating a no-win situation. The continuation *or* termination of treatment means failure.

Self-esteem becomes damaged when a couple notices the flood of emotions that overtakes them, emotions they may not be accustomed to, which rule their lives. There are periods of calmness and then explosions of the underlying distress and emotional upheaval similar to a psychological volcano. The ups and downs are due to extended treatment, monthly reminders of failure, and the inability to make clear plans (Frank, 1984). Everything in life is subject to: "What if we are pregnant/have a child?" Couples plan their entire lives around conception of this child that may not come.

Losing control over when or whether one becomes a parent—a loss most people never even consider, much less face—enrages most infertile couples. How could they be deprived of something so basic and yet so significant to their lives? The question "why" gets asked over and over. When there is no answer, anger, in response to the helplessness and hopelessness they feel, is conceived instead (Mahlstedt, 1985).

The couple is angry at both the situation and themselves. As daily lives become fragmented by personal and work obligations and treatment demands, the anger grows. It is an internal war that can destroy their sense of peace and harmony. It is fed by other people's insensitivity, criticism from families, limited treatment options, inconclusive diagnosis, and the violation of an external sense of justice.

This type of anger is very difficult to handle. At whom does one get mad? Indirect channeling of anger may cause marital tension to surface. The couple may spend more time arguing over false issues than coping with their feelings about their shared problem. Internal rage may be repressed because there is no one to blame. It may manifest as depression, or it may build until it eventually is unleashed on the physician, the spouse, family, friends, or God. Even if done appropriately, direct expression of anger may further isolate the couple from medical/emotional support (Shapiro, 1982).

Finally, for most women, the wound to their ego that infertility causes is deep and long lasting. One woman who conceived and delivered a child after eight years of infertility said:

> Even now, I feel like an infertile woman. It is a wound that never heals . . . or maybe it heals but it has a thin scab that can be penetrated very easily. I still feel less than most people – not as valuable – different.

Loss of status or prestige (in the eyes of others). Since the dawn of civilization, religious, cultural, social, and personal values all have placed a premium on fertility. Genesis tells adults to "be fruitful and multiply." Having children is seen as part of ordinary adult life; peers expect each other to join in parenthood; and parents want the joy of becoming grandparents. Having children follows naturally growing up and getting married. Not doing so seems unnatural.

In a study that examined the reasons individuals give for wanting children, Payne found that the respondents (1) had always expected to have children and (2) saw children as a means of identifying and communicating with significant others (Payne, 1978). It was a means of becoming ordinary adults. Childless couples feel reminded of these cultural, social, and personal expectations. They feel different, abnormal, out of place. Some feel that divorce would be more socially acceptable. Others think their worth to society is lessened by their inability to have children.

The infertile couple stands out in a gathering of families. They are often left out of social affairs that involve children. Because they feel awkward about their own children, friends and relatives may avoid the infertile couple and isolate them even more. They are embarrassed by the infertile couple's distress and do not know what to say. Feelings of inadequacy and injured pride result. Even when included, the infertile couple feels left out emotionally.

> Our infertility has destroyed our social life. We can't win. When left out, we feel lonely and sad. When invited, everyone talks about their children and we feel lonely and sad.

On some occasions parents of infertile men and women are unfairly critical, offering painful advice or implying that their identities as adults are incomplete. Ironically, these are often adults who, until being childless, had fulfilled everyone's expectations. Couples who feel well liked, accepted, and respected by others prior to their infertility may lose the certainty that others appreciate them. Attention and respect are given to those who have children. The infertile couple feels different, less acceptable, and left out.

The loss of self-confidence or an adequate sense of competence or control. Loss of control is a primary theme in the despair of the infertility patient. Plans, goals, and values are tossed aside to make room for the all-pervasive treatment process. Vacation plans are put on hold; job changes are avoided; and visits with friends and family are canceled. Men and women have trouble concentrating on short- or long-term goals when they are taking medication, recuperating from surgery, dealing with the emotional consequences of infertility, and hoping daily that the process will end soon. They have become controlled by the drive to conceive.

Not only does the process seem to take over one's life, but also the physicians seem to have complete control of the treatment, wanting little or no input from the couple. One man said:

> One discussion with my doctor really heightened my awareness that he was calling all the shots, not caring what I wanted. He went through a litany of procedures he planned to complete without explaining why or asking for my opinion. He thought he could plan my life . . . so to speak. I was furious.

This man's wife was upset by the husband's anger at the physician, fearing that the physician would be offended and not help them if they spoke up for themselves. Both felt afraid and out of control.

In another vein, nothing can be as intimidating to a reasonably well-educated person as medical facilities, treatments, and even the personnel. Patients are in "foreign territory" facing the unknown.

> I've always wanted to understand what goes on around me and take charge of shaping my life. But when you enter infertility treatment, you truly do relinquish control of a big part of your life. Despite all my reading and my thousands of questions, I still don't understand what is happening.

There is also a loss of control over one's body — "Why won't my body do
what it's supposed to?" Despite the enormous price paid in terms of money,
time, persistence, commitment to a schedule, and sacrifice of self and marriage, infertile couples cannot do what everyone else can do with little effort:
get pregnant. Competence in this task is beyond their grasp — no matter what
they do or how hard they try. This failure leads to another as the pain and
frustration overwhelm them emotionally.

> I've found that losing control of the events in my life has been frustrating, but
> not nearly as much as losing control over my emotions. If only I could control
> my rage and my rivers of tears, maybe these other losses would be easier to take.
> At least I wouldn't question my emotional stability.

Infertility also involves innumerable decisions concerning the medical treatment and the alternatives to continuing treatment which might include adopt-
ing or accepting childlessness. Individuals struggle with a multitude of questions for which there are no definitive answers or right decisions. This brings
uncertainty about judgment and insecurity about decisions in this very significant area. The result is great fear, procrastination, and continuation of
treatment.

In their attempts to gain control, many individuals become obsessed with
the many facets of the medical treatment. It consumes their entire lives.
Individuals who cope in this way are desperate. Many will do anything to get
a child — even if it is not in their best interest, legally, personally, or financially.
Family and friends can feed the obsession by implying that the couple is not
competent in their handling of the matter. Moreover, if a focus is needed in
the relationship to cover up psychological problems, obsessing about infertility
can enable the couple to avoid reaching resolution and making other decisions.

The whole process of trying to conceive takes over the infertile person's
life, eliminating the sense of self-confidence, competence, and control that
comes from familiarity with and success in accomplishing a particular challenge.

Loss of security (occupational, financial, social, or cultural). Obviously
the loss of important relationships, the loss of self-esteem and a positive body
image, and the loss of self-confidence all contribute to a feeling of insecurity
and instability in one's personal life. The infertility patient wonders if anything
is predictable, definitive, or secure.

Affecting all components of a couple's life, infertility often interferes with
career activities and subsequent financial remuneration. Job performance,
relationships with co-workers, ability to concentrate, decisions to move,

acceptance of a promotion, and decisions to resign or change jobs are affected by infertility treatment (Mahlstedt & Macduff, 1985).

Couples may become insecure about the financial burden of repeated appointments, surgeries, and medication. For example, one ampule of Pergonal at this time costs approximately $40. Some women take two or three a day for 10 to 14 days a month. They must also receive HCG injections, which cost approximately $28 per injection. Traditional treatment alternatives such as *in vitro* fertilization are also very expensive (approximately $5,000 per cycle treated), are often not covered by insurance, and have low success rates. When this is their only choice, couples sometimes sacrifice life savings to take that one in five chance that they will conceive. Regardless of success, they are less secure financially after the procedure is over.

At a deeper level, there is a loss of security about the fairness of life. Couples struggle to determine what they have done to deserve infertility and how they could have prevented it from happening. They fear, "If this could happen, so could anything else" (Berg, 1981). And finally, for some, there is a loss of religious or spiritual faith, something that previously may have formed a cornerstone of their life.

Loss of a fantasy, or, more precisely, the loss of hope of fulfilling an important fantasy. Becoming a parent is both a lifelong fantasy and a developmental need of most people. It is a part of one's core identity and so taken for granted that most do not realize its significance. The dream is that children will enable one to become an adult in the eyes of the previous generation, to project the best of oneself in someone else, and to be respected by one's peers. The friendships that are formed through the activities of children's lives are long-lasting and enrich the personal lives of adults. These are lost to the infertile couple.

After years of trying unsuccessfully to conceive, many individuals experience tremendous despair. They are both frustrated and sad that they have been unable to have a child and at times hopeless that they will be successful in the future. They feel incomplete. They may never be parents and thus never experience all that accompanies parenthood: from being pregnant and giving birth, to preparing for baptism and sharing that experience with extended family, to watching kids play baseball and experiencing the pride of their achievement, to escorting a daughter down the aisle—and so beginning again the continuous cycle of life. Infertility disrupts the life plan.

Evidence suggests that although many beliefs are drawn upon in people's desires to have children, the underlying reasons are concerned with beliefs about the nature of adult life. Having a child is tantamount to growing up, becoming an adult, and being like others. Without this experience, individuals may not believe they have accomplished that unique psychological passage to adulthood. Being a parent is a part of one's vision of an idealized adult self; losing that vision hurts deeply.

Loss of something or someone of great symbolic value. Unlike others who conceive easily, the infertility patient has to examine his/her reasons for wanting children and thus can identify many of the taken-for-granted philosophical values of having children: links to the future; sources of pleasure, pride, and challenge; meaning in life. A childless person lives indefinitely with the fear that the hoped-for child is dead. Paradoxically, the infertile couple yearns for the child that may never be and mourns the child that never was. This loss is as tangible to the infertile couple as if the child had been born, lived, and died.

Because there is no tangible or clearly defined loss for family and friends to see, no sense of finality as in death or divorce, it is difficult for others to truly empathize. Even the couple finds it hard to comprehend this intangible loss. Other children acutely remind them of the children they do not have. The hurt returns often as they watch beautiful children on television commercials, receive birth announcements from friends, buy birthday presents for nieces and nephews, and notice their friends slipping away and developing different interests. They long for the sense of family that children embody.

This loss is especially painful for the couple who loses a child through miscarriage. Responses of disbelief, anger, guilt, and depression follow the traumatic physical experiences as the couple try to understand and cope with the loss (Pizer & Palinski, 1980). The responses of others often overlook the couple's need to answer *why* this has happened and what they should do now. Others make light of miscarriage, offer superficial explanations, and discount the couple's pain. The fact that there are no socially accepted rituals for mourning the loss of a child after miscarriage makes the decision to conceive again very risky. Many become afraid to try again, and if pregnancy occurs, they are cautious, reserved, and worried throughout the nine months.

The diagnosis and treatment of infertility have a profound impact on people's lives. Couples experience multiple losses as they struggle to integrate this crisis into their lives. They commit to a treatment plan with no definite resolution or time frame. Common emotional responses due to this stressful life experience are depression, anger, guilt, frustration, and sadness. The grief associated with infertility is similar to the grief caused by the death of a child. But it is the child who was never born, and there is no funeral. For some the pain and loss of infertility will be with them throughout their lives. It may never end.

These are issues that need to be addressed by all infertile couples. Some couples get stuck and some choose to get the assistance of a therapist who can help them work through the pain and the losses of infertility.

THERAPEUTIC INTERVENTIONS

> What matters above all is the attitude we take toward suffering. Suffering ceases to be suffering in some way the moment it finds a meaning. (Victor Frankl, *Will to Meaning*)

The crisis of infertility shatters dreams at a time when people are most hopeful. If not worked through, the losses and subsequent wounds could impede emotional growth for the individual and the couple.

The extent to which the emotional responses incapacitate the life of an individual facing infertility depends on a number of factors. These factors include family history, the level of differentiation in the marriage, the couple's ability to communicate with and to understand each other, his/her usual coping strategies (or lack of them), and the significance of the hoped-for child to the marriage. Resolution of this crisis is an emotional task. It involves recognizing the multiple losses and the ways in which they affect lives, coming to terms with both the existence and consequences of these losses, and making positive decisions about alternatives to achieving parenthood or remaining childless.

There are several alternative approaches for helping couples who are going through the infertility crisis. An assessment of each person's ego strength and level of functioning is necessary to decide the appropriate treatment modality. Differentiating between healthy, neurotic, and borderline functioning helps the therapist to plan appropriate treatment goals (Batterman, 1985).

In general, conjoint therapy sessions offer the optimum opportunities for both spouses to share feelings and needs, learn effective coping strategies, work through the losses, and make appropriate decisions. However, when one spouse does not want to come to therapy sessions, individual therapy is a viable option. There are times when infertility reactivates unresolved issues for one spouse and the other feels no need for therapeutic support.

Another option is infertility support groups. Resolve, a national support organization, has local chapters in over 30 cities which offer welcome resources for individuals and couples struggling with infertility.* There are also local support groups in many communities which offer group meetings, seminars, and workshops for the infertile couple. Group meetings enable

---

*Resolve, Inc., P.O. Box 494, Belmont, Massachusetts 02178.

members to offer each other special comfort, encouragement, and shared experience.

Working Through the Losses of Infertility

Couples must work toward reframing the losses of infertility into a positive concept of themselves as individuals and as a couple. This reframing begins with a discussion of the general impact that infertility has had on their lives and moves to a more detailed examination of the losses it entails and the ways in which husband and wife are affected by them. In accomplishing this goal, they can understand more fully the meaning of this crisis, thus creating an opportunity for personal growth. Resolution is accomplished in degrees and over a long period of time. For those who never conceive, it may be a lifelong process.

Loss of a relationship with an emotionally important person because of death, divorce, the waning of affection. To varying degrees, the infertility crisis creates changes in the infertile couple's relationships with fertile friends and family as well as in their relationship with each other. These changes often involve a lessening of the trust and understanding that characterized their relationship prior to the knowledge of infertility. Whether these changes destroy the relationship or are merely building blocks for a stronger relationship will depend on the couple's willingness and ability to examine the process.

Since a lack of information is often the reason for increased tension in relationships, the therapist can provide articles on infertility from popular magazines and journals as well as helpful books. By doing so, the therapist is educating both the couple and significant people in their lives with whom the couple can share this material. These materials often become a basis for the beginning or renewal of damaged communication between an infertile couple and family or friends.

The couple is often most confused about the intensity of their own responses. Difficulty dealing with anger and rage is a common reason for seeking counseling. The therapist should allow ventilation and encourage clarification. Another very important task of the therapist is to explain *very early* that many others experience these same feelings. Knowing that these types of responses are common and, in most cases, normal is comforting and validating.

If the couple is estranged from family and friends because of infertility, the therapist should encourage them to restore these relationships with significant others, through sharing the pain involved and asking clearly for what they need and want from them. People are sometimes afraid to voice their needs, but doing so gives others a better chance of meeting them.

Couples may appreciate a therapist's help in identifying social situations that are especially difficult to handle and in developing ways to respond appropriately. Many individuals find that attending baby showers, christenings, and holiday functions is too painful for them when their wounds are unhealed. Moreover, attendance at a party with a group of pregnant women may evoke a sense of despair that is overwhelming. In handling potentially painful events, infertile couples can use assertive statements that help them to be honest about their own feelings while confirming the feelings of others. Educating others about the medical and emotional aspects of infertility and asking for what they need can greatly enhance the depth of relationships and remove the loss that may have developed. Role playing is often helpful.

Because couples can lose one another in this attempt to create another human being, the therapist can help them to differentiate their feelings and needs during this process. Individuals within a relationship often struggle over differences, expecting their spouse to respond like they do and wanting only a certain kind of support. One woman said:

> I do not feel I understand my spouse's feelings fully. I wanted having a baby to be as important to him as it was to me. I wanted him to show his pain, too. Instead he just held it in.

This woman must learn that a couple is two individuals and that to expect both to feel the same about infertility or to express their feelings in the same way causes considerable stress.

A common loss in marriages is fun and enjoyment. Couples living with infertility struggle with their partner's feelings, often believing that if one spouse is depressed, the other must be depressed, also.

An important goal of therapy is to help these couples stop sharing misery so that they can nurture their marriage. They can learn to live for what is present and not for what is missing in the relationship, to celebrate what they are and what they *can* do. The challenge is to create a sense of humor, playfulness, intimacy, and enjoyment in their marriage by going out on dates and talking about the love they feel for each other. The burden can be lessened by creating a balance between the sadness of infertility and the joy of being married.

The therapist can help the couple communicate in order to investigate the deep emotional impact of this crisis on each other. Each partner should be encouraged to *listen carefully*. If one person is feeling pain, the other can show understanding. Instead of saying, "You're taking all of this too seriously," encourage patients to say, "It worries me when you are so upset. Is there anything I can do to help?" Through more effective communication, the couple should be able to help each other successfully grieve the real losses of this crisis.

In order for grieving to be facilitated, individuals need to give themselves permission to grieve, understanding that a loss of great magnitude has occurred and that grieving is appropriate. They also need a social support system to comfort them as they grieve and an awareness that grieving runs a time-limited course.

Finally, the greatest gift couples can give their future children is a strong marriage based on each partner having a positive sense of self. By helping the couple to communicate more effectively and to differentiate their needs, the therapist may enable them to achieve a higher level of functioning in their marriage and in their relationships with family and friends.

Loss of health, important body functions, or physical attractiveness due to disease, injury, aging—in short, some loss of acceptable body image. The therapist can provide an opportunity for individuals to regain these losses in several ways. First, both individuals need to express their feelings about the damage to their body image created by the diagnosis of infertility. They must look deeply into themselves and speak freely about the wounds that infertility has dealt to their image. Couples need to grieve over the medical shortcomings that contribute to their infertility. Every physical component that has been removed or is not functioning as it should needs to be talked about and mourned. The therapist can help couples to separate infertility from their body image and sexuality and to view infertility as an experience outside themselves, not an inherent defect.

The therapist can also help couples to discuss their feelings about scheduled and monitored sexual intercourse, as well as diminished spontaneity and satisfaction in their sexual relationship. Discussion should include the loss of control as well as the loss of privacy concerning such intimate aspects of their lives.

The couple must also be encouraged to examine each partner's fears of performance for themselves and their partner. Individuals can understand that such fears are very personal and not determined by the presence or absence of love. Moreover, learning ways that they can be supportive of each other when sexual failures do occur may lessen the apprehension and serious doubts about sexual adequacy. The therapist might also suggest that the couple have a romantic evening out that does not end in intercourse, thereby enriching their relationship without adding pressures to perform.

Working through feelings about sexuality includes discussions about what being a man or woman means to the individual client. This process is facilitated by examining societal role conditioning, childhood experiences, and the meaning of pregnancy within the concept of sexuality. An important goal is to redefine womanhood or manhood excluding childbearing and involving a positive self-concept (Batterman, 1985).

Each individual would profit from identifying satisfying aspects of sexual interaction to be incorporated into their sexual activity for both scheduled and spontaneous lovemaking. Such openness would enhance their sexual relationships as well as their feelings of closeness and concern (Frank, 1984). And finally, the couple might profit from a vacation from the day-to-day struggles of infertility. A "time-out" can make it possible to put infertility into the appropriate perspective—that it is only a part of the relationship.

The therapist can provide reassurance that lack of interest, failure to perform, decreased pleasure, and sometimes abstinence are normal responses to infertility and need not be seen as permanent conditions in their relationship. However, in those cases in which sexual dysfunction is a primary cause for their infertility, or in which sexual problems preceded infertility, sexual issues should become a focus of the therapy. Short-term therapeutic techniques include support, education, and encouragement (Berger, 1977).

Loss of self-esteem (or pride in oneself). Part of the resolution of infertility involves addressing the loss of self-esteem and how it is tied to the infertility crisis. The time, energy, and money dedicated to solving the infertility depletes people's emotional reservoirs, leaving them vulnerable to self-doubt and criticism. The degree of lost pride depends, in part, on the level of pride prior to the awareness of infertility problems.

Having experienced a wound to their self-esteem, couples must be encouraged to examine the wound itself. How does it feel? What is it like? Has it brought changes? How does the couple cope with it? Looking at themselves and talking about these changes enables individuals to see the many ways in which infertility has hurt their lives. The therapist can support this task by first legitimizing and normalizing their feelings. With this comfort, couples can then proceed to talk about the ways in which they feel self-doubt, shame, and disappointment. After attending a support group, one man said:

> Talking about my feelings helped me to work out solutions. It was important for me to know that I was not alone or singled out for punishment. I was finally able to accept my feelings and go on.

Feelings of anger at both self and others are the hardest to accept, as individuals are afraid to even talk about them. Many are taught that "good" people do not have such feelings and to admit them is tantamount to saying one is "bad." Expressing anger during therapy sessions and communicating openly with one another will facilitate resolution.

Couples must also learn how to assertively express their frustrations to family, friends, and the physicians with whom they work. Assertive communication involves communicating openly without violating the other person's rights (Shapiro, 1982). Since this type of sharing involves respect — not deference — its use can enable the infertile individual to maintain self-respect while clearly communicating their needs to those who can help. By so doing, individuals often find that they feel greater integrity and more fulfillment in their relationships.

Within a marriage, couples need to validate each other and support open expression of feelings. *Accepting differences* in feelings and attitudes as well as in ways of coping is important for each to feel cared about and respected. Moreover, the infertile couple can be helped to broaden their perspective, remembering that there is more to life than infertility. It is easy to get stuck in infertility. Since the quest for parenthood and advancement in other areas are not mutually exclusive, a person could use advancement in other areas to enhance his/her self-esteem.

Loss of status or prestige (in the eyes of others). Unlike most adults, the infertile couple has to examine with greater depth their reasons for wanting children. The therapist can facilitate this process by helping them to reevaluate the religious and cultural values of parenthood. Do children enable adults to feel "grown-up"? Do children enrich relationships with parents? Do children give adult life greater depth and meaning? Are children the only way to identify and communicate with others? Is reliving one's childhood through children a positive experience?

In order to examine these issues, a couple will first need to grieve over the real or perceived loss of status. There is disappointment and pain in being left out of a group, in being seen as less valuable because of something out of one's control. Paradoxically, to gain status through children is no validation of one's personal value or importance, but rather merely a confirmation of one's fertility. If fertility (and not the character of the individual) is the value of one's peers, perhaps an examination of the group's significance in one's life should follow. The question is: "Why must a person have children to be an important part of a group?"

For those whose own status is dependent on having children, another plan of action must be developed. The therapist can help them to speak frankly and openly to family and friends about their needs to be included and to be given the choice of coming or not. Honest sharing about the events, attitudes, and comments that are hard for them to handle might make it easier for others to relate to their crisis.

The infertile couple must have a positive attitude toward themselves in order to expect others to do the same. To accept one's physical limitations as being only a *part* of the total self and to recognize the positive attributes they possess in other areas of their lives will enhance their self-confidence and thus their importance in the eyes of others.

The loss of self-confidence or an adequate sense of competence or control. Many couples report that the loss of control is the most stressful aspect of the infertility crisis. One woman sums it up eloquently:

> The waiting and uncertainty was the most stressful aspect of the infertility treatment—not knowing if any of the time, money, or pain would pay off. It's bad enough if you can never achieve a pregnancy, but having no end to the quest is the worst. You just want someone to tell you to forget it because it's hopeless or to hang in there because you will finally be successful.

She felt incompetent and out of control in relation to her own body, her medical treatment, and her day-to-day life.

The therapist can help people regain competence in and control of their lives in several ways. First, he/she can encourage study of both the medical and psychological aspects of infertility. Access to information will broaden the couple's understanding and reduce some anxiety about the whole process. Education and information may help the couple develop realistic expectations about the treatment process. As mentioned earlier, knowing what to expect during a particular procedure allows the couple to prepare for the test and hence to feel more confidence and control.

Patient studies have shown that those who receive information *and* support fare better in recovery than those who receive just one or none at all. They feel less anxiety, their immune and nervous systems are improved, and healing is much quicker. They feel more in control of their bodies and their treatment (Frankl & Holman, 1985). Therefore, therapists should encourage couples to ask for information and support from their physicians and to be prepared emotionally and physically for their surgery. The following suggestions might be made.

- Be sure you understand completely what the physician is going to do and why.
- Make sure your spouse knows what you want done if pertinent decisions need to be made while you are under anesthesia.
- Find out approximately what the surgery will cost and how much your insurance will cover.
- Talk to your anesthesiologist.
- Prepare for emotional and physical support following hospitalization.

Couples might also profit from knowing about self-help groups and coping techniques like relaxation and deep breathing, both of which can help them feel a sense of control and can ease the ordeal of hospitalization.

For the same reasons, couples should be encouraged to communicate openly with their physicians. In fact, they do have control over their choice of physicians, and they must choose one who is sensitive to their emotional needs. The couple needs to express their fears and concerns during different phases of the evaluation and treatment and to ask questions and receive answers for the parts of the treatment that are unclear. Doing so will probably lessen the frustration with or lack of faith in a treatment.

In an attempt to do everything possible and thus to gain control, individuals sometimes obsess about infertility. Therapy should help couples become focused not obsessed and broad not narrow in their view of infertility and the rest of their lives.

After a painful, uncomfortable, ineffective treatment, many couples cannot "let go." The growing research on infertility offers a cruel sense of hope that next month or next year there will be a solution to one's problem. Many people live with the myth that if they just *try* hard enough, eventually things will work out. When is it enough? One client said:

> My life has been a series of goals — very ordered — and very hierarchical. But that chain of goals was broken when we couldn't achieve our plan for a family. It isn't just that I can't have that second child. I can't move on to all those other goals later in my master plan. At least I can't move on until I can give up the dream of the child.

People often associate stopping treatment with "quitting" and are adamant about not being "quitters." So, they hang on . . . until their resources and coping skills are depleted. A therapist can help a couple make a decision about stopping treatment by directing some attention to their primary goal: Is it to be pregnant or to become a parent? The two are not mutually exclusive. If it is the latter, perhaps the couple should seriously consider other means of achieving the goal. Each individual must examine him/herself and determine how much he/she is willing to put into this goal. When considering an end to treatment, the couple might set a reasonable goal in terms of time and, if the goal of pregnancy has not been achieved, move on to other options.

Couples need to be reminded that stopping treatment is not an admission of failure. It is simply a recognition of one's own limitations and needs to go on with other aspects of life. Individuals must be encouraged to see themselves as more than people who want a baby. They have worked hard and done all they can. They must also be cautioned that sadness will not go away when the decision is made and that grief work will still be needed.

Loss of security (occupational, social, or cultural). Every couple has their own set of security needs. Working to attain them consumes a large proportion of one's waking hours. Failure to achieve any of them creates insecurity.

The infertile couple learns early in the process that having children is a need they may not fulfill. A therapist can help them to discuss how a child will solidify their security and what they will lose if conception does not occur. As with other losses, the loss of fulfilling the security need should be mourned and buried, and other means of fulfilling it must be explored.

The crisis of infertility interferes with meeting security needs in jobs and educational pursuits, as well as in financial planning and home buying. Decisions that seem straightforward to other couples are complicated for the infertile couple. What type of home should they buy? Should they take a trip or should they save their money for adoption or treatment options? The therapist can help couples to set goals in all areas of their lives and to integrate treatment demands into that schedule. Priorities must be established periodically so that changing needs can be communicated and met.

When couples begin to feel a pervasive sense of bitterness and resentment, they have probably gone for too long concentrating on infertility and denying needs in other areas of their lives. Guidance and encouragement to reexamine their situation might help them to build a broader base of commitment which involves finding ways to identify and meet other personal, social, and financial needs.

Loss of a fantasy or, more precisely, loss of hope of fulfilling an important fantasy. Many important fantasies are potentially crushed by this crisis: the natural ability to conceive, the childbearing experience, and parenthood. Though often taken for granted, these fantasies frequently form a part of the core of adult personality. To lose them is to lose a significant part of oneself. It is as if part of the person has died.

Support for grieving the death of these fantasies is a major part of the resolution process. The couple might need help crystallizing and verbalizing their own unique fantasies of what their lives would be like if this crisis had not occurred or were over. The loss must then be appropriately mourned. They must assess the importance of parenthood and determine whether other activities could substitute for having a biological child. They must also explore what is fulfilling for them and determine what goals they want to accomplish in adulthood. Couples can then consider alternatives to a natural child, including adoption, artificial insemination, *in vitro* fertilization, surrogate motherhood, or child-free living. Creating new fantasies, sharing and evaluating them with each other, and making new plans will then enable the couple to find new meaning and hope for fulfilling another important fantasy.

Loss of something or someone of great symbolic value. For many, this is the most difficult to mourn. The difficulty stems from the fact that it is abstract or potential loss. Whether through miscarriage or the inability to conceive, there is no tangible loss — nothing that others can see. There is, to others, nothing to cry about. Moreover, there is no socially accepted ritual, such as a funeral, to mourn this loss. And there is often no support group to help as there is in a death or divorce — often because others do not know.

Grieving is also made difficult if there is no definitive diagnosis of infertility to enable the couple to know for sure that they will not be able to have children. It is hard to grieve when there is still hope, hard to start planning for the future. The couple might be encouraged to imagine or create an actual ceremony in which they give up the dream and say good-by to the unborn babies they will never have. Such symbolic rituals can enable the couple to "let go" and pave the way for the emergence of new hopes and plans for the future.

For the couple who has had a miscarriage, remarks from others such as "There was a reason for it," "It happens all the time" slow down the grieving process. Often after a miscarriage, a woman has the extra weight and no baby as a consequence. The sadness is profound as is the fear about getting pregnant again. The therapist can reaffirm the appropriateness of the couple's deep feelings, encourage them to learn as much as they can from their doctor, and help them to say good-by to their baby, perhaps employing a ritual similar to that noted above.

In addition, if the couple has a relationship with a church or synagogue, they can be encouraged to seek an appropriate memorial service to facilitate the grieving process. Many clergy are sensitive to the needs of individual church members with these issues and are willing to provide pastoral care and a memorial service for the bereaved. Such a service permits the immediate and extended families to share their grief and give and receive needed support. It "normalizes" the grief of these couples and families and places it within a social context, affirming a "real" death has occurred and facilitating the resolution of the pain, anger, and loss. If the couple feels awkward seeking such unorthodox support, the therapist can express a willingness to make an initial contact with the clergyperson.

CONCLUSION

The crisis of infertility becomes an opportunity for growth when the couple begins the grieving process. This often occurs when their own coping mechanisms begin to fail and unexpected problems begin to develop. Friends and relatives cannot help, and the couple look to themselves, infertility support groups, and mental health professionals to support them through this process.

Grieving involves expression of feelings about the multiple losses and subsequent depression, anger, disappointment, guilt, and fear, as well as an examination of the impact infertility has had and will continue to have on the couple. Grieving is difficult because there is no recognized loss, no certainty over the loss, social negation of the loss, and little support. Individuals in the marriage may feel that they have to be strong for each other and therefore conceal their feelings. As long as there is hope of conceiving, it is difficult to feel that the issue is finished or resolved.

Expressing one's feelings and letting time help with healing contribute to the completion of the grieving. Most infertile couples believe that it takes a long time to resolve the losses involved and to arrive with mutual understanding at decisions about parenthood. One woman explained:

> Resolving our infertility took years. Even though we had 'accepted' that we would not have children, the desire to have a child was still there. Those feelings never go away. We just had control of them after making the decision to stop treatment.

In other words, resolution does not occur when one stops treatment, nor necessarily when one gets a baby by birth or adoption. Feelings not only do not go away with the arrival of a child; they may never go away.

A complete or final resolution of the infertility crisis is not absolute. As in grieving due to death, the issue continues to reverberate and can be revived even though it may be essentially worked through. However, by working through the multiple problems created by this crisis, many couples get to know each other in deeper ways than may have occurred if they had not been infertile. They may resolve marital issues that would otherwise have interfered with effective parenting. For these couples, infertility can be seen as a sad and painful experience of their lives which, because of their determination and hard work, provided an opportunity for them to grow and increase intimacy.

REFERENCES

American Fertility Society (1980). What you should know about infertility. *Contemporary OB/GYN, 15*, 101–105.

Batterman, R. (1985). A comprehensive approach to treating infertility. *Health and Social Work, Winter*, 46–54.

Berg, B. (1981). *Nothing to cry about*. New York: Seaview Books.

Berger, D. (1977). The role of the psychiatrist in a reproductive biology clinic. *Fertility and Sterility, 28*, 141–145.

Berger, D. (1980). Couples' reactions to male infertility and donor insemination. *American Journal of Psychiatry, 137*, 1047–1049.

Frank, D. I. (1984). Counseling the infertile couple. *Journal of Psychosocial Nursing, 22*, 17–23.

Frankl, V. (1969). *Will to meaning*. New York: World Publishing Company.

Frankl, V., & Holman, M. (1985, September 24). Get prepped for surgery—Psychologically and physically. *Executive Fitness Newsletter*.

Keye, W. R. (1984). Psychosexual responses to infertility. *Clinical Obstetrics and Gynecology, 27*, 760–766.
Kraft, A. D., Palombo, J., Mitchell, D., Dean, C., Meyers, S., & Schmidt, A. W. (1980). The psychological dimensions of infertility. *American Journal of Orthopsychiatry, 50*, 618–628.
Mahlstedt, P. (1985). The psychological component of infertility. *Fertility and Sterility, 43*, 335–346.
Mahlstedt, P., & Macduff, S. (1985). Emotional factors and the IVF-ET process. Unpublished research presented at the American Fertility Society Annual Meeting, September.
Menning, B. (1977). *Infertility: A guide for the childless couple.* Englewood Cliffs, NJ: Prentice-Hall.
Payne, J. (1978). Talking about children: An examination of accounts about reproduction and family life. *Journal of Biosocial Science, 10*, 367–374.
Pizer, H., & Palinski, C. O. (1980). *Coping with a miscarriage.* New York: The Dial Press.
Shapiro, C. H. (1982). The impact of infertility on the marital relationship. *Social Casework: The Journal of Contemporary Social Work, 63*, 387–393.
White, R. B., Davis, H. K., & Cantrell, W. A. (1977). Psychodynamics of depression: Implications for treatment. In G. Usdin (Ed.), *Depression: Clinical, biological, and psychological perspectives.* (pp. 309–322). New York: Brunner/Mazel.

Chapter 8

Treating Extramarital Sexual Relationships in Sex and Couples Therapy

Frederick G. Humphrey

DEFINITIONS AND PREVALENCE OF EXTRAMARITAL SEXUAL RELATIONSHIPS

The relationship between a couple's overall marital satisfaction and their sexual adjustment has long been debated. Some theorists see good marriage leading to good sex; others see good sex being a prime ingredient of good marriage; and, finally, some hold that these two factors are so inextricably intertwined that only in exceptional cases does one exist positively without the other. However, when extramarital sex (EMS) is introduced into the couple's marital-sexual system by one or both of the partners, the complexities of couples dynamics and sexual therapy soar geometrically. The therapist must consider a variety of issues: the couple's sexual adjustment, their total marriage relationship, the EMS partner him or herself (and their spouse, in turn, if s/he is married), children, family kin, work associates, etc. EMS relationships, almost invariably, unleash a hurricane of emotions into the lives of the couple. These emotions, like the winds of a hurricane, appear to be virtually uncontrollable, capable of enormous destruction, unpredictable as to precisely how and where they will strike, and often demonstrate moments of serene calm and beauty in between the devastating blows that are wrought.

Therapists engaging in sex and marital therapy need to be aware of the implications that EMS plays in marriage and in sexual adjustment. We shall refer to therapy here dealing primarily with married persons, but almost any type of couples therapy will be similarly affected by one or the other partner in a committed relationship engaging in a sexual affair with one or more third parties, regardless of whether the couple is heterosexual or homosexual, or whether they are living together or just seriously dating. The impact on married couples will vary somewhat, however, from nonmarital relationships inasmuch as marriage is formalized by religious and civil contracts, obligations, and restrictions which tend to support conventional (i.e., non-EMS) behavior and condemn and punish unconventional (i.e., EMS) behavior. Couples in the other alliances tend to lack both social supports and sanctions. For example, it frequently happens that a nonparticipating spouse (the one not engaged in EMS) will call on the service of their clergyperson to admonish or otherwise attempt to persuade the "errant" (participating in EMS) spouse to "come to their senses" and "do their duty" to break off the offending EMS relationship. Such community supports are rarely available to the unmarried couple facing couple-sexual problems complicated by extra-"marital" sex.

Defining Extramarital Sex

EMS is not monolithic and should never be considered by therapists to be so, even though legally and religiously there may exist only one model. It occurs in a variety of patterns, dimensions, and constellations. Some of the criteria used to evaluate EMS and its impact on a couple's marital/sexual relationship are the following.

Time. EMS may occur in fleeting "one-night stands" such as at a convention, as "quickies" stolen in the bathroom at a New Year's Eve party, or as a single act of paid sex purchased from a prostitute. At the other end of the time spectrum, couples sometimes report extramarital affairs (EMAs), with or without sex, lasting years or even decades. Brecher (1984) reports one couple who carried on their EMA for 52 years while each went through three marriages. For research analysis, however, EMAs shall be referred to here as "short term," meaning under six months in duration, or as "long term," meaning over six months in duration. In actual therapeutic practice, however, these distinctions sometimes hold little meaning. A husband may be as angry about his wife engaging just once in EMS with his "best buddy" at a party as another may feel about his wife having a summer-long romance with a man on Martha's Vineyard while the cuckolded husband toils in the hot, humid city.

Degree of emotional involvement. EMS may involve the deepest level of intimate, caring love, or consist of recreational sex, or demonstrate total indifference, or even hate and contempt, such as occurs in sexual assaults. Therapists should assess the level and the quality of emotional involvement between the EMS partners and, just as important to the sex-marital therapist, the level and quality of the emotional involvement as perceived by the nonparticipating spouse. EMS involvement without "love" appears to represent less of a threat to the marriage than EMS with love. The participating spouse who is not emotionally involved with his/her EMS partner will find the process of disengagement much easier, if they choose this route, than will the person in love. The perceptions and beliefs of the nonparticipating spouse on this matter deserve serious attention due to the concept that "feelings are facts." If a nonparticipating person feels and believes that his/her spouse is participating in EMS and cares about his/her "lover," then that truly becomes a "fact" to the nonparticipating spouse and he/she will respond and act accordingly. Clients may express dismay that they are being accused of adultery (a legal term) when they are "only" having an EMA with no intercourse or even sex pleasuring involved. Such technical niceties, it should be noted, may have little meaning to a hurt and angry nonparticipating spouse.

Sexual intercourse or abstinence. Although some aggrieved spouses may care little about whether or not the EMA partners actually engaged in sexual intercourse or pleasuring, for many clients this is a significant issue. The participating spouse believes he/she has engaged in less serious violations of the marital vows if a penis has not entered a vagina. This has been labeled by Laura Sarrel as the "nonpenetrating affair" (Sarrel, 1984). Again, EMAs occur on a continuum in this regard. At one end are "cerebral" affairs where no sex activity occurs (the "brother-sister" model), and at the other end are EMS relationships where all sexual activity has been shifted to the EMS partner and none occurs with the spouse. Some of the latter clearly represent collusion between the married pair either on an overt, conscious, verbalized level or at an unconscious level. The participating spouse doesn't "bother" his/her spouse for sex and the latter never complains about its absence. A classic example of the latter was a couple where it had been established that the husband was sterile. The wife, however, had two children during their marriage, without going to any medical facility for artificial insemination by donor, and the husband never raised the issue of her obvious EMS. Significantly, he was, during this time, keeping his own homosexual EMS activities secret from her. Together their collusion enabled both of them to avoid confronting the marital-sex issues that were so obvious, particularly in the wife's situation.

Secret or not. Therapists who perform both individual therapy and couples therapy often state that the married clients they see exclusively for individual treatment report higher rates of EMS than do clients treated only as couples. This demonstrates the issue of the secret versus the known affair. As will be reported later, some couples "complete" marital therapy without the nonparticipating spouse ever knowing that the partner was or had been engaged in EMS. Indeed, many of these cases even elude the awareness of the therapists, particularly those who demand a purely conjoint interviewing format in conducting couples therapy. Some of these (cuckolded) therapists state that the presence or absence of an EMA or EMS is of little interest to them as their particular systems approach to couples therapy deals only with what occurs with the here and now of the therapeutic hour (Teissman, 1983). Others, particularly if they are psychodynamically oriented and/or engaged primarily in sex therapy, will want to know about secret affairs. For instance, some individuals may be sexually dysfunctional with their legal mate, but not with their EMS partner (Humphrey, 1985a). Such a finding will significantly influence the question of organicity in a sexual dysfunction.

Another specific area of concern deals with disorders of sexual desire. A married person regularly engaging in sexual intercourse with an EMS partner may have little or no desire for intercourse with his/her spouse. Hence what may appear to represent a need for sex therapy dealing with a lack of desire is actually a case requiring a couples therapy approach. Even if no regular sex is occurring with the EMS partner, the participating spouse may refrain from intercourse with the mate out of guilt, out of a sense of loyalty to the EMS person, or because he/she has lost all feeling for the legal partner. In assessing disorders of sexual desire, it appears to be essential that inquiry always be made about the existence of EMS. Even when intercourse regularly continues with both the spouse and the EMS partner concurrently, a secret EMS may mask the source of marital conflict or disinvolvement if the therapist is unaware of the outside relationship.

Single or bilateral EMS. EMS is most typically spoken of as if only one of the marital partners engages in it. Frequently, and perhaps most often, this is true. Either the husband or the wife may remain absolutely and totally faithful, while the mate engages in one or more EMS relationships. In these instances, the nonparticipating spouse tends to maintain an attitude of innocence and righteous indignation, a position often reinforced by children, family, friends, and anyone else aware of the participating person's "sins." It must be recognized, however, that in many cases both partners may have been engaging in EMS (Humphrey, 1985b). These instances cover all types of EMS and can vary, for each spouse, in respect to time, emotional commitment, level of sexual activity, and secrecy. Some couples are involved in "alternative life-style" phases in their lives and regularly participate together in mate swapping or in group sex orgies. At the other extreme are the instances where each partner's EMS is kept a total secret. If, in the course of therapy, one partner discloses his/her EMS, the other one would appear to be more likely to also "confess" than would be true if he/she was not also participating. Couples involved in idealistic alternative life-styles invariably evoke strong countertransference reactions from conventional sex/marital therapists and may require referral to a different therapist (Constantine, Constantine, &

Edelman, 1972). Another common pattern is for one spouse to engage in EMS only after learning that the mate is doing it. Motives here may include revenge, curiosity, or the seeking of support at a time of crisis.

Heterosexual or homosexual. One is again tempted to believe from discussions of EMS that it always occurs with heterosexual partners. This myth may stem from a lack of understanding regarding human sexual orientation. Over four decades ago, the first Kinsey reports (Kinsey, Pomeroy, & Martin, 1948) illustrated that few persons behave 100% heterosexually or 100% homosexually during their lifetimes. This fact, coupled with Kinsey's later volume (Kinsey, Pomeroy, Martin, & Gebhard, 1953) on female sexual behavior and with subsequent work by developmental psychologists, biologists, endocrinologists, and sexologists, should be borne in mind when performing all sexual/ marital therapy. A person may be primarily oriented toward heterosexuality so that s/he chooses to marry a member of the opposite sex or s/he may be responding primarily to social pressure when doing this. Either way there is never a guarantee that heterosexual marriage will stop all homosexual behaviors so that "heterosexuals" having "homosexual" EMS affairs should hardly come as a surprise, but it does, and with a special impact. In these instances the nonparticipating spouse not only feels rejected as a marital partner, but also feels a rejection of the very core of his/her self-identity: one's sexuality. Therapists will hear these clients offer such laments as "I could handle it to lose him to another woman, but to another MAN, NEVER!" Heterosexual infidelity often threatens a nonparticipating spouse's sense of sexual adequacy, but homosexual infidelity in heterosexual marriages (or heterosexual infidelity in homosexual couples) strikes an even more threatening blow at one's basic sexuality. Special therapeutic emphasis in these instances should be directed to exploring and assisting both husbands and wives with these issues regarding each one's own sexual identity and orientation.

Summary. Both EMA and EMS relationships have been defined here in terms of time, emotional involvement, level of sexual activity, secrecy, bilateral involvement, and sexual orientation. Other criteria obviously exist, but for marital/sexual therapists these six components will be found to present the primary issues ordinarily requiring the therapist's assessment in order to successfully treat these cases (Humphrey, in preparation).

Prevalence of EMS in the Population

For centuries, writers, clergy, politicians, and others have speculated about the existence of EMAs and EMS. It remained for Kinsey and his co-workers, however, to make systematic attempts to find out how common these phenomena were in American society. They estimated that "half of all the married males have intercourse with women other than their wives at some time while they are married" (Kinsey et al., 1948, p. 585). Considerable variation was reported according to age, education, religiosity, and geographical location. Later, in their volume on women's sexual behavior, the Kinsey group reported that 26% of all married women also engaged in EMS (Kinsey et al., 1953, p. 416). Although studies on the scale of Kinsey's have never been performed since, other studies in more recent times have suggested that EMS has remained a common occurrence in American marriages. Included in these findings are those of Athanasiou, Shaver, and Tavris (1970), 40% male EMS and 36% female EMS; Johnson (1970), 20% men, 10% women; Hunt (1974), 41% men, 18% women; Bell, Turner, and Rosen (1975), 26% women; Levin (1975), 39% women; Maykovich (1976), 32% women; Pietropinto and Simenauer (1978), 47% men; Yablonsky (1979), 47% men; Wolfe (1980), 69% women; and Hite (1981), 66% men. Caution should be observed regarding conclusions about some of these studies as sampling techniques were often quite selective, for example limiting testing to readers of magazines, such as *Redbook* (Levin, 1975) and *Cosmopolitan* (Wolfe, 1980). Since these studies, other writers have attempted to offer projected rates for EMS, but these offer us, at best, educated guesses. What it would seem reasonable to conclude, however, is that EMS probably occurs in a majority of all marriages. The findings for men alone hover around the fiftieth percentile, and when we consider that much EMS is participated in solely by wives, it appears that over half, or a majority, of American marriages are so affected. Based on this conclusion alone, marital-sexual therapists could reasonably anticipate that at least every other married pair entering their offices contains at least one spouse who has, is, or will participate in one or more EMAs and/or EMS relationships.

The Prevalence of EMS in Clinical Populations

As noted above, at least every other American marriage appears to be affected by one or both partners engaging in EMS at some time. Is the same thing true for clinical populations? Apparently yes, at least for clients seeking therapeutic help from marriage and family therapists. A 1976 study of a random sample of the clients being treated by clinical members of the American Association of Marriage and Family Therapy (Humphrey & Strong, 1976) revealed that approximately 46% of all clients coming to marital and family therapists sought help for issues concerning one or both partners' EMS. When this study was replicated in 1984, similar or higher proportions of EMS were found, with some therapists reporting up to almost their total client loads consisting of EMS cases (Humphrey, 1985b). In a pilot study of clients seeking sex therapy from therapists trained at the Yale University Sex Therapy Program under Philip and Lorna Sarrel, the therapists reported only 6% of husbands, 6% of wives, and 2% of both spouses engaging in EMS (Humphrey, 1985a). These same therapists reported, however, that among their clients seeking "individual, marital, and/or family therapy," 26% of husbands, 11% of wives, and no cases of both having EMS were reported. This suggests that clients seeking "sex therapy" as opposed to "individual, marital, and/or family therapy" may present fewer cases of EMS (Humphrey, 1985a).

Comparable studies have not been published for clients of clinical practitioners in psychology, medicine (including psychiatry, obstetrics-gynecology, and urology), and pastoral counseling. Beck and Jones (1973), reviewing client requests for casework help at family agencies, reported 25.6% of their marriage counseling cases involved in EMS issues. The conclusion to be drawn from these studies, coupled with responses from a separate, open-ended questionnaire sent by the author to 50 prominent therapists in the United States and Canada, is that EMS cases represent a very significant proportion of those couples seeking help for individual, marital, family, and, perhaps to a lesser extent, sexual problems. As such, every practitioner needs to alert him/herself to the special issues these situations present in therapy.

MARITAL-SEXUAL INTERACTIONS AND EXTRAMARITAL RELATIONSHIPS

Sexual and Marital Health

Although nearly everyone is born with adequate physiological sexual potential, many individuals undergo such negative sexual learning and socialization experiences that they reach adulthood with widely varying capacities to fulfill their sexual destinies. In addition, sexual intercourse requires mutual surrender and involvement by two uniquely different persons, each with his/her own separate sexual value system (SVS).

Achieving successful adult sexual interaction is a formidable developmental task. When one adds this sexual task to all the others the couple face in living their life together in a marriage relationship, one may be surprised not that so many experience marital/sexual problems, but rather that so many successfully achieve this without professional help. Educators talk about family life and sex education, clergypersons preach countless sermons on these topics, and parents hope for the best. When one examines the average person's preparation for marriage and sexual interaction, however, the conclusion must be drawn that each person and each couple are left up to their own devices in these areas. These learning opportunities come from their parents' role modeling (and close to 50% of them are now divorcing and/or having EMAs, while their children are growing up), from their peers (where the majority of teens are engaging in sexual intercourse and producing one of world's largest ratios of youthful illegitimate births and abortions), and from the mass media, especially television, which teaches about sex and family life by offering everything from soap operas to late-night porno shows on cable. If family life and sex educational programs were oriented to the real world, they would place greater stress on both divorce and extramarital sex since the majority of people will experience one or both of these during their lifetimes. In this respect, soap operas may be one of the most realistic preparations for adulthood being offered to children and youth as sex, EMS, out-of-wedlock pregnancies, and divorce appear to be their most prominent themes.

Regardless of where and how they received their family life/sex education, men and women alike react to sexual interaction, both in and out of marriage, both at a concrete, behavioral level and, more important, at a symbolic level. Sexuality, highlighted in sexual intercourse, is both felt and perceived on a continuum. At its most positive, sex represents love, intimacy, trust, need, happiness, fun, pleasure, creativity, and ecstasy; at the negative end of the continuum, it represents rejection, distance, hurt, evil, filth, and subjugation. Hence the same act or actions may be simultaneously experienced by both of the participants as mostly positive or mostly negative, or it is just as possible to be experienced by one partner as positive while simultaneously being felt by the other as negative. These symbolic meanings, when added to the strong biological and libidinal sexual pressures experienced in healthy adults, contribute to sexual interaction being one of the most emotionally charged areas of all possible couple interactions.

Part of most individuals' socialization processes are the messages that when they grow up they will fall in love, marry, engage in 4200 sexual copulations together over their lifetime (figures reached by extrapolations from Kinsey's findings of 1948 and 1953), and be faithful to each other during all of the 50 years currently predicted for their adult life-spans. With these expectations, added to religious teachings that define marriage vows as sacred, it is possible to see why sex often fails to fulfill couples' expectations of it, why marriage likewise fails, and why an EMS relationship evokes the strongest levels of shattered trust, hurt, and anger. It may symbolically represent a "failure" of both individuals as sexual beings, as competent married adults, and as a pair.

These issues are further complicated by the different socialization process received by males and females regarding sex, sexual fidelity, and marriage. Males are encouraged to "get all they can"; to demonstrate their "manliness" by making multiple sexual conquests, before, during, outside of, and after marriage; and to be genitally oriented. Females, on the other hand, are encouraged to remain virgins or at least to limit their sexual activities to their serious premarital lovers and then to their husbands, to be sexually submissive, and to enjoy their sexuality "but not to overdo it." These differential processes, which have, broadly speaking, characterized American sexual training for generations, may be changing under the influence of the women's movement and other modern, egalitarian influences, but clients currently seen in therapists' offices still tend to hold to the earlier values. Only a small minority of current clients demonstrate both conscious and unconscious emancipation from these traditional male-female differences. Consequently, male EMS is often viewed by both of the married partners as more common (which, statistically, it is), as more to be expected, and as more acceptable, or at least less unacceptable, than female infidelity. This shows up when motivations for therapy are considered. If a wife has EMS, the husband's highest motivation for therapy will be to save the marriage. This is less true for wives (Humphrey, 1985b).

Etiology of Extramarital Sexual Relationships

Therapists and clients alike may ask, "Why did the EMS happen?" The reasons are many, complex, often overlapping, and rarely specific and definitive. "Pure" systems therapists may express little interest in the "whys" of EMS, but psychodynamically and behaviorally oriented therapists will wish to explore this area. They will seek to determine what aspects of the clients' intrapsychic and interpersonal systems contributed to the EMS, what defense mechanisms were operating for both spouses, and how therapy may be organized to help the couple cope with the total situation and to assist them, if possible, to resolve the EMS or the marriage or both. Reasons reported by clients for engaging in EMS include: variety; curiosity; retaliation; rebellion; love; friendship; spouse encouragement or permission; reassurance of aging sexuality; pleasure and recreation; combatting depression; infrequent or absent marital coitus; unhappy or boring marriage; poor marital coitus; preserving the marriage; commitment failure; conquest; compensating for feeling inferior or inadequate; learning a new sex technique; being drunk or otherwise under the influence of drugs; gaining social status; getting promoted; frustration; escapism; "curing" sexual dysfunction; "helping out" a sexually deprived friend; asserting one's independence; hurting or challenging a spouse; unavailability of spouse; being neurotic, mentally ill, or retarded; feeling vulnerable; being emancipated from conventional standards; clarifying sexual orientation; creating jealousy and gaining attention; becoming pregnant; earning money; rekindling a former romance with old beau or previous spouse; and reducing marital intimacy. Therapists, not wishing to struggle with such an enormous category of reasons, should consider a smaller number of broader issues. These include: (1) the quality of the overall marital relationship; (2) the quality and quantity of the couple's sexual relationship; (3) the presence of any sexual dysfunctions; (4) both spouses' emotional-mental health; and (5) the presence of any unusual circumstances such as health problems, partner absences, alternative life-style ideologies, or other unusual circumstances.

Thompson (1983) reviewed much of the research literature on EMS and closely examined several studies that reported on the contextual and qualitative characteristics of marriage in respect to EMS. He concluded that "the lower the evaluation of aspects of the marital relationship related to marital satisfaction and the lower the frequency and quality of marital intercourse, the more likely the occurrence of EMS" (Thompson, 1983, p. 10). Although a few studies fail to support this hypothesis, the majority do. When this finding is considered in the light of extensive clinical experience, the evidence appears impressive. We conclude that poor marital adjustment and/or poor marital sexual adjustment is a significant factor in whether or not EMS will occur within a particular marriage.

Looking at the other side of the phenomenon, the evidence appears incontrovertible that EMS leads to severe marital/sexual discord. Clients in treatment for EMS issues report anger and shock as the most common emotional response to the discovery of a partner's EMS. Divorce rates for these couples, even while they are in therapy, have been found to be 10% for husbands' EMAs to 17% for wives; in addition, marital separations occurred in 45% of the husbands' EMS cases and 31% of the wives' (Humphrey, 1985b). However, these figures for divorce are down from 29% and 31%, respectively, reported from a study done in the mid-1970s (Humphrey & Strong, 1976). This may suggest an increasing tolerance by American married couples of their partners' infidelities.

A variety of more individualized explanations for EMS also exist. These include a sense of alienation (Maykovich, 1976); the need for intimacy, emotional independence, and sex role equalitarianism (Buunk, 1980); and, for women at least, possibly knowing someone who had engaged in EMS, talking to another person about the subject, and thinking a lot about it (Atwater, 1979). Although social background factors, in general, are unreliable or varied in explaining the occurrence of EMS (Thompson, 1983), prior knowledge of the EMS partner may play a role. Both research and clinical impressions suggest that wives are more inclined than husbands (41% to 26%) to have EMS with a "friend" and that the working place may be a fertile breeding ground for EMS in today's world, 39% of husbands and 36% of wives in treatment reporting their EMS partner was a co-worker (Humphrey, 1985b). Given the changing roles of women and their ever-increasing participation in the working world outside of their homes, one can predict that the EMS rate for women will rise in the future. Working outside the home raises a woman's "availability quotient," exposes her to more "risks" and opportunities, and may correlate with personality factors that reflect her increasing emancipation from traditional, double-standard, sex mores.

The impact of sexual dysfunction on marital interaction is considered to be consistently negative (Masters & Johnson, 1970; Kaplan, 1983). Regular sexual expression is considered to be the norm for marriage in American society. When dysfunctions prevent this from occurring, or when they interfere with the quality of marital sex, couple discord may be expected to follow almost immediately. This discord may result from blaming the partner for one's own dysfunction or unconsciously displacing the blame into some other aspect of the relationship. Contemporary approaches to sex therapy place high value on the importance of working with both partners (Masters & Johnson, 1970). Sometimes, however, one person refuses to cooperate and may act out in an EMS relationship. As American couples become more sophisticated about sexuality, more and more individuals are realizing that sexual dysfunction may be partner specific (Kaplan, 1983). Faced with erectile dysfunction, a male may decide he needs to utilize the "Coolidge effect" and seek out a new, younger female partner. The pilot study of sex therapy cases referred to earlier in this chapter found that in five cases out of six, sex therapy clients reported sex dysfunction with their spouse but not with their EMS partner(s) (Humphrey, 1985a). This needs to be interpreted with much caution, however. Kinsey reported that 24% of females had not reached coital orgasm in their EMS as often as they had reached it during marital coitus, 34% reached it with about equal frequency, and 42% of his married female subjects reported that orgasm had occurred more often with their EMS partners than it did with the women's husbands (Kinsey et al., 1953, p. 432). This suggests that the Coolidge effect of EMS works for some women with orgasm phase disorders, but it is hardly the cure-all a woman may imagine it to be. Indeed, for the 24% who reached orgasm less often with their EMS partners than they did with their husbands, questions they may have harbored about their sexual adequacy from sex with their husbands may have been reinforced—not diminished—by the EMS activity.

Disorders of sexual desire should be viewed as especially sensitive to the issue of EMS. If a client is actively engaging in EMS, his/her need and desire for marital coitus may become adversely affected. Sexual needs may be satisfied by the EMS, guilt over the EMS may lead the client to unconsciously punish himself by depriving him of the positives of marital sex, and, as previously noted, the lack of sexual desire may be only one of several factors that suggest "dead" marriages, ones that exist in legal and religious fiction only. These factors highlight the desirability of therapists following interviewing and assessment procedures that are most likely to reveal the presence of EMS in a couple (Humphrey, 1983). Amazingly, however, only scant attention has been paid by sex therapists writing on this subject. In her volume on *Disorders of Sexual Desire* Kaplan (1979) mentioned EMS only once. Similarly, LoPiccolo (1980), writing on low sexual desire, examined a wide variety of physiological and psychological issues for low sexual desire, but also mentioned EMS only once. Crenshaw (1985) did likewise. What we appear to be dealing with here is a case of professional tunnel vision. Experts zeroing in on their own special areas of concern may not see or give adequate attention to issues seemingly peripheral to their main concerns. Therapists performing sexual/marital therapy, however, should be ever alert to the possibility of EMS as a significant factor and presence in their cases lest they overlook highly emotional issues directly impacting on all types of sexual dysfunctions, especially low sexual. desire.

In earlier decades it was common to find participants engaged in EMS diagnosed as immature or personality disorders (Caprio, 1953). These may still be considered salient factors in some EMS, but their ipso facto presence is no longer held to be tenable. Profoundly immature individuals usually demonstrate strong narcissistic trends with little compassion for others' feelings. If they want something, they persistently seek to obtain it, including EMS relationships. A variety of neurotic disorders contribute to persons unconsciously acting out their needs for acceptance, attention, power, and other dynamic factors through the satisfactions gained in EMS (Strean, 1980). For personality disorders, individuals who characteristically demonstrate inadequate superego inhibitions, EMS presents little discomfort or worry for their behavior is ego syntonic. Additional mental health considerations would include examination for mental retardation and for the presence of an active psychotic process. Persons in the latter diagnostic categories have to be evaluated from a different perspective than other clients. Treatment for these persons should be in accordance with accepted psychotherapeutic practices for their primary disorders before specialized marital and/or sexual therapies are applied (Kaplan, 1983).

It was noted earlier that, in assessing EMS relationships and their etiology, the presence of any unusual circumstances needs to be considered. Physical and mental health problems of marital partners may interfere with or totally preclude their regular and full participation in marital sex. A young wife, suddenly faced because of a tragic auto accident with a husband with profound and extensive neurological injuries which hospitalize him for months and then leave him a quadraplegic, may have extreme difficulty in maintaining her sexual fidelity vows in the face of such overwhelming problems. Society will condemn her if she resorts to EMS for periodic sexual satisfaction, but therapists, unless blinded by their own moralistic countertransferences, will want to help both her and the husband cope with the realities and feelings of their situation. Periodic spousal absence is another fact of life in contemporary marriage. This ranges from the husband or wife who is "on the road" several days and nights per week or month to the families of nuclear submariners who are separated from each other routinely for months at a time and unable to call each other during this period. Other "dual-career" couples opt for "weekend" marriages while each pursues his/her career in separate cities and states. These absences increase loneliness, sexual frustrations, and vulnerability to other sexual partners who may be immediately available. Many couples in EMS might have been more able to cope with exclusive monogamy were one or both of them not caught up in frustrations of spousal absence.

A third major type of "unusual" circumstance to consider in assessing EMS is made up of those couples who choose to live, or at least experiment with, what have been termed "alternative life-styles." Mate swapping, communal and group marriage, and sexually "open" marriages are examples of these. A common factor in all these life-styles is that lifelong sexual fidelity to one's legal mate is not required as it is in the case of conventional marriage. The sexual activities of participants in these systems have been described as consensual adultery. Proponents of these variations include religious leaders, idealists, futurists, anarchists, and psychotherapists (Cuber & Harroff, 1966; Bartel, 1971; Constantine & Constantine, 1971; Denfield, 1974; Ellis, 1972; English, 1971; Kephart, 1976; Myers & Leggitt, 1968; Rimmer, 1968; Smith & Smith, 1974; Taylor, 1982). When EMS is truly consensual and ego syntonic for both husbands and wives, little marital or sexual discord would be expected. Problems, when they do emerge, arise from several issues. These include coercion by one mate or the other to engage in EMS against his/her wishes, public condemnation, secrecy, bisexuality, sexually transmitted diseases, and "intellectual" consent followed by reactions to unconscious guilt. Many of these couples, if facing marital/sexual problems, avoid "conventional" therapists as they believe them to be prejudiced against these life-styles and, hence, the participants themselves (Constantine, Constantine, & Edelman, 1972).

Negative Consequences of Extramarital Sex

Proponents of EMS, including those vociferously defending alternative life-styles, civil-rights defenders supporting the rights of consenting adults to live their sexual lives without government interference, and some therapists, have been accused of only talking about benefits of EMS. Marital/sexual therapists, along with individual therapists, social workers, attorneys, and police, however, most commonly find clients reporting on EMS with regard to their negative consequences for the marital couple, their children and family, the EMS partner(s) and his/her/their families, and the broader social consequences. A list of the consequences that clients report includes the breaking of religious teachings; the breaking of trust; guilt; dishonesty; lies; anger; humiliation; depression; suicide; homicide; marital conflict; separation; divorce; anxiety; regret; lost respect and love; disruption of careers, marriages, and families; their illegality; loss of reputation; unwanted pregnancies; abortions; sexually transmitted diseases; time and money lost; fears; masking of the need for individual, marital, family, or sexual therapy; exploitation; jealousy; the length of time needed to "heal" their repercussions; and sexual conflicts and dysfunctions. Such a list could probably be considerably expanded. The negative consequences of EMS are many and serious.

In a clinical sample of clients' reactions to learning that their spouses were engaged in EMS, the most common negative emotion experienced by husbands over their wives' EMS was anger (38% ranked it first) and shock (19%) (Humphrey, 1985b). Wives ranked shock first (45%) and 35% responded with anger. Therapists noted that 8% of husbands and 7% of wives first reacted to their spouses' infidelity with denial, suggesting this defense may not be common in EMS cases. No wives responded first with calm acceptance of their husband's EMS and only 3% of husbands responded to their wives' EMS this way. At the other end of this spectrum of responses to spouse's EMS, in 6% of husbands' EMS and in 14% of wives' EMS, their spouses never knew about the EMS even after marital therapy was completed. It should also be noted that in 26% of cases with husbands' EMS and 21% of cases of wives' EMS therapists reported couples' marital relationships as improved at the end of therapy. It is not possible to ascertain whether this is due to the EMS, the therapy, both, or neither. Yet, in 46% of the husbands' EMS and 48% of the wives', the couple were either separated or divorced at the end of therapy, illustrating the high toll that EMS takes, at least on those who seek therapy. However, 24% of husbands and 23% of wives were still involved in EMS at the end of therapy, suggesting the strong involvement many persons have with their EMS partners (Humphrey, 1985b).

If the study reported above may be considered representative of clients who seek out professional therapy to help them cope with the consequences of EMS, EMS must be viewed as one of the most significant threats to marriage that exists. It strikes at the very existence of the continuation of the marriage, and even for those that survive, clinical evidence suggests that recovery for the marital pair must be anticipated to take months or years before trust, comfort, and stability have fully returned. Some clients report they never completely recover from the aftereffects of the EMS. These marriages may appear stable, but much of the joy and happiness in them is permanently lost. Sometimes the EMS, seemingly forgotten, emerges as a contributor to marital friction or divorce years later.

Little or no research evidence is available on the direct impact of EMS on couples' sexual adjustments and functions. However, earlier references to the impact of marital distress on sexual adjustment appears to support clinical impressions that EMS always impacts on marital sex. The impacts frequently create polar opposite effects, however. Some spouses react to their mates'

EMS by overcompensating in their sexual activities. Marital sex frequencies may increase dramatically, techniques or positions previously rejected may now be initiated by the nonparticipating spouses, sex and love "manuals" appear in the bedrooms, and, at least for a time, strenuous efforts may be made to prove to the "errant" spouse that the husband or wife is just as "sexy," if not more so, than the EMS outside partner. Some married couples that survive EMS report that their sexual adjustments permanently improve, although they settle down to a more average norm after the immediate scare of the EMS has worn off. At the other end of this spectrum, some marital sex adjustments are permanently negatively affected. Spouses, on learning of their mate's EMS, may terminate forever all marital sex. Others may develop an immediate secondary sexual dysfunction. Perhaps no other event so dramatically demonstrates the impact of emotions on sexual desire and functioning. Couples who previously enjoyed satisfactory sexual lives find that within the space of a few hours after learning of the partner's EMS, their marital sex is drastically harmed. Sex therapy in these instances, according to Kaplan (1983), should be held off until the marital distress is reasonably resolved. If, however, the impact of the EMS has less negative impact on the marriage than these severe responses, combined sex/marital therapy may ensue (Kaplan, 1974).

SPECIFIC THERAPEUTIC CONSIDERATIONS IN COUPLES/SEX THERAPY CASES INVOLVING EXTRAMARITAL SEX

Unit of Treatment

Marriage, in its simplest terms, may be thought of as a two-person system. As such it may be open or closed according to the permeability of the boundaries established by each member of the couple. Ordinarily, in respect to sexual activity and adult love, couples initially act, think, and feel that the boundary lines for these attributes will be clear, mutually agreed upon, and maintained in such a manner that the system is closed for life. The violation of this line instantly changes a two-person system into a minimum of a three-person system. If, as many therapists postulate, all significant persons in a system should, or must, be involved in any therapeutic activities, all therapists dealing with an EMS case should demand, at the very least, the inclusion of the EMS person(s) into the therapy room with the husband and the wife. For marital/sexual therapists with these therapeutic philosophies, ethical and practical problems immediately emerge when it comes to specific therapeutic considerations. Who is (are) the client(s)? Who pays for the treatment hour? How do you bill whose insurance carrier? Will all three (or more) of these people work together? If a sex dysfunction exists for one part of the triangle but not another part, which part does the therapist focus on? The answers to these questions preclude rational explanation; hence "pure" systems therapy is ordinarily not practical for EMS marital/sex cases.

In actual practice, it appears that marital therapists (information is lacking about sex therapists) tend to ignore the EMS "outside" person. In studying treatment units it was reported that almost never did therapists see the participating spouse and his/her EMS partner(s) conjointly. The number of therapists seeing the husband, wife, and his/her/their partner(s) all together was infinitesimal (Humphrey, 1985b). Reasons given for these "failures" to include these "outside" significant EMS persons include the following: therapists' loyalty to the marriages, refusal of one or more clients to sit in the same room with "those" persons, problems of professional ethics, and a lack of therapeutic models to encompass the divergent goals that would be presented in such groups. Therapists may feel it desirable to refer these outside EMS partners to therapists of their own choosing to work on their own issues. These outside EMS partners have been treated by much of the literature as forgotten persons, for they are rarely mentioned. They too, however, are often married so that marital/sexual therapy should be encouraged for them. Treatment of the whole family in EMS cases has been reported as averaging 1.5 sessions for husbands' EMAs, 1.8 for wives', and 3.9 when both have EMAs. Conjoint interviews have averaged 9 to 10 sessions for all types of EMS, and two to seven individual interviews have been held with one or both spouses (Humphrey, 1985b). From these reports, one would conclude that conjoint sessions are the most common treatment unit utilized by marital and family therapists. This is not surprising, given the outcome research studies that support the effectiveness of this approach. At the same time it should be noted that numerous individual sessions are conducted, thus allowing therapists to concentrate on specific issues partners may have without the deterrent of their spouse's presence. Issues of guilt, blame, ambivalence, and unresolved attractions to outside EMS partners may be addressed at these times. Family sessions are utilized infrequently, and when they do occur, they are likely to be during the assessment process, before the EMS is known to the therapist, and again when the circular impact of the affair on the children is dealt with, especially if there are teen-agers in the family.

Therapeutic Goals

When an EMS case first enters therapy, therapy goals frequently vary between participating and nonparticipating spouses. The person not participating in the EMS seeks rapid resolution of the crisis that almost invariably exists and the immediate cessation of the affair, if that has not yet occurred. The spouse participating in the EMS, however, is often unclear about what s/he expects from therapy. Couples may expect the therapists to demand, as a condition of therapy, that the EMS stop. Therapeutic resistance in these cases may be high, at least initially, especially on the part of the spouse engaging in EMS. Some EMS participants may set as their goals the utilization of therapy to work through their ambivalences about both their EMS and their marriages. Many see their only "solutions" as bigamy for they feel in love with both their legal spouses and extralegal partners. The dilemma for therapists is to determine just where to start, with whom, and on what. Decisions about treatment goals need to be made quite promptly, however, as the caldrons of emotions couples experience at these times are often boiling near the point of explosion.

Prioritizing Goals and Approaches

Marital/sexual EMS problems present therapists with a challenging array of issues on which to focus. What is most needed? Individual, marital, or family therapy? Education? Surgery? The administration of various drugs? Referral to other specialists? Pinsof (1983), Kaplan (1983), and Humphrey and Eldridge (1984) have addressed the prioritizing of therapeutic approaches. Their contributions consist of accessing the presenting complaints in a manner wherein issues are examined according to their need for sex therapy (psychogenic, organic, and/or surgical considerations), individual therapy (counseling, education, or psychiatric treatment), or marital therapy, or combinations of all three of these. The rationale for these priority systems rests in the issues of crisis management, degree of impairment that each complaint presents to the person/couple, source of the difficulty, and motivations of the clients. A psychiatrically "normal" couple in a satisfactory marriage with a sexual dysfunction would ordinarily be candidates for "regular" sex therapy; a couple experiencing extreme marital distress (such as so often accompanies EMS cases) would first be offered marital therapy even if sexual dysfunction(s) existed; and a person seriously psychiatrically impaired would have to be treated for this before either marital or sexual therapy could be considered. Although concurrent marital/sexual/individual therapy may be considered in some cases (Kaplan, 1974), the high anger, rage, and distrust levels present in EMS cases usually dictate that treatment of the EMS issues be resolved, or at least significantly mitigated, before sex therapy commences.

Stopping the EMS:
Therapists' Dictates or Clients' Choices

Therapists are divided on whether or not any type of therapy should be initiated if an EMS is ongoing. One school of thought holds that marital therapy is impossible in the face of an ongoing EMS, regardless of whether or not the nonparticipating spouse knows about it. They point to the guilt, the ambivalence, the hurt, and distrust — or the imminent possibility of these occurring — to the divided loyalties, and to triangulated systems and, therefore, refuse to treat couples when the EMS is ongoing. If these couples are accepted for treatment, the therapists demand that the EMS stop. This demand is made in 25% of husbands' EMS cases, 20% of wives' and 15% of the cases when both marital partners are having affairs (Humphrey, 1985b). Another stance is taken by therapists who do not necessarily require the EMS to stop but who do demand that the participating spouses tell their marital partners about these outside relationships (3.4% of husbands' EMS cases, 1.6% of wives', and 3.7% if both are having EMS; Humphrey, 1985b). The largest proportion of therapists, however, take issue with these more dogmatic positions and maintain neutrality on the issue of stopping or continuing the EMS and of telling or not telling one's spouse about the EMS. This neutrality occurs in 33 to 37% of all cases (Humphrey, 1985b). These therapists take the stance that therapists involved in all types of systems therapy should remain neutral, that they have no right to impose their own values or standards on clients, and that all clients have a right to make their own decisions. In addition, it may be argued that until any particular behavior becomes ego syntonic, its cessation due to the imposition of an outside authority will, at best, be temporary and may very well contribute to therapeutic resistance, including dropping out of therapy.

When an EMS relationship remains ongoing, therapists should grant the participating spouses ample private, individual session time to explore with them feelings about both their regular mates and their outside partners, to explore and attempt to help them resolve probable ambivalences toward each of the persons they are involved with, to produce insights into the individual and couple dynamics that led to the EMS, to reflect on how the EMS currently impacts on them and their marital partners, and, finally, to reach a decision regarding the continuance or ending of either the EMS relationship or the marriage, or both. At the same time the nonparticipating mates need a great deal of cathartic support and help with their anger, broken trust, depressions, ambivalences, and future plans. If the EMS remains secret, therapists must be able to keep confidentiality intact and to handle their own countertransference feelings about what is going on. Some therapists choose not to have to contend with their discomforts in these situations and take one of several steps to change things. They may refuse to handle the case, demand the EMS stop or at least that the nonparticipating spouse be told, or they may restrict the couple exclusively to conjoint sessions where everyone knows what is being discussed. This may handle the problem for the therapists, but it may leave one or both of the marital partners feeling blocked from therapeutic discussions of their own, individualized concerns.

When confidential, individual sessions are combined with conjoint sessions, therapeutic work in these couple interviews can be focused on the issues directly impacting on the couple's daily lives (Humphrey, 1983). It is during these conjoint sessions that, ultimately, couples must reach consensus between themselves in respect to the EMS, to the sexual issues within the marriage, and to the future of the marriage itself. If consensus is not reached, an impasse of conflicting goals, behaviors, and feelings will create continued stress and conflict. This will make the future both of sexual functioning and of the marriage itself precarious. In many cases this will lead to the abandoning of the goals of marital/sexual improvement, and a switch to divorce therapy is indicated.

Marital Therapy After EMS Has Ended

At first glance it may appear that once outside EMS relationships are terminated, couples are free to focus directly on the remaining sexual/marital issues. Such a belief is a great oversimplification, however, for much healing needs to occur before the necessary ingredients for satisfactory sexual/marital interaction can occur. As noted, trust is invariably shattered when EMS occurs, and trust is a cornerstone upon which all human relationships are built. Therapeutic strategies should be focused, therefore, on behaviors and communications that permit each member of the marital unit to earn the other's trust and respect. Anger must be dissipated, both through cathartic ventilation within the sessions and in the couple's home life. Guilt must be addressed, both the guilt of the participating spouse about what s/he has done and that of the nonparticipating spouse about what s/he may have contributed to the breakdown of the couple's system.

Loss is another theme at this time. The participating spouse may give up his/her outside EMS partner but, if strong positive emotional feeling has existed for that person, the spouse may easily become depressed, grieve, and have intense feelings of loneliness and isolation. When an adult loses a loved one by death, society provides many types of support, including rituals at funerals, visits and support from relatives and friends, and general community recognition of the loss. When an EMS lover is lost, however, no such support exists and the therapist may be the only person who is aware of the problem and in a position to offer supportive help. Due to the crisis that often occurs when an EMS is discovered and/or dissolved, the participating marital partner may not only have to contend with the loss of the loved one but may also experience the outside partner's rejection as that person moves to protect his/her own loss. Or, in other cases, the outside person may continue his/her attempts to maintain or resume the relationship, thus complicating the spouse's struggle with guilt, rejection, and the confusion of finding contentment back in his/her own marriage. Months of therapy are frequently required before couples can begin to relax in their marriages with any reasonable sense of confidence and trust.

Sex Therapy After an EMS Has Ended

When can sex therapy be attempted after an explosive EMS relationship has disrupted the marriage? No definite answers can be given. In marital therapy, this therapeutic quandary does not exist, as EMS produces an immediate crisis, both marital partners are affected by it, and therapy must move quickly to deal with the consequences. Ordinarily, however, sex therapy cannot be successfully undertaken without the existence of a reasonably committed couple relationship. Kaplan (1983) writes,

> The success of treatment depends on eliminating or modifying the immediate, currently operating psychobehavioral antecedents which are impairing the patient's functioning. This is the crucial ingredient for cure and the basic strategy of sex therapy. When therapy succeeds in modifying the immediate cause of the patient's symptom, his sexual functioning will improve no matter what other psychological or relationship problems remain (p. 42).

Although her remarks were focused primarily on individual, intrapsychic issues, they appear to be highly relevant here as all marital partners in the crisis of EMS experience high levels of psychic and behavioral disequilibrium. They must be helped to reach more normal, stable levels of functioning before they can concentrate on specific sex-functioning issues. Consistent with Kaplan's (1983) statements, many couples report an increase in both sexual functioning and sexual pleasure when their EMS issues are successfully resolved. Indeed, it may be speculated that, from a systems perspective, EMS relationships may be interpreted as cries for help from distressed marital/sexual relationships. This is not to say, however, that specific sex therapy techniques are not going to be required after EMS is resolved. What the resolution of the affairs does is to unleash couples' motivations, strengths, and sense of commitment so that they can more fully invest themselves in addressing the specific sexual dysfunctions that exist. Standard sex therapy can now be undertaken, but therapists need to remain continuously alert to the repercussions that the EMS will persistently introject into couples' relationships for months or even years afterward.

SUMMARY AND CONCLUSIONS

Extramarital sexual relationships exist in American marriages in large numbers. Surveys and clinical experience indicate that half or more of all distressed couples coming to therapists for help with their marital/sexual lives may be so affected. The psychological and systems repercussions of EMS are so intense and invasive that couples may expect both their marital and their sexual functioning to be adversely affected until the EMS issues are successfully resolved. This will result either in improved marriages or in separations/divorces. In the former cases treatment strategies must be focused on the EMS and marriage issues before specific therapies can be undertaken for the sexual dysfunctions. In the case of separations/divorces, sex therapy will ordinarily become a moot issue, at least in respect to the marital unit.

REFERENCES

Athanasiou, R., Shaver, P., & Tavris, C. (1970, July). *Psychology Today*, 37–52.

Atwater, L. (1979). Getting involved: Women's transition to first extramarital sex. *Alternative Lifestyles, 2*, 33–38.

Bartel, G. (1971). *Group sex: An eye witness report on the American way of swinging.* New York: Signet, New American Library.

Beck, D. F., & Jones, M. (1973). *Progress in family problems.* New York: Family Service Association of America.

Bell, R. R., Turner, S., & Rosen, L. (1975). A multivariate analysis of female extramarital coitus. *Journal of Marriage and the Family, 37*, 375–384.

Brecher, E. M. (1984). *Love, sex, and aging: A Consumers Union report.* Boston: Little, Brown.

Buunk, B. (1980). Extramarital sex in the Netherlands: Motivation in social and marital context. *Alternative Lifestyles, 40*, 11–39.

Caprio, F. (1953). *Marital infidelity.* New York: Citadel.

Constantine, L. L., & Constantine, J. M. (1971). Sexual aspects of multilateral relations. *Journal of Sex Research, 7*(3), 204–290.

Constantine, L. L., Constantine, J. M., & Edelman, S. K. (1972). Counseling implications of comarital and multilateral relations. *The Family Coordinator, 21*(3), 267–273.

Crenshaw, T. (1985). The sexual aversion syndrome. *Journal of Sex and Marital Therapy, 11*(4), 285–292.

Cuber, J. F., & Harroff, P. B. (1966). *Sex and the significant Americans: A study of sexual behavior among the affluent.* Baltimore: Penguin.

Denfield, D. (1974). Dropouts from swinging. *The Family Coordinator, 23*(1), 45–49.

Ellis, A. (1972). *The civilized couple's guide to extramarital adventure.* New York: Wyden.

English, O. S. (1971). Positive values of the affair. In H. Otto (Ed.), *The new sexuality* (pp. 173–192). Palo Alto, CA: Science and Behavior.

Hite, S. (1981). *The Hite report on male sexuality.* New York: Knopf.

Humphrey, F. G. (1983). *Marital therapy.* Englewood Cliffs, NJ: Prentice-Hall.

Humphrey, F. G. (1985a). Sexual dysfunction and/or enhancement interactions with extramarital affairs. Paper presented at Yale University Sex Therapy Program, New Haven, CT, January 9, 1985.

Humphrey, F. G. (1985b). Extramarital affairs and their treatment by AAMFT therapists. Paper presented at American Association of Marriage and Family Therapy, New York, October 19, 1985.

Humphrey, F. G. (In preparation). *Extramarital affairs: History, etiology, and treatment.* Englewood Cliffs, NJ: Prentice-Hall.

Humphrey, F. G., & Eldridge, S. (1984). Unraveling and treating interlocking dynamics of sexual and marital complaints. Paper presented at American Association of Marriage and Family Therapy, San Francisco, CA, October 20, 1984.

Humphrey, F. G., & Strong, F. (1976). Treatment of extramarital sexual relationships as reported by clinical members of AAMFC. Paper presented at Northeastern American Association of Marriage and Family Counselors, Hartford, CT, May 22, 1976.

Hunt, M. (1974). *Sexual behavior in the 70's*. Chicago: Playboy.

Johnson, R. E. (1970). Some correlations of extramarital coitus. *Journal of Marriage and the Family, 32*, 449–456.

Kaplan, H. S. (1974). *The new sex therapy*. New York: Brunner/Mazel.

Kaplan, H. S. (1979). *The new sex therapy*. Vol. II: *Disorders of sexual desire*. New York: Brunner/Mazel.

Kaplan, H. S. (1983). *The evaluation of sexual disorders: Psychological and medical aspects*. New York: Brunner/Mazel.

Kephart, W. H. (1976). *Extraordinary groups: The sociology of unconventional life styles*. New York: St. Martin's Press.

Kinsey, A. C., Pomeroy, W. B., & Martin, C. E. (1953). *Sexual behavior in the human female*. Philadelphia: Saunders.

Kinsey, A. C., Pomeroy, W. B., Martin, C. E., & Gebhard, P. H. (1953). *Sexual behavior in the human female*. Philadelphia: Saunders.

Levin, R. J. (1975, October). The *Redbook* report on premarital and extramarital sex. *Redbook*, 38, 40, 42, 190, 192.

LoPiccolo, L. (1980). Low sexual desire. In S. Leiblum and L. Pervin (Eds.), *Principles and practice of sex therapy*. New York: Guilford.

Masters, W. H., & Johnson, V. (1970). *Human sexual inadequacy*. Boston: Little, Brown.

Maykovich, M. D. (1976). Attitudes versus behavior in extramarital sexual relations. *Journal of Marriage and the Family, 38*, 693–699.

Myers, L., & Leggitt, H. (1975). A positive view of adultery. In L. Gross (Ed.), *Sexual issues in marriage*. New York: Signet.

Pietropinto, A., & Simenauer, J. (1978). *Beyond the male myth*. New York: New American Library.

Pinsof, W. (1983). Integrative problem centered therapy: Toward the synthesis of family and individual psychotherapies. *Journal of Marital and Family Therapy, 9*(1), 19–35.

Rimmer, R. (1968). *Proposition 31*. New York: Signet.

Sarrel, L. (1984). Personal conversation, December 7.

Smith, J. R., & Smith, L. G. (1974). *Beyond monogamy: Recent studies of sexual alternatives in marriage*. Baltimore: Johns Hopkins.

Strean, H. (1980). *The extramarital affair*. New York: The Free Press.

Taylor, R. (1982). *Having love affairs*. Buffalo, NY: Prometheus.

Teissman, M. (1983). Institute on Extramarital Relationships. Presented at the American Association of Marriage and Family Therapy, Washington, DC, October 6, 1983.

Thompson, A. T. (1983). Extramarital sex: A review of research literature. *Journal of Sex Research, 19*(1), 1–22.

Wolfe, L. (1980, September). The sexual profile of that Cosmopolitan girl. *Cosmopolitan*, 254–265.

Yablonsky, L. (1979). *The extra-sex factor: Why over half of America's married men play around*. New York: Times Books.

Chapter 9

Effects of Rape on the Marital Relationship

William R. Miller

It is well known that rape can leave deep and long-lasting psychological scars on the victim. Less well understood are the effects of rape victimization on the spouses, lovers, and families of women who are raped. The purpose of this chapter is to discuss the types of marital and sexual dysfunctions that result from rape and to describe treatment approaches for these dysfunctions.

Rape is a legal term whose definition varies across legal jurisdictions. Rape, as legally defined, requires vaginal penetration with the use of threat of force and nonconsent of the victim. The author agrees, however, with others (cf. Brownmiller, 1975) who broaden the definition of rape to include any sexual intimacy forced on another person. In this chapter, therefore, the terms rape and sexual assault will be used interchangeably. We will begin our discussion by briefly reviewing the characteristics of the rape victim population.

VICTIMS OF RAPE

In spite of the many recent studies and surveys of rape, there continues to be great controversy regarding the frequency of rape. The crime rate for rape varies from the FBI statistic of 47 per 100,000 to an estimate of 200 per 100,000 (Sutherland & Scherl, 1970). One major source of the variance in estimates of the frequency of rape is the unwillingness of many victims to report rape to the police. The findings of studies of unreported rape differ widely (Amir, 1971; Sutherland & Scherl, 1970).

Rape victims are predominantly female adolescents and young adults (Amir, 1971). Male victimization by means of homosexual rape occurs, but it is relatively uncommon except in institutional settings. Child victims of sexual assault, particularly victims of incest, have received special attention in the rape literature. Our focus here, however, will be on the adolescent and adult victims of rape.

A consistent finding in the rape research literature is that blacks are over-represented in rape statistics and also that victims are mainly from the lower socioeconomic classes. For example, Amir (1971) reports a frequency of rape 12 times higher for blacks than for whites.

PSYCHOLOGICAL IMPACT OF RAPE

The Victim

Burgess and Holmstrom (1974) labeled the typical psychological effects of rape as the "rape trauma syndrome." This syndrome entails two postrape stages — the acute disorganized phase and the long-term reorganization phase. Burgess and Holmstrom (1974) also identify two types of victim response. The expressed style is one in which the victim is visibly emotional and upset, whereas the controlled style is characterized by more denial and reaction formation and less emotionality.

In the immediate phase of acute response the victim experiences a variety of physical and emotional symptoms. A shock reaction occurs with fear as the primary emotional response. At first, the most common fear is of death. With the passage of time, however, fear of men, sex, and locations associated with the rape often emerge. Consistent with this fear response is the occurrence of obsessive thoughts about the attack.

Other acute emotional reactions include somatic complaints, depression, changes in sleep patterns and nightmares, changes in eating habits, and shame and guilt.

As the acute reaction subsides, the victims attempt to cope with their anxiety through a number of mechanisms. Some turn to alcohol and/or drugs. Others develop a phobic avoidance of feared objects and situations. Sexual intercourse, discussion of sex, and sometimes even nonsexual physical affection and touching are avoided.

If the rape occurred in the victim's home or neighborhood, she may change her place of residence. The need to relocate is so great that the victim sometimes moves within days after the rape. All too often, however, changing the place of residence has mixed effects. Changing her surroundings may make the victim feel more safe and secure from retaliation by the rapist. However, since she is usually terrified of being alone, the sudden separation from friends and neighbors may increase her feelings of aloneness and isolation. The victim's fear often leads to heightened feelings of dependency, an outcome that can have damaging consequences for the victim's intimate relationships.

The passage of time reduces the level of disorganization experienced by most victims. A variety of residual symptoms, such as phobias, compulsive rituals, avoidance of sex, and excessive dependency, may continue, however, to interfere with a complete return to the prerape adjustment. Changes in lifestyle with deficits in functioning at home, work, and in school are common. The intensity of the symptoms during this reorganization process is a function of the victim's prior coping mechanisms and personality and the support she receives from others.

The Partner

Little attention has been given to the male response to the rape of his partner. One study suggested that boyfriends and husbands often have strong negative reactions toward the victim (Silverman, 1978). Male partners were reported to be angry and resentful toward the victim. The males were seen as feeling personally wronged, since they typically endorsed the attitude that the woman was the male's exclusive property. This response has, however, been found to be atypical in other studies (Miller & Williams, 1984; Miller, Williams, & Bernstein, 1982).

In fact, the author has observed some strong similarities between the reactions of the victim and the reactions of her male partner. Like the victims, some of the men experience an immediate fear response. For the men, however, the fear is usually short-lived, probably because the men have not personally experienced a life-threatening situation. Overt fear and anxiety usually subside quickly, but other signs of anxiety, such as sleeping and eating disturbances and difficulties in concentration, may remain for days or weeks. Male partners typically do not develop phobias or compulsive behaviors after the rape. The rather quick resolution of the fear/anxiety components in the men limits the association of anxiety with environmental stimuli, making the development of phobias less likely. Also, the need for defense mechanisms against anxiety, such as compulsive rituals, is lower when the anxiety and fear are briefer and/or less intense as they are in the male partners.

Usually, the men feel some degree of responsibility for their wives or girlfriends having been raped. The men berate themselves for not having protected their partner. These guilt feelings usually subside gradually over a period of weeks, although some men continue to feel quite guilty for long periods of time. During the fear and guilt stage, the men often spend much more time with their partners than had been the case prior to the rape. Taking extra time to be with the victim sometimes causes additional problems for the male. For example, some male partners have lost jobs or suffered poor performance in school due to lack of attention to work or school responsibilities, outcomes that seriously aggravate the husband's feelings of helplessness.

A rage response, emerging with the quick dissipation of fear, is the most dramatic emotional response of the male partner of rape victims. Many men become consumed by anger and rage, their waking hours and their dreams filled with fantasies of confronting the rapist and killing or hurting him.

In cases where the rapist has not been arrested, the male partner's inability to vent his anger on an appropriate target increases his feelings of powerlessness, feelings that are shared by the victim. To counter these feelings, the men attempt to reestablish control through indirect means. Some men spend many hours either thinking of ways to apprehend the rapist or searching for the attacker. Others sublimate their aggressive impulses with the male directing enormous energy into work, presumably to gain power through greater authority and a higher income. In cases where a suspect has been arrested, the male partner often pressures the victim to prosecute, even when she's reluctant because of her fears of retaliation or of rekindling her nightmares.

It may be, of course, that the male's rage response is unconsciously directed at the victim and derives from the feeling that the male's property has been damaged (cf. Silverman, 1978). My own clinical observations suggest, however, that more commonly the male *identifies* with his partner and shares to some extent her pain and trauma. His rage is thus seen as resulting from a sense of injustice and a powerlessness at altering the situation.

The Couple

Since a variety of factors act to modify a couple's reaction to rape, there is no standard, invariant response pattern for all couples. Nevertheless, we are able to identify responses to sexual assaults that seem to be typical. These include problems in empathic understanding, communication disturbances, excessive dependency, and a variety of sexual dysfunctions.

In spite of the previously described similarities in response to rape of the male and female partners, the partners frequently lack an empathic understanding of each other. A difficulty in distancing oneself sufficiently from one's own feelings to appropriately respond to the feelings of the other results, in part, from the simultaneous experience of both partners' intense feelings, such as fear, guilt, and rage. Another factor interfering with the experience of accurate empathy is the different timing of the sequential emergence of emotions in the partners. Since the male's stage of fear and guilt tends to be much briefer than the female's, the male begins to experience the rage response at the same time that the victim is still very fearful and anxious. Thus, the female's main concern is for safety and security, whereas the male's primary concern is for revenge and retribution.

To gain revenge, the male partner may discuss, plan, and think about a variety of methods—either through legal routes or by direct confrontation—to inflict pain and punishment on the rapist. This aggressive and confrontative stance is in direct opposition to the victim's seeking of safety and anxiety reduction by means of avoidance, withdrawal, denial, and repression. As the partners focus on their individual need for revenge or for safety, they tend to become less understanding of their partner's opposite need.

The communication disturbances that occur are perhaps the most damaging consequences of rape for the couple. The victim does not want to talk about—or even think about—the assault. The victim avoids discussion of her thoughts and feelings, and the male partner is left to guess at what she needs from him.

Of course, the male partner is enduring his own disturbing thoughts and feelings. Yet, he knows that his partner is in pain and avoids burdening her with his feelings. The tragedy is that the partners consequently fail to give and receive the mutual support and sharing that they need so much.

As was mentioned above, high levels of fear typically lead the victim into a more dependent role *vis-à-vis* her partner. Although the male initially tries to give the needed support, his efforts are undermined by his own emotional trauma and by the external pressures of commitments to his job. Also, the continuation for weeks or months of heightened emotionality in the victim often erodes the partner's resolve to be supportive. Thus, the victim's increased dependency needs are felt by the male as a drain. He becomes resentful, and the victim's needs go unfulfilled.

As the male's rage response emerges, the male partner becomes even less able to meet the victim's dependency needs. Furthermore, this rage tends to increase the victim's anxiety. She fears that her partner may get into trouble or that the rage will be turned back onto herself. The rage is often a reminder to the victim of the violence of the rape and may reinforce the victim's fear of men as violent and dangerous.

The communication difficulties and increased dependency finally lead to mutual resentment. Resentment develops in the woman for needing her partner so much and for feeling that he is not fulfilling her needs. The male's resentment results from his being placed in a position where he can never be as supportive and protective as his partner requires.

Sexual Problems

Sexual problems and dysfunctions are among the most common sequelae to rape, and the sexual disturbances may arise in a number of ways. Most commonly, the victim avoids all sexual contact for a period of a few weeks (although, in some cases, months of avoidance are seen). Usually, the male partner is understanding of this initial sexual avoidance and waits for some sign of readiness for sex from the victim.

A major source of problems at this point is the previously described communication disturbance, which tends to interfere with the partners' understanding of each other's needs and desires. Each partner may be waiting for signs of sexual interest before initiating sexual activity. Obviously, though, if both partners are waiting for a signal from the other to initiate and if the partners are not openly talking about their desires, no initiation occurs. Thus, continued sexual avoidance results with resentment and anger eventually becoming overt. This process is intensified in couples where, prior to the rape, the female had seldom taken the sexual initiative.

In a majority of cases, the male or female partner may attempt sexual activity very soon after the rape. The motivation for such a quick resumption of sexual activity may be to replace the horrible memory of the rape with a pleasant memory of shared and loving sex or to somehow confirm one's femininity, masculinity, or love of the partner. There are several problems with this approach.

First, sex is being initiated in an attempt to serve some need other than mutual caring and love; it is to prove a point of sorts. Second, sex is being initiated at a time when the predominant emotions in both partners are fear and perhaps guilt or anger. Finally, there is a "testing" quality to the sex. That is, one or often both partners are observing each other's sexual responses to see whether "things are still right." This is a form of spectatoring that inevitably is associated with performance anxiety and, thus, very likely with performance difficulties.

When sexual relations are resumed — with or without a period of sexual avoidance — many couples are anxious and tentative in their responses. Many victims find that although they are sexually interested, certain sexual behaviors are reminders of the rape and lead to anxiety and/or withdrawal. Often the males respond to this anxiety and pulling back with fear or with anger for the presumed rejection. This atmosphere of self-observance, spectatoring, hurt, anger, and anxiety may lead to the development of any of the female or male sexual dysfunctions, although female dysfunctions occur much more commonly.

TREATMENT OF MARITAL/SEXUAL DYSFUNCTIONS

Rapists obviously do not select their victims on the basis of the victim's individual, marital, and sexual adjustment. Virtually any woman can become a victim of rape. Consequently, the observed psychological reactions to rape will depend not only on the occurrence of the rape, but also on the preexisting individual and relationship strengths and weaknesses of the victim and partner.

Some rape victims and their male partners recover rather quickly and completely from the rape experience. For these couples, no long-lasting negative effects are seen. These couples are comprised of psychologically healthy and resilient individuals in loving, unconflicted relationships. Typically, these couples have also been fortunate in receiving support from families and friends after the rape and in avoiding traumatization in dealing with institutional reactions to rape (Holmstrom & Burgess, 1978).

Most couples are neither so well adjusted nor so fortunate. For these couples, a variety of individual and relationship disturbances will remain after recovery from the acute disorganization stage. As we have seen, there are a number of common themes in a couple's long-term responses to rape. Yet, clinicians must be prepared to deal with the fact that each couple has its own unique set of coping strategies, defenses, and dysfunctions. Further complicating the clinical picture are various preexisting conditions, such as individual psychopathology, alcoholism, and marital and family conflict. These factors not only affect the couple's reaction to the rape, but also continue as ongoing problems in their own right.

As a result of this complexity and variety of individual and relationship dynamics, there is no univariant approach to the treatment of all rape victim couples. Rather, the therapist needs to address the problems with what can be referred to as "informed eclecticism." That is, the therapist needs to make a careful assessment of the needs of each couple and then to apply any of a wide variety of treatment approaches, techniques, and modalities to the issues at hand.

The first step in developing a treatment plan is, of course, obtaining a thorough individual and relationship history. The same general approach to obtaining this history as would be used in other cases of marital and/or sexual dysfunction is used (cf. Martin, 1976). The clinician must be very sensitive, though, to the particular difficulty that many rape victims have with discussions of the details of the rape. Some basic information about the rape incident needs to be acquired during the initial history taking, but a focused discussion of the details of the rape can be, if necessary, postponed until a good therapeutic rapport has been developed with the couple.

Decisions need to be made in regard to the use of male/female cotherapy teams and of individual, conjoint, and group sessions. My experience has been that the complicated, gender-related issues in rape-victim couples make the use of male/female cotherapy teams especially beneficial.

Rape victims, because of their special fear of men, often find it very difficult to establish a good, therapeutic relationship with a male therapist. Some of these male partners also have difficulty relating to a male therapist, fearing that the therapist will judge him negatively for not having "protected" his wife. Other male partners are concerned that a female therapist will be aligned too closely to the victim and fail to understand his pain. With an awareness of these gender-related issues, the cotherapists can adjust the style of the cotherapy to deal with these concerns.

Since, for example, fear of men is usually intense in rape victims, the female member of the cotherapy team can initially take primary responsibility for questioning and exploring issues with the victim, while the male therapist reflects feeling statements back to the victim. As the victim begins to see the male therapist as less threatening, he begins to interact more actively with the victim.

Another advantage of cotherapy teams is that the therapists are modeling for the couple a method of communication and interaction. As therapy progresses, the therapists can use their relationship as a vehicle not only for modeling, but also for more direct demonstration of new communication patterns.

Both marital and sex therapy are typically conducted conjointly. There are advantages with rape victim couples, however, to more blending of individual and conjoint sessions than is usually the case. In addition, there are some powerful benefits to group treatment sessions.

Individual sessions allow for greater freedom in dealing with the secrecy about thoughts and feelings that characterizes many rape victim couples. The members of the couple experience a greater sense of safety and freedom in being able to "open up" with the therapist in the absence of the spouse. Since individual sessions eliminate the worry about a negative reaction from a spouse who is listening, the therapist can also be more confrontive in exploring secrets in the individual session.

When secrets are uncovered during an individual session, the therapist can explore with the individual the consequences of revealing versus keeping the secret. Often, the individual has erroneously concluded that revealing certain thoughts or feelings will elicit negative reactions from the spouse. In one case, for example, the husband made no sexual advances for fear that the wife would feel anxious or pressured, while the wife assumed that the absence of sexual initiations by her husband indicated a lack of interest on his part. Both partners were keeping secret the fact that each was interested in resuming their sexual relationship.

Of course, partners' reactions to secrets can be powerfully negative. Nevertheless, members of the couple tend to overestimate the costs of telling the secret while underestimating the costs of keeping the secret. Within the context of the individual session, the therapist assists with the analysis of these costs. When members of the couple decide to be more open, the therapist then helps the individual to identify the most helpful and least threatening ways of revealing previously hidden thoughts and feelings.

A note of caution here is that when many individual sessions are held or when there is not a balance between individual and conjoint sessions, there is a danger that therapist-individual patient alliances may interfere with the goals of therapy. This is particularly a concern where members of the couple are very angry with one another. Separating such couples too much via individual sessions tends to reinforce an adversarial posture.

As was mentioned above, group sessions can be very useful with rape victim couples. These groups may be for victims, spouses, or mixed groups of victims and husbands. The primary advantages of group sessions are the additional support provided by group members with similar problems and the demonstration to the group members that they are not alone in the experience of and reaction to rape.

Establishment of rapport with the couple is one of the most critical therapeutic tasks. Some couples have been eagerly awaiting the opportunity to discuss their problems with someone, and for these couples the establishment of rapport tends not to be a serious problem. For most couples, however, establishing rapport is a major hurdle that must be overcome if therapy is to be helpful. Many rape victims have developed a deep distrust of new people, especially of those who may be probing at thoughts and feelings the victim has worked hard to repress and deny.

Therapists need to have the good sense not to press too hard or too fast for the information victims have repressed. For the most part, however, no particularly different techniques for developing rapport are needed with rape victim couples than for other couples in marital or sex therapy. Therapists need to be empathic, warm, respectful, accepting, and nonjudgmental.

Generally, rape victim couples present with some mixture of marital and sexual disturbances. Because sexual issues are so sensitized with these couples, it is usually better to address the more general marital issues and conflict before directing the therapy at the sexual issues. This approach makes sure also that progress in treatment of sexual problems and dysfunctions is more likely when the couple is otherwise reasonably conflict-free and capable of good communication.

Since a very eclectic approach to treating marital and sexual disturbances in rape victim couples is advocated here, a cataloguing of treatment interventions is not appropriate. Rather, a descriptive example of how different techniques may be integrated will be given, followed by a summary of approaches specifically aimed at sexual problems in this population.

Helen is a 28-year-old homemaker. She and her husband Jerry, a 30-year-old pharmacist, have been married for six years. They have two children, aged four and two. Helen was raped in her home in the evening by an assailant who broke a door to gain entry. Jerry was at work at the time of the rape. The couple presented for treatment about one year after the rape occurred.

The couple's relationship seemed to have been quite good prior to the rape, and even now signs of real affection and caring could be seen. Nevertheless, significant problems had emerged.

Helen's desire for sex had dropped to near zero after the rape, and her sexual interest had not returned. At first, Jerry was understanding of this change, but he was becoming increasingly impatient and angry. Helen and Jerry were withdrawing from one another and becoming more uncommunicative. Finally, Helen was suffering from generalized anxiety, accompanied by occasional panic attacks.

After establishing rapport with the couple, the male/female cotherapy team began to work on the communication disturbances in conjoint session, and the female therapist worked with Helen in individual sessions on the anxiety problem. These two problem areas were targeted first because it was thought that improved communication and lowered anxiety would be most beneficial for restoring to the couple their mutual supportiveness. The lack of communication and heightened anxiety were seen as blocking the ability of the two partners to empathically understand and support the other.

Communication training, patterned after Stuart (1976) and using specific instructions, behavioral rehearsal, and practice, was successful in getting the couple to increase the quantity and quality of their verbal interactions. At the same time, relaxation training and brief cognitive therapy were used to markedly lower Helen's anxiety level.

With these positive changes, there was a small spontaneous improvement in the sexual relationship. Helen's sexual desire was improved, although far below what had been normal for her prior to the rape. The couple was pleased that they had had sexual intercourse for the first time in months.

At this point, the treatment began to focus on the sexual problems. It was learned that Helen had, prior to the rape, rarely engaged in sexual fantasies. Since the rape, thoughts about sex were quickly followed by sexual images reminiscent of the rape. The anxiety elicited by these images quickly dampened Helen's sexual interest.

The decision was made to use sensate focus (Masters & Johnson, 1970) exercises to assist the couple in gradually resuming physical contact in a nondemanding, nonthreatening atmosphere. Also, it was thought that encouraging sexual fantasies would help Helen to block out her negative images while simultaneously enhancing her desire and pleasure. The fantasy work included "permission giving" for the use of sexual fantasies, the reading of fantasy material (Friday, 1973), and the development of personal fantasies that Helen found to be acceptable as well as arousing.

Because of the communication improvements already attained, the couple was able to clearly let each other know what types of stimulation were most pleasurable. The sensate focus exercises led to a decrease in general sexual anxiety and, combined with the fantasy training, to an increase in Helen's sexual interest.

The purpose of the case history above is to illustrate the ways in which a variety of therapy techniques can be employed, depending on the specific needs of the individual couple. In this particular illustration, behavioral and cognitive techniques were used. In other cases, particularly those with pre-existing individual psychopathology or marital dysfunction, more dynamically oriented approaches might be seen as more appropriate.

One very useful approach to the specific sexual problems and dysfunctions of rape victim couples has been described by Becker and Skinner (1984). Their approach, based on the P-LI-SS-IT model of Annon (1976), also incorporates components from a wide variety of treatment techniques. The P-LI-SS-IT model refers to different levels of intervention that may be used in treating sexual problems and dysfunctions. There are four basic levels of intervention, and the notion is to vary the level of intervention depending on the intensity and complexity of the sexual problems. These levels of intervention are permission (P), limited information (LI), specific suggestion (SS), and intensive therapy (IT).

The treatment package of Becker and Skinner (1984) differs from the approach used by the author primarily in the use of groups composed of rape victims only. Apparently, the population treated by Becker and Skinner had a large proportion of rape victims without male partners. The sexual problem areas included in this treatment package are: negative body image, interference of sexual arousal by intruding/distracting thoughts, difficulties in having sexual fantasies, inadequate sexual information, sexual performance anxiety, poor sexual communication, and lack of sexual assertiveness. This treatment approach has much to offer, although in my experience the inclusion of male partners if at all possible is likely to enhance the treatment effects considerably.

As we have seen, rape victims and their male partners endure a great deal of suffering. It is my hope that more clinicians will become familiar with the particular needs of this population and will begin to develop additional, innovative approaches to treating the marital and sexual dysfunctions of rape victim couples.

REFERENCES

Amir, M. (1971). *Patterns in forcible rape.* Chicago: University of Chicago Press.
Annon, J. S. (1976). *Behavioral treatment of sexual problems: Brief therapy.* New York: Harper & Row.
Becker, J. V., & Skinner, L. J. (1984). Behavioral treatment of sexual dysfunctions in sexual assault survivors. In I. R. Stuart & J. G. Greer (Eds.), *Victims of sexual aggression: Treatment of children, women, and men.* New York: Van Nostrand Reinhold Co.
Brownmiller, S. (1975). *Against our will: Men, women, and rape.* New York: Bantam Books.
Burgess, A. W., & Holmstrom, L. L. (1974). *Rape: Victims of crisis.* Bowie, MD: Brady.
Friday, N. (1973). *My secret garden: Women's sexual fantasies.* New York: Pocket Books.
Holmstrom, L. L., & Burgess, A. W. (1978). *The victim of rape: Institutional reactions.* New York: John Wiley.
Martin, P. A. (1976). *A marital therapy manual.* New York: Brunner/Mazel.

Masters, W., & Johnson, V. E. (1970). *Human sexual inadequacy*. Boston: Little, Brown.

Miller, W. R., & Williams, A. M. (1984). Marital and sexual dysfunction following rape: Identification and treatment. In I. R. Stuart & J. G. Greer (Eds.), *Victims of sexual aggression: Treatment of children, women, and men*. New York: Van Nostrand Reinhold Co.

Miller, W. R., Williams, A. M., & Bernstein, M. H. (1982). The effects of rape on marital and sexual adjustment. *American Journal of Family Therapy, 10*, 51–88.

Silverman, D. (1978). Sharing the crisis of rape: Counseling the mates and families of victims. *American Journal of Orthopsychiatry, 48*, 166–173.

Stuart, R. B. (1976). An operant interpersonal program for couples. In D. H. L. Olson (Ed.), *Treating relationships*. Lake Mills, IA: Graphic Publishing.

Sutherland, S., & Scherl, D. J. (1970). Patterns of response among victims of rape. *American Journal of Orthopsychiatry, 40*, 503–511.

Chapter 10

Systematic Treatment of Inhibited Sexual Desire

Gerald R. Weeks

The diagnosis and treatment of inhibited sexual desire (ISD) in the clinical literature as a separate and distinct disorder is fairly recent. Although Masters and Johnson (1970) used the term "sexual avoidance" to refer to women experiencing low sexual desire, it was not until 1979 that Helen Kaplan published a landmark book describing this disorder. Kaplan (1979) proposed that low sexual desire could be caused by psychological factors. She described this disorder in terms of the rapid, active, and unconscious suppression of sexual desire. She also developed a fourfold classification for ISD similar to Masters and Johnson's concept of primary or secondary problems.

In her classification, primary ISD referred to those individuals who had never experienced sexual desire; secondary ISD referred to those individuals who had experienced desire but currently experienced no or reduced desire; global ISD referred to those individuals experiencing low desire with all partners in all situations; and situational ISD referred to those individuals who experienced desire with some partners in some situations. This definition and classification scheme clearly focused ISD on or, more correctly, in the individual. In short, the disorder was conceptualized within the intrapsychic framework.

Zilbergeld and Ellison (1982) reconceptualized ISD in interactional terms. According to them, ISD referred to a discrepancy in the levels of desire experienced by the couple. They stated, "It is not that one person has too much desire and another too little on an absolute scale; it is rather a discrepancy in two people's styles or interest" (p. 68).

These two definitions reflect the differences found in intrapsychic versus interpersonal conceptualizations of problems in general, conceptualizations that appear to compete with each other and are frequently proposed as being mutually exclusive. In fact, both approaches are useful in understanding ISD.

Most clients presenting with ISD experience two discrepancies. The individual experiences a discrepancy in self in the sense of wanting to experience sexual desire but not being able to, and the couple experience a discrepancy in their levels of desire.

The purpose of this chapter is to help clarify, integrate, and extend current explanations and treatments for ISD. A systematic model of approaching the problems is used. In this model, three major views of symptom formation and resolution are integrated. This model grew from the recent philosophical work of Bopp and Weeks (1984) and Weeks (1986) on dialectic metatheory in systems theory. Dialectic metatheory allows us to see the person across four dimensions of human development simultaneously: inner-biological, inner-psychological, outer-cultural, and outer-physical (Riegel, 1976). A dialectical analysis of this problem suggested that the disorder be understood at three levels of analysis—individual, interactional, and intergenerational. This chapter will discuss both the etiology and treatment from these three perspectives simultaneously.

INCIDENCE OF ISD

The actual incidence of ISD is difficult to determine. It is a newly defined psychiatric disorder and has not been extensively researched. Various authors have established the incidence among couples in therapy to be 40% and higher (Kaplan, 1979). Several studies have attempted to assess the frequency of this complaint in couples. Lief (1977) found that 28% of the clients seen at the Marriage Council of Philadelphia had a primary diagnosis of ISD, 37% for women and 18.7% for men. Schover and LoPiccolo (1982) reanalyzed data from 1974–1981 collected at the sex therapy center at Stony Brook. Of 152 couples with intake data, 38% of the husbands and 49% of the wives were diagnosed with low desire. In addition, 18% of the women and none of the men reported sexual aversion (i.e., revulsion to sex). These researchers also found an increase in the incidence of ISD from 1974 to 1981 and an increasing prevalence of the disorder in males. Frank, Anderson, and Rubinstein (1978) examined the sexual functioning of normal couples as part of a larger study on couples relationships. They recruited 100 couples who defined themselves as being in marriages that were "working." These couples were far from a random sample. They were self-selected, mostly white, highly educated, and many were working in high-level occupations. In addition, in response to a global question on marital satisfaction, over 80% stated they rated their marriages from happy to very happy. On the basis of these demographics and stated level of marital happiness, a researcher would not expect to find much sexual dysfunctioning. However, their analysis revealed that 40% of the men had had an erectile or ejaculatory problem, 63% of the women an arousal or orgasmic problem. These figures reflected a surprisingly high incidence of major sexual problems. When the researchers examined the frequency of minor problems or difficulties, 50% of the men and 77% of the women reported problems.

Perhaps because of the time period in which this study was conducted, ISD was not included as a major sexual problem. There were, however, two categories which were informative: 35% of the women and 16% of the men reported disinterest, and 28% of the men and 10% of the women reported being "turned off." If we combine the percentages for men and women, it becomes apparent that at least 40% of these nonclinical or healthy couples have experienced desire phase problems. In addition, correlations between the problems and perceptions of levels of sexual happiness showed that these two problems did significantly lower perceptions of sexual happiness, whereas other problems did not make a significant difference. One explanation for this last finding is that couples expect each other to be desiring and implicitly expect that desire is something which is controllable.

Couples appear to be able to tolerate major sexual problems and be sympathetic and empathetic if they believe the problem is something over which the partner has little, if any, control. However, couples act on the assumption that desire is controllable, which in turn means it is not easily tolerated in the relationship.

The ISD then acquires a special meaning. The partner sees the lack of desire as a deliberate, sometimes malicious attempt to control the sexual relationship. Such a view may generate feelings of hurt, anger, and rejection in the partner. Many couples will present for help with this problem directly, others will mention it after a few sessions in which work has been focused on the relationship, the others will not reveal the fact until the therapist begins to assess the sexual part of the relationship. Knowing that this problem is very likely to be present should direct the therapist to assess the presence of sexual problems in the marriage early in treatment according to the guidelines provided by Hof in Chapter 1.

The sexual area of the relationship should not be probed, however, until the therapist feels s/he has been able to join with the couple. This process may take a few seconds to a few sessions to accomplish. Most couples are embarrassed talking about their sexual lives and may believe this area of their relationship is too private to discuss with a therapist.

A final point should be made about the incidence of ISD for men versus women. In the past, ISD has been stereotyped as a woman's problem. Clinicians who treat sexual problems have noted that more and more men are presenting with ISD. The author's personal experience has been that men and women are presenting with equal frequency. This trend may reflect the fact that women are becoming more sexually assertive. As long as men were primarily the initiators and women the noninitiators, a lack of desire in the male produced less of a discrepancy in who initiated. In short, both partners would be initiating infrequently or never. This pattern would have created a situation in which the male's lack of desire would have been unquestioned. The couple would not talk about the fact that the male desired sex less often. As women have become more sexually assertive, men have had to confront their sexual responsiveness more directly. Moreover, a man who fails to initiate or rejects the advances of his partner would be more likely to be questioned about his level of desire and participation.

ETIOLOGY

Several attempts have been made to understand the causes of ISD. Kaplan (1979) attempted to explain the disorder from a psychodynamic perspective. She described intrapsychic conflicts, such as the following, to be major contributing factors: anger; fear of loss of control; fear of pleasure, romantic success, and love; and fear of rejection and performance.

Verhulst and Heiman (1979) approached the problem of etiology of all sexual dysfunction from an interactional perspective. They identified four types of interactional patterns that could become problematic. The first pattern dealt with territorial interactions. Basically, this pattern concerns one's right to one's body—to be approached and touched in a way that allows the person to feel in control. For example, a woman might feel "invaded" if her partner touches her in a certain place, in a particular way, or at a particular time in the sequence of a lovemaking encounter. The second pattern is related to the issue of control over the relationship and over communication. These interactions, which help define status and hierarchy in the relationship, or how power is distributed, are called rank-order interactions. A rank-order interaction problem might center around who initiates sex. If one spouse initiates and insists on having sex, undue control or power is being exercised in the relationship. Attachment interactions constituted the third area. These interactions pertain to care, tenderness, and the affiliative bond. The main problem in this area is how sex is used to express attachment. For example, if the husband views sex alone as an expression of attachment and his wife does not share this view, a struggle emerges over sex.

Fourth, problems may arise in exploratory interactions. These interactions refer to feelings about being explored by another or exploring another. A man might, for example, experience sexual repulsion simply at the thought of exploring his wife's genitals. Such blocks raise the level of anxiety and prevent one from being able to function effectively. In order to function effectively, the couple must negotiate how they will allow exploration to occur. They develop a "sexual dance" (see Chapter 4). The four factors identified were not directed specifically toward ISD, but were intended as a general model to help explain all the sexual dysfunctions. However, they appear to be especially salient in understanding ISD.

In addition to these two major models of explanation, Fish, Fish, and Sprenkle (1984) reviewed other theorists who have described ISD as attempts to protect an impotent husband and serve as a distance regulator in the relationship. The explanations these theorists have presented are all useful in diagnosing ISD, but the major problem is that these ideas emerged from compartmentalized models, appear fragmented and simplistic, and are not linked to each other systematically.

AN INTEGRATED ETIOLOGICAL MODEL

The model of understanding being proposed in this chapter consists of three perspectives — the individual, interactional, and intergenerational. All parts of this model are inextricably linked to all other parts. It is only for ease of conceptual understanding that factors are listed under each category separately.

This model can be visualized as:

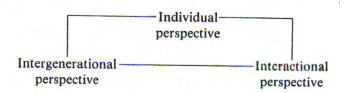

Individual Factors

Biological functioning and health. Kaplan (1979) has focused on the individual-intrapsychic factors more than any other theorist. She has identified a number of factors that she treats as both intrapsychic and psychodynamic phenomena. These factors will be discussed from an interactional perspective in this chapter. The reader who is interested in Kaplan's psychodynamic formulations should consult her book. Whenever an individual presents with low sexual desire, biological factors such as hormonal imbalances and use of medication must first be ruled out. ISD, however, refers to low desire having a psychological basis. The person's health may be a factor in ISD according to how the individual perceives his or her health.

A person who appears healthy may have experienced or may be experiencing a fear of loss of health. Such fears may be exaggerated, suppressed, displaced, and the object of obsessive concern in the individual and/or the relationship. The therapist must assess not only the client's physical health, but also the perceptions of health. In addition, age may also be related. Fears of death and dying may be factors along with misconceptions about the relationship between age and sexual interest (e.g., you lose it after 40), vitality, and ability to perform.

Body image. The client's perceptions of the real versus ideal body image may be a factor in ISD. Sexual functioning is dependent on having an adequate body image and believing that one is attractive to one's partner and that one's partner is physically attractive. In many of our cases, the individual presenting with ISD believed he/she was unattractive.

This idea is usually manifested as obsessive concern with a body part (e.g., breasts, legs, too much hair, too little hair) which does not fit the current cultural stereotype of beauty. In many such cases, the partner will contribute to this concern by expressing overt or covert disapproval.

Information. A factor in practically every case of sexual dysfunction is lack of education and factual information. Research has now shown that a lack of factual information leads to sexual misinformation and mythology, which in turn increases sexual guilt and anxiety (Mosher, 1979). Anxiety and guilt are effective barriers to becoming sexually aroused. The therapist should, therefore, attempt to assess the information level by asking about the client's former sex education and parental education and listening for negative sexual attitudes and thoughts.

Fantasies. A common factor observed in both men and women with ISD is the absence of sexual fantasies. Sue (1979) found that the most common use of sexual fantasies was to become aroused or to increase the level of sexual arousal. The absence of fantasies in ISD clients supports the idea that sexual desire is not being facilitated in a way most people find normal (Loren & Weeks, in press). Only one empirical study has examined the lack of fantasies in ISD versus a normal control group. Nutter and Condron (1983) investigated the sexual fantasies of 25 women presenting at a sex therapy clinic with the ISD diagnosis. These researchers found that ISD clients had significantly fewer fantasies during foreplay, coitus, masturbation, and general daydreaming. The content of the fantasies that they did have was quite similar to that of the control group, and there was not a total lack of fantasy. Many of the clients treated by the author report no fantasies whatsoever. An interesting finding of this study was that the females with ISD did not masturbate less or have fewer orgasms via masturbation than the control group of women. This finding supports the idea that ISD is related to the relationship and not simply an intrapsychic disorder. If it were an individual-intrapsychic disorder, it would be difficult to explain the ability to enjoy sex with oneself.

Conceptual confusion between sex and affection. An area of confusion noted in every sex therapy case, including ISD, is the problem of separating and negotiating sex and affection. One partner, usually the male, believes affection is expressed through the sexual act. The other partner, usually the female, believes affection has value in itself and sees any move by the partner, including attempts to express affection, as an attempt at sexual seduction. This occurs because she has seen how the partner frequently links sex and affection. She then begins to believe affection has only one meaning in the relationship. Couples caught in this confusion have been trading sex to get affection, and affection to get sex, with neither one being happy with the outcome of the interchange. Eventually, each one begins to feel angry over this situation and begins to withdraw. The most common pattern seen is when the husband pursues his wife for sexual release without giving affection. The wife attempts to find affection by being sexual but feels frustrated in her attempts to be responded to affectionately. As the frustration builds, so do anger and resentment, leading to an inhibition of sexual desire. In assessing this problem, the therapist should ask what sex and affection mean in the context of the relationship and whether each one is happy with the expressions of these behaviors.

Interactional Factors

Kaplan (1979) identified several factors that lead to the development of ISD. Unfortunately, her psychodynamic bias was so strong that she was not able to place these factors in the context of the new systems therapies. Kaplan's basic approach had been to combine her psychodynamic training with behaviorally oriented sex therapy. Although behavioral sex therapists work with couples and appear to be systems therapists, they are not. This fact is probably one of the most difficult concepts to explain to a "sex therapist." They argue that because they work with couples, they are doing couples therapy. The fact is that sex therapists such as Masters and Johnson do individual, behaviorally oriented therapy with couples. The interventions they described in *Human Sexual Inadequacy* (1970) tend to be noninteractional and nonsystemic in spite of the fact that they state "there is no such entity as an uninvolved partner in a marriage contending with any form of sexual inadequacy" (p. 188). However, Masters and Johnson have recently changed their perspective in the treatment approach they have developed for inhibited sexual desire (Schwartz, 1986). They stress the interactional nature of this problem and use a variety of marital interventions, especially couples skill training. The fact that both approaches are so similar supports the validity of this model.

This criticism should not be construed as an attempt to diminish the contributions of these pioneers. It simply means we must build on their work and shift to a more systemic theoretical framework. The framework proposed in this chapter is interactional or systems oriented. Rather than view ISD as an individual-intrapsychic problem, it should be seen as a dyadic-interactional problem. Each partner is viewed as playing a role in the lack of desire. This view is sometimes difficult to operationalize because the partner who appears to be desirous may not be aware of the subtle ways in which he contributes to the problem and the therapist may be inclined to focus on just one person.

Kaplan's (1979) individually oriented analysis of the etiology of ISD represented a major contribution. She identified many of the major causes of ISD, which can now be reconceptualized in an interactional framework. The major interactional factors being proposed here are:

Anger. Dealing with anger is one of the most difficult tasks confronted in an intimate relationship (L'Abate & McHenry, 1983). It is not difficult to understand how anger can temporarily cause an individual to lose sexual interest. The problem in ISD is not simple anger. It is anger that has been dealt with poorly over a long period of time, resulting in chronic suppressed anger or resentment. In the ISD cases the author has treated, this cause is the most common. Interestingly, it appears to be somewhat more common for men than women. The men state that they do not believe a direct expression of anger will change anything or that peace should be maintained at all costs. They have adopted an attitude of resignation, consisting of depressed/anxious affect and withdrawn sexual behavior. However, the problem with anger is not just in one individual. Couples develop an interlocking way of relating to each other which meets their individual needs and the need to preserve and protect the relationship. When this attitude is found in the husband, the wife's contribution may be her fear of anger, need to criticize, or need to be in control of the relationship. These couples may share similar or have complementary irrational ideas about anger. They may both believe in conflict-avoidance and believe "Anger is bad for a relationship," "One should not express anger openly," or "If you pretend it's [anger] not there, it will go away," or they may have complementary ideas, such as the following:

Anger won't change anything so why say anything.	Let it all out (feeling) and it will be better.
I shouldn't ever be angry with my partner.	It would be awful and a fearful situation if my partner ever became angry with me.
Anger only leads to destruction in a relationship.	I must withdraw whenever anger begins to emerge in our relationship.

The unexpressed anger and ISD may also lead to feelings of rejection in the partner not experiencing the ISD and feelings of needing to be taken care of in the spouse with the ISD. These conflicted couples may lack the cognitive and behavioral skills they need to resolve conflicts. They do not view anger in a realistic way and they do not know how to negotiate differences. Over the years, and with the advent of events that increase conflict, the problem of ISD emerges.

Control. The issue of control may manifest in several ways. However, in each case the ISD represents a way for the individual to control the relationship and, hence, control self. One of the patterns observed is the overcontrolling husband and undercontrolling wife with ISD. In this relationship, the ISD allows the wife to sense some power or control in the relationship. The wife's experience is that of lacking an identity she can call her own. In traditional marriages of some duration, women have been socialized to believe they are extensions of their partner. When these women begin to struggle with who they are and what they want, they discover a feeling of emptiness. A common reaction is to blame their spouse for their dilemma and begin to reject the relationship entirely. Being sexual with their partner represents a return to the old relationship in which they were nonentities.

The root of this type of problem is actually a lack of differentiation in the partners. L'Abate (1976) has defined differentiation in terms of how we define ourselves vis-à-vis others. The differentiated individual sees herself or himself as both similar to and different from others. Those individuals are able to act autonomously. As one moves to the less differentiated part of his scale, the individuals see themselves in terms of sameness or oppositeness. Behavior becomes more reactive—determined by others. The undifferentiated individual in the oppositeness part of the continuum would respond oppositionally to her or his partner being aroused. He/she would see the lack of responsivity as a way to assert identity. The undifferentiated individual in the sameness part of the continuum would be in the dilemma of deciding whether to comply behaviorally and have sex or, in the struggle for differentiation, reject sexual arousal toward the partner because it represents a lack of autonomy. The fears of pleasure, love, and performance described by Kaplan (1979) are all related to some lack of differentiation. The individual is not able to make choices for herself or himself because of earlier experiences which dictated following a script.

The idea of a sexual script refers to the idea that the child has been sexually programmed by the parents and/or other significant socializing forces to think, feel, and act in a stereotyped fashion. This programming takes place over a long period of time and is insidious. The individual is unaware of being scripted and does not have the defenses to reject this regimented type of thinking. The result is an adult who thinks, feels, and acts the way that was dictated by the sexual programming.

Intimacy. Intimacy has been defined in a number of ways in the literature, and each couple has their own definition of what it means to be in an intimate relationship and how intimacy is to be expressed. In ISD, the type of intimacy that is problematic has to do with emotional intimacy. In these cases, the partners experience fears associated with the idea of getting closer. These fears may include fear of hurt, rejection, abandonment, and even the fear of one's own feelings. It is important to help the client define intimacy and identify any fears he/she may have. Some unusual fears may be manifested in this category. For example, one woman believed she would lose control of her feelings completely if she were to reach orgasm. In order to avoid orgasm, she would suppress her feelings of arousal. Another woman believed she would appear ugly, repulsive, and animalistic should she let go of her feelings. Men tend to deal with the fear of being hurt by being angry and resentful. They find it unacceptable to show hurt feelings. Hurt has been equated with vulnerability. Vulnerability, in turn, symbolizes weakness — an unmanly trait. In each case, the fears in one partner are part of an interlocking pattern of a similar or complementary problem in the spouse. It is easy to become overfocused on the symptom bearer and forget the role played by the partner. Assessment must remain relationship focused in order to avoid the traditional trait-type individual diagnosis.

Intergenerational Factors

The idea of intergenerational messages as salient factors in sexual dysfunctions has never been systematically examined in the literature on sex therapy or treatment of ISD. Intergenerational messages are internalized by the individual early in the life-cycle and later become a part of the person's interactional set. If the therapist attempts to deal with these messages as they appear in the "here and now," he/she may miss an important component of diagnosis and treatment. The value of exploring intergenerational messages and events is so important that the reader is referred to the chapters by Berman and Hof (Chapter 3) and Hof (Chapter 1).

An example of a case where intergenerational messages were critical involved a couple who received the injunction to remain loyal to their respective families of origin by being asexual. After doing the sexual genogram, the wife realized that her script was to not grow up and leave home. Her mother had warned that sex with men was dangerous in part because her father acted seductively toward her. The husband was also treated seductively by his mother. The husband's mother would say that women exercise "pussy power" over him in pulling him away from her partner. In this particular case, the wife appeared to be the one with all the relationship problems, including ISD. The sexual genogram was extremely useful in showing the husband's part in the problem. This couple was locked in an intergenerational struggle which they had initially tried to resolve by forming their own pathological interlocking system of sexual avoidance.

TREATMENT

The one point on which all sex therapists agree is that ISD is a difficult problem to treat. Kaplan (1979) reported a success rate of only 10 to 15% after 15 sessions. Her model of treatment consisted of combining behaviorally oriented sex therapy with a psychodynamic approach. Of course, the psychodynamic approach is individualistic and insight-oriented and the behavioral approach is individualistic and behavior-oriented.

Three other models of treatment for ISD have been developed since the publication of Kaplan's book in 1979. McCarthy (1984) developed a cognitive-behavioral approach which utilized semistructural written behavioral exercises. He developed four sets of exercises for individuals and four sets for couples. The individual exercises helped the client develop the following: (1) a positive self-concept; (2) a positive body image and attractiveness; (3) positive sexual thoughts, images, and fantasies; and (4) a positive sexual scenario which can be acted out. The couples exercises help the client couple: (1) work on expressing affection; (2) discuss what they find attractive about each other; (3) explore how much trust and vulnerability they desire; and (4) design and implement a sexual scenario they are to act out. Thus, McCarthy departed from Kaplan's (1979) position to assert that ISD must be viewed as a system problem which requires an understanding of the cognitive, behavioral, and affective inhibitions.

Regas and Sprenkle (1984) presented the first of two approaches to treating ISD from the Purdue Department of Child Development and Family Studies. They described how functional family therapy (Alexander & Parsons, 1982) could be used in treating ISD and presented a case study. Their approach to treatment advocated the use of : (1) relabeling; (2) shifting the focus of treatment to the relationship; (3) identifying the functions of the ISD for the couple; and (4) using educational strategies (e.g., sensate focus, relaxation, systematic desensitization, and bibliotherapy).

Fish, Fish, and Sprenkle (1984) published another paper which purported to offer a marital therapy approach. In this paper ISD is clearly conceptualized in system concepts. The key issues they address are power, intimacy, and boundaries. However, rather than present a marital therapy approach, they show how Minuchin (1974) and Minuchin and Fishman's (1981) structural family therapy could be applied in treating one case. Although it is clear that this approach was useful in the case presented, the use of one model of treatment is obviously not appropriate for a disorder as complex and multifaceted as ISD.

A SYSTEMATIC APPROACH TO TREATMENT

The systematic approach to treatment stems from the multicausal model of understanding of ISD at the individual, interactional, and intergenerational levels. The model is complex, yet elegant in the sense that assessment leads directly into a systematic program of treatment, which is specifically tailored for each couple. Treatment begins with an extended assessment session, lasting from one and a half to two hours. During this interview, the couple will be seen together initially, then apart for 30 to 45 minutes, and then together again. Aside from information collection, the therapist should set the stage for therapy. The therapist should point out that ISD is not an uncommon problem and give the couple a positive rationale for treatment. In other words, the couple should be reinforced for caring enough to want to eliminate the problem from their relationship rather than avoiding it in the hope that it will disappear. The therapist should also point out that, although this problem is difficult and will require a number of sessions, treatment can work. They should be warned that progress may be slow because a number of factors may need to be changed before desire is at an acceptable level. Finally, the therapist should point out that ISD is a couple or relationship problem. This means the sessions will be conjoint and the partner without the ISD will be fully involved in treatment. No blame should ever be assigned to either party. The therapist's position must be one of deliberate neutrality and balance unless strategy otherwise dictates. The partner's role is initially defined as one of helpfulness, although this definition may later change as the partner becomes more aware of her or his part in the problem.

It is not necessary to describe the total assessment procedure in this chapter since this material was covered in Chapter 1. Only the essentials and new procedures will be described for this approach. Five specific questions should be asked from the outset of treatment. First, the history of sexual frequency should be examined. The therapist needs to find out what the frequency of sexual contact has been, both within the current relationship and across all other relationships. Because frequency refers to behavior, the therapist should also inquire about who initiated the sexual experience in their relationship. Second, when a sexual encounter does occur, is it physically satisfying or are there any "mechanical" problems that interfere with pleasure? Third, the history of sexual desire should be examined in the same way sexual frequency was explored. Fourth, desire can be conceptualized along a scale from very turned off to very turned on, with a midpoint of no sexual interest. This concept is explained to the client and a scale of − 10 (very turned off) to + 10 (very turned on) is suggested as a subjective way of quantifying her or his experience. The client is asked to rate the level of desire experienced for the current partner. Fifth, the client is asked whether and under what circumstances desire is felt. Some clients will report never being turned on, others will say they feel desire but some specific event happens (e.g., husband arriving home, partner getting ready for bed) that causes them to lose their desire, and others report that desire occurs only after drinking and receiving physical stimulation.

The next step is to explain the primary assessment procedure. The couple is asked how people become turned on. Most couples will talk about physical stimulation and sexual fantasy. The therapist then adds that another way people become aroused is by engaging in positive sexual self-talk (+ SST). The therapist explains that + SST is saying sexy things to oneself about oneself, one's partner, and the relationship. These thoughts may be consciously experienced or they may be unconscious. The therapist then follows with the question "If this is how people turn on, then how do they become turned off?" The clients are then guided in understanding that this process sometimes involves negative sexual fantasies, frequently involves the lack of fantasies, and always involves negative sexual self-talk (− SST). In addition to pointing out how − SST affects one's sexuality, Ellis and Harper's (1975) RET model is described so the client can see how these thoughts will be treated. However, the therapist should not suggest that this model is sufficient to remedy the problem. This work is only one part of the more general relationship work.

Clients find this idea simple and easy to accept. The process of sexual arousal is being demystified for them. The therapist would then ask about whether there are any negative fantasies or an absence of fantasies. Negative fantasies have been rare in our experience, but a lack of sexual fantasy has been an almost universal characteristic of individuals with ISD. Many of these individuals have never experienced sexual fantasies. The therapist then elaborates on the idea of − SST. S/he points out that thoughts may occur in four categories. There may be negative thoughts about self, other, relationship, or from the family of origin. The client is told these thoughts must be fully categorized and that they will be examined in the context of the relationship because most of them either are the result of the couple's interaction or are maintained by the relationship.

At this point in the session, the couple will be split and interviewed separately in order to explore how each one experiences the problem individually. When men present with ISD, there are two issues which need to be discussed in the individual sessions with their wives. For many women, the only way they can explain their partner's lack of desire is to believe he is either having an affair or has become gay. The woman should be encouraged to express these suspicions, and information can be given to help allay these fears if they are unfounded. Humphrey (Chapter 8) has discussed the role of extramarital sex (EMS) in sexual desire and the problems associated with the treatment of EMS.

The interview with the person experiencing the ISD focuses on the − SST. By the end of this session the client has usually talked about a number of negative sexual thoughts. The reason for gathering these ideas in an individual meeting is because of the editing that occurs when the partner is present. Some of the ideas are irrational and embarrassing and only indirectly related to one's partner, and others have become a part of the system. Some of the negative sexual statements may be worked on in a brief individual session; however, most of the ideas need to be brought back to the relationship. The assessment of the negative sexual sex talk provides an enormous amount of information and is the major component of the rapid assessment method used in these cases.

Following the individual sessions, the couples will be reunited and a homework assignment will be given. The traditional sex therapy techniques described by Kaplan (1979) are useful. Their first homework exercise is to do pleasuring I (nongenital massage), with the rationale that it will facilitate communication, remove the pressure to perform sexually, and help to bring into focus other − SST. This exercise is also a useful way to begin the discussion about sex and affection. In this discussion, the goal of therapy is to help the couple differentiate and learn to appreciate affection for the sake of affection. This problem area needs to be monitored throughout therapy. The clients should be told that homework may be given after each session. In addition to the pleasuring I task, the couple is asked to catalogue their − SST. The therapist should be sensitive to the use of language in assigning the work to be done at home. The therapist has the choice of calling this work "assignments," "exercises," "experiments," "homework," or "tasks." A client who did poorly in school and disliked homework should not be given "homework." The use of this term triggers unpleasant associations and feelings of being graded or judged. Clients who need to feel they are in control of the therapy can be given "experiments." The word experiment is associated with creativity and with learning new facts. The other terms have a more neutral quality.

The second session begins by discussing the homework and asking whether any new negative thoughts were discovered. The partner manifesting the lack of desire then begins to go over this list with two goals in mind. First, for each negative thought, a positive thought which can be reinforced in the relationship is to be found or created. Second, those thoughts which represent relational issues (e.g., "All we ever do is fight, which means we don't really love each other") must be carefully reframed for the couple, so that the problem is truly seen as a relationship problem, rather than an individual problem (Weeks & L'Abate, 1982). For example, a man might believe his wife's criticism is an individual problem of hers. The therapist's task is to show how her criticism is a reaction to his behavior, perhaps withdrawn. She may, in fact, be angry and frustrated over his lack of involvement and be trying to gain some attention through the use of this behavior. In addition, the therapist determines whether this idea is shared by both partners or when the partner has a complementary thought. As each thought is examined, the partners talk *with each other* about how to change the thought and their relationship with the therapist acting as facilitator. In order to give the reader an idea of what kinds of thoughts are commonly described, the following case material is presented. In this case, the 32-year-old husband presented with the ISD. The information presented below was gathered in the first session from the husband in the individual interview.

NEGATIVE SEXUAL SELF-TALK

Self

1. I don't like my skin. I have psoriasis and I feel embarrassed about it.
2. I come too fast. I usually come right after I enter her.
3. I think my penis is too small. My wife tells me my penis is smaller than that of her previous boyfriends.
4. I put my business first. I'm always worrying about money when I'm trying to have sex.

Partner

1. She is always talking about previous relationships, especially how great sex was.
2. She is somewhat overweight, especially her hips, and that really turns me off.
3. She is insecure. She doesn't like it when I want to go off with my friends. She gets jealous.
4. She doesn't like my friends.
5. She isn't willing to do things on her own. I have to entertain her all the time.

Relationship

1. We can't agree on when to have children. She wants them right now and I'm not ready. She's stopped using birth control.

2. We are always fighting about money and my business. She wants me to sell my business and get a job with a steady income.
3. We don't know how to deal with anger. I have given up trying to express my feelings. The anger and resentment just keep building up.

The information gathered in this brief period of time reveals the complexity of many ISD cases. There are usually many problems that contribute to the problem. When clients can see these problems early on and so clearly in treatment, they have a better sense of what will be required to resolve the problem.

A few other general procedures are also helpful in treating these cases. Almost all couples presenting with sexual problems find sex education useful. Books that give a general understanding of human sexuality, such as *Shared Intimacies* (Barbach & Levine, 1980), and books on sexual fantasies, such as *My Secret Garden* and *Forbidden Flowers* (Friday, 1973, 1975) are useful psychoeducational reading.

The client experiencing the ISD is encouraged to begin developing sexual fantasies along with +SST from the first or second session. The behavioral/sexual exercises listed by Kaplan (1979) are also useful: (1) pleasuring I, (2) pleasuring II, (3) self-stimulation, (4) nondemand intercourse, and (5) having sex only when both agree.

In addition to countering the −SST with directly related positive thoughts, the therapist can also have the client list two or three positive thoughts for self, partner, and relationship. The following examples will give the reader an idea of how the clients' homework will appear.

−SST	Counterideas	Positive thoughts
Self		
I hate my breasts. They look like dried prunes.	I would prefer that my breasts be larger. They are soft, small, firm, and very sensitive.	I have nice legs.
Partner		
He never shows me any affection so he must not care about me.	I wish he were more affectionate. He is sometimes affectionate and I know he is trying to show me more of the affection he feels.	He has a good sense of humor and he can be a good lover.

Relationship

We disagree all the time over our daughter.	We do disagree sometimes, but that means we both care about how our daughter is reared. It is OK to disagree as long as we can get together before we talk to our daughter.	When we do make love, it is a wonderful experience.

The combination of these ideas early in therapy will, in many cases, produce greater desire. However, these techniques alone are not sufficient to sustain change unless the relationship issues are resolved through the use of other therapeutic modalities.

The therapy proceeds with the framework of integrating the individual (cognitive therapy), interactional (marital therapy), and intergenerational (family-of-origin therapy) dimensions of the problem. The intergenerational part of the work will not be discussed in this chapter because of its extensive treatment in Chapter 3. The individual-cognitive part of the therapy has already been described in earlier parts of this chapter. The marital work must be fully integrated with the other dimensions of treatment. The specific types of marital intervention must be *tailored to the each of the contributing problems* (e.g., fear of intimacy, lack of communication skill, different relationship expectations).

In order to be effective with a problem as complex as ISD, the therapist should be familiar with the communications, behavioral, structural, strategic, and family-of-origin approaches to working with couples. The communications approach is especially useful in many cases because of the fact that suppressed anger is often the main contributing factor to ISD. The use of conflict resolution programs, problem solving, and contracting (L'Abate & McHenry, 1983) is essential in working with these cases.

CONCLUSION

Inhibited sexual desire is rapidly becoming one of the most common problems treated by sex and marital therapists. Unlike many of the more traditional sexual problems, ISD is not treatable using behaviorally oriented sex therapy. The sex therapist who has limited his or her training to sex therapy or a narrow range of therapeutic modalities is especially challenged in treating this problem because of its multicausal etiology.

This chapter has demonstrated that treatment and assessment should be conceptualized broadly. Assessment must include an understanding from three perspectives that have largely been treated as being mutually exclusive: individual, interactional, and intergenerational. Once ISD is understood within this context, therapy proceeds by integrating several therapeutic approaches: for the individual factors, cognitive/behavioral and psychodynamic therapy; for the interactional, marital therapy with an emphasis on communications, behavioral marital therapy, contracting, problem solving or conflict resolution, structural, and strategic therapy; and for intergenerational factors, family-of-origin work.

The therapist who attempts to treat ISD must be thoroughly trained in all the major approaches to marital therapy, have some knowledge of individual therapy (especially, cognitive therapy), and be a competent sex therapist. A therapist who is wedded to only one approach to treatment will not be effective with these types of cases. Even with this arsenal of techniques and a solid understanding of the etiology, treatment can be extended and difficult. The therapist must be prepared to carefully map out the course of treatment. Doing one session at a time within a process-oriented model does not work unless the therapist has an overall concept of the problem and strategy for working through the problems. Each problem must then be tracked and resolved within the larger matrix of problems. The usual treatment formats sex therapists have learned do not apply to treating ISD. The clinician must now create and tailor formats for specific clients with specific etiological factors. This process is indeed a challenge for the clinician and an impossible task for the sex therapist who has become a technician.

REFERENCES

Alexander, J., & Parsons, B. (1982). *Functional family therapy.* Monterey, CA: Brooks/Cole.

Barbach, L., & Levine, L. (1980). *Shared intimacies.* Garden City, NY: Archer/Doubleday.

Bopp, M., & Weeks, G. (1984). Dialectical metatheory in family therapy. *Family Process, 23,* 49–61.

Ellis, A., & Harper, R. (1975). *A new guide to rational living.* Englewood Cliffs, NJ: Prentice-Hall.

Fish, L., Fish, R., & Sprenkle, D. (1984). Treating inhibited sexual desire: A marital therapy approach. *American Journal of Family Therapy, 12,* 3–12.

Frank, E., Anderson, G., & Rubinstein, D. (1978). Frequency of sexual dysfunctions in normal couples. *New England Journal of Medicine, 3,* 111–115.

Friday, N. (1973). *My secret garden.* New York: Trident Press.

Friday, N. (1975). *Forbidden flowers.* New York: Pocket Books.

Kaplan, H. (1979). *Disorders of sexual desire.* New York: Brunner/Mazel.

L'Abate, L. (1976). *Understanding and helping the individual in the family.* New York: Grune & Stratton.

L'Abate, L., & McHenry, S. (1983). *Handbook of marital interventions*. New York: Grune & Stratton.

Lief, H. (1977). Inhibited sexual desire. *Medical Aspects of Human Sexuality, 11*, 94–95.

Loren, R., & Weeks, G. (In press). Comparison of the sexual fantasies of undergraduates and their perceptions of the sexual fantasies of the opposite sex. *Journal of Sex Education and Therapy*.

Masters, W., & Johnson, V. (1970). *Human sexual inadequacy*. Boston: Little, Brown.

McCarthy, B. (1984). Strategies and techniques for the treatment of inhibited sexual desire. *Journal of Sex and Marital Therapy, 10*, 97–104.

Minuchin, S. (1974). *Families and family therapy*. Cambridge, MA: Harvard University Press.

Minuchin, S., & Fishman, H. (1981). *Family therapy techniques*. Cambridge, MA: Harvard University Press.

Mosher, D. (1979). Sex guilt and sex myths in college men and women. *Journal of Sex Research, 15*, 224–234.

Nutter, P., & Condron, M. (1983). Sexual fantasy and activity patterns of females with inhibited sexual desire versus normal controls. *Journal of Sex and Marital Therapy, 9*, 276–282.

Regas, S., & Sprenkle, D. (1984). Functional family therapy and treatment of inhibited sexual desire. *Journal of Marital and Family Therapy, 10*, 63–72.

Riegel, K. (1976). The dialectics of human developments. *American Psychologist, 31*, 689–710.

Schover, L., & LoPiccolo, J. (1982). Treatment effectiveness for dysfunctions of sexual desire. *Journal of Sex and Marital Therapy, 8*, 179–197.

Schwartz, M. (1986, March). The Masters and Johnson treatment approach for inhibited sexual desire. Paper presented at the meeting of the Society for Sex Therapy & Research, Philadelphia, Pa.

Sue, D. (1979). Erotic fantasies of college students during coitus. *Journal of Sex Research, 15*, 299–305.

Verhulst, J., & Heiman, J. (1979). An interactional approach to sexual dysfunction. *The American Journal of Family Therapy, 7*, 19–36.

Weeks, G. (1986). Individual-system dialectic. *American Journal of Family Therapy, 14*, 5–12.

Weeks, G., & L'Abate, L. (1982). *Paradoxical psychotherapy: Theory and practice with individual couples and families*. New York: Brunner/Mazel.

Zilbergeld, B., & Ellison, L. (1982). Desire discrepancies and arousal problems. In S. Leiblum and L. Pervin (Eds.), *Principles and practice of sex therapy*. New York: Guilford Press.

Chapter 11

Understanding Hypersexuality in Men and Women

Martin Goldberg

In recent years, much attention has been paid to the sexual dysfunction which is designated as *inhibited sexual desire*, and which is defined as "persistent and pervasive inhibition of sexual desire" in the American Psychiatric Association's *Diagnostic and Statistical Manual of Mental Disorders* (DSM-III, p. 278). It is worthy of note, however, that the dysfunction which might be termed *exaggerated* or *excessive sexual desire* has been virtually disregarded in clinical and scientific circles and is not even listed as a separate entity in the APA Manual. Unquestionably, one reason for this oversight is the difficulty in defining this dysfunction in a satisfactory manner. Such terms as satyriasis, nymphomania, and Don Juanism have been used to loosely and inaccurately refer to conditions that may or may not represent excessive sexual desire (Levine, 1982). Even more pertinent is the difficulty in establishing what degree of sexual desire can be regarded as exaggerated or excessive. Levine (1984) has pointed out that sexual desire or "the propensity to behave sexually . . . is not a discrete, quantifiable phenomenon," and that it cannot be equated with the frequency of sexual behavior.

Clearly, then, a number of basic factors must be considered in attempting to delineate excessive sexual desire and/or hypersexuality:

1. Excessive sexual desire is a relative term, and someone has to take the responsibility of defining what is excessive in any given case. The most reliable witness, in these terms, is that person himself or herself. Surely if he or she complains of excessive desire, we must accept that as being the case. Less reliable are the reports of others, although the "significant other" is often the one who brings this complaint to the physician's attention. The wife who tells us that her husband is a "sex maniac" may do so because he demands sexual intercourse twice daily — or, in some cases, because he desires sex twice a week

Portions of this chapter are reprinted from *Physician and Patient*, Vol. IV, No. 6, June 1985. Reprinted by permission.

(i.e., she may be identifying her husband's excessive sexual desire or she may be mislabeling her own inhibited sexual drive).

2. Excessive sexual desire may or may not result in excessive overt sexual behavior. Some people who indulge in relatively little or no overt sexual activity may still suffer from excessive sexual desire as manifested by constant preoccupation and rumination over matters sexual, to the point where other thinking and activity is impaired.

3. When excessive sexual desire does result in excessive sexual activity, such activity may be heterosexual or homosexual; it may be genital, oral, or anal; it may involve another person or be strictly masturbatory; it may be normal/usual; or it may be deviant/paraphiliac (i.e., voyeurism, exhibitionism, fetishism, etc.).

4. Excessive sexual activity may result from excessive desire or it may result from inadequate restraint due to poor impulse control, faulty judgment, or neurological disinhibition.

5. The psychic effects of excessive sexual desire may be described in terms of obsession and compulsion. The individual is *obsessed* with sexual thoughts and sexual feelings, often to the virtual exclusion of other matters. And excessive sexual activity, when it is present, is *compulsive* in nature: the person is driven or compelled to sexual activity over and over and over again in a manner that produces only very temporary gratification or sometimes is devoid of any gratification at all. (The terms *sexual addict* and *sexual addiction* have achieved some popularity in the last few years and are used by some to describe at least some of the phenomena detailed here (Orford, 1978).

6. Quantitative judgment of sexual desire and activity is based on cultural norms, social norms, gender differences, and age appropriateness. Some of these judgments are unquestionably sound; a level of sexual desire that may be excessive in a 40-year-old man may be entirely appropriate in an 18-year-old boy. Other judgments simply reflect social biases, and thus the extreme sexual desire that we see as normal and appropriate in the 18-year-old boy may be labeled as excessive or pathological should it be encountered in a young woman of the same age.

Case Examples

Sarah R. is a 39-year-old artist who has never been married and who is affluent both from family inheritance and from professional income. She has been sexually active ever since her junior year in high school and has rarely been without at least one or two lovers during that time. In those periods of her life wherein, for one reason or another, she has had to do without sexual intercourse for several weeks or more she has become quite uncomfortable and has definitely felt, in her own words, "horny and hard-up." Over the years, she has had two unwanted pregnancies, resulting in abortions. She has several times suffered from infestations of pubic lice. In addition, she has had gonorrhea on three different occasions and is troubled with recurrent episodes of genital herpes. Most of the time, Sarah limits her sexual relationships to one or two partners, although on some occasions she has had concurrent sexual relationships with three or four men. On an average, she may have sexual intercourse two or three times a week, and when this is not possible, she may or may not resort to occasional masturbation for relief of her sexual drive.

Perhaps the most noteworthy aspect of Sarah's situation is the attitude she engenders in her physicians. Her family practitioner and her gynecologist, both of whom have been involved in Sarah's medical problems over the years, regard her as a "nymphomaniac." The gynecologist, speaking of Sarah, said, "Of course she has herpes. What can you expect with the kind of sexual excesses she indulges in? She's a real nympho." Whether or not there is validity in this viewpoint is perhaps a matter of definition of terms. However, the reader is invited to go back and peruse the details of Sarah's situation and consider what diagnostic label would be appropriate if Sarah were a male. In all likelihood, a 39-year-old man living the sort of life that Sarah is living would not be regarded as suffering from satyriasis or, indeed, as being sexually abnormal in any way. Obviously, Sarah is regarded by her physicians as suffering from hypersexuality simply because her behavior does not meet their expectations of female sexuality.

Arthur C., an 80-year-old business executive, has a situation not too different from Sarah's. He is a widower who is still quite active in the company he founded 50 years ago. Very much alert and alive to the world, this vigorous 80-year-old man works a full 40- or 50-hour week, enjoys good health, and is still very much interested in sex. Customarily he has a "steady friend," usually a woman 30 or 40 years younger than himself, with whom he shares interests and shares his bed. On at least two occasions, members of his family have tried to raise questions about his legal and mental competence, citing the fact that he is a "dirty old man" as evidence of some presumed senility. Here again, Arthur's behavior would certainly not be seen as abnormal for a 40-year-old or 50-year-old widower. His sexual desire, rather than being labeled as excessive for his age, might more appropriately be recognized as *unimpaired*, just as his general vigor, health, and work capacity are unimpaired.

TYPICAL COMPLAINTS RELATED
TO EXCESSIVE SEXUAL DESIRE

As indicated previously, complaints relating to excessive sexual desire may be presented by the person experiencing them or, at least as commonly, by the "significant other" (spouse, lover, or parent). Consequently, this type of complaint is quite often presented in any kind of couples therapy or sex therapy.

The patient may complain that constant sexual feelings and urges interfere with relaxation and productivity, that judgment is badly affected thereby, and that impulsive actions are taken that cause various difficulties. Currently, not a few patients complain that excessive sexual desire with resulting excessive sexual activity causes them to risk exposure to venereal disease such as herpes and AIDS, of which they are extremely frightened.

"Significant others" complain that the individual's hypersexuality overshadows all other common interests and makes him or her demanding, inconsiderate, and—at times—socially embarrassing.

One of the most common of all complaints relevant to excessive sexual desire is repeated, compulsive infidelity. This complaint is presented at times by patients who are concerned that such activity is jeopardizing their marriages or love relationships. Far more commonly, it is presented by the "innocent" spouse or lover, who is tortured by the steady recurrence of sexual dalliances on the other's part. Such situations are encountered all too frequently among all sorts of couples: heterosexual, bisexual, gay, and lesbian.

The simplest complaints engendered by excessive sexual desire are those in which a marriage or other relationship is conflicted because of the differing levels of sexual desire in the two partners. Needless to say, it is often very difficult in such cases to determine whether one partner is suffering from excessive sexual desire, whether one is suffering from inhibited sexual desire, or—as is perhaps most often the case—whether the problem is only one manifestation of a general struggle for control and power being reflected in the sexual arena.

ETIOLOGY

Examples of sexually hyperactive individuals abound in history and in fiction (cf.: Casanova, Don Juan, Catherine the Great of Russia, and the Roman Empress Valeria Messalina). Obviously, we are all somewhat fascinated by tales of those whose sexual appetites and/or sexual capabilities are gargantuan in proportions. Yet, there is little hard evidence pertinent to the etiology of excessive sexual desire.

That organic factors are of any great importance in the etiology is a possibility, but other than in a few very specific conditions, this remains to be demonstrated. We know that a certain level of androgens is necessary in men for normal sexual appetite, but there is no evidence that levels higher than normal produce increased desire. With women, the evidence of a hormonal basis for desire is quite tenuous. The female hormones do not appear to play any part in libido. "High-testosterone" (or high-androgen) women are sometimes described as quite sexually responsive, but it is unclear whether this connects with increased sexual desire or whether it has to do with more assertive behavior, both sexually and generally (Bancroft, 1984).

Some organic conditions and some drugs are capable of producing a disinhibiting effect on the central nervous system, with a resultant increase in sexual behavior.

Case Example

George C., a 50-year-old salesman, had been successful in his work and in his family life for many years. He was known as a hard-driving, serious person who generally played by the rules. His co-workers, customers, family, and friends all found him to be generally rather dignified and decorous in his manners and conduct.

Under these circumstances, George's wife was particularly upset when she noted a change in his behavior. He began to make very frequent reference, often couched in gutter language, to all sorts of sexual material. Even in his wife's presence, he would make passes — verbal or more than verbal — at almost any attractive woman he encountered. His sexual demands on his wife also increased, but she noted that his actual sexual performance was, if anything, less than before in both quantity and quality.

After talking this over with friends and relatives, George's wife came to the conclusion that he was "suffering from male menopause" and that he needed psychiatric help. Since he would not accept the idea of seeing a psychiatrist by and for himself, she went with him in the guise of obtaining help for their marital relationship.

In the course of two conjoint interviews with the psychiatrist, George displayed repeated references to sex and talked almost incessantly about sexual activities in which he wanted to be involved. However, it was also noted that his grooming was less than one would expect of a successful salesman, that he appeared careless and forgetful about all sorts of details, and that he exhibited mental confusion and confabulation. A neurological referral was made and insisted on, and the diagnosis was subsequently made and confirmed surgically: George had a sizable meningioma impinging on his frontal lobes. His postsurgical recovery was uneventful, and his hypersexuality evaporated with the removal of his tumor. Cases such as this are not common but they do occur from time to time, and it is of special importance to note that a marital or sex therapist may often be the first clinician consulted and may be confronted with the necessity of at least suspecting the possibility of such a diagnosis.

The Kluver-Bucy syndrome (Gerstenbrand et al., 1983; Lilly et al., 1983; Nakada et al., 1984), first described in rhesus monkeys after bitemporal lobectomy and subsequently identified in humans, consists of hypersexuality along with prominent oral tendencies, emotional blunting, altered dietary habits, visual and auditory agnosia, and a decrease in fear reactions with aggressive behavior. It results from bilateral temporal lobe damage and has been observed in patients suffering from Pick's disease and Alzheimer's disease and as a sequela to head trauma and herpes simplex encephalitis (Cummings & Duchen, 1981). Despite these occurrences of hypersexuality associated with temporal lobe lesions, *decreased* sexual desire is probably the more usual concomitant of such pathology (Cogen et al., 1979; Levine, 1984). Hypersexuality induced by dopaminergic drug treatment in parkinsonian patients is a rarely reported side effect of such therapy (Vogel & Schiffter, 1983). It has, however, led to some clinical trials of dopamine agonists in attempts to find a successful drug treatment for inhibited sexual desire.

Far more common than any of the above as a cause of disinhibition with resultant excessive sexual desire is the abuse of certain drugs, particularly alcohol, the amphetamines, and cocaine. It should be noted, however, that although these drugs may thus serve to increase sexual appetite in some instances, there is no evidence that they increase sexual performance. In fact, the effect of drugs on the latter is almost always deleterious.

Among the more psychological conditions that may give rise to excessive sexual desire are certain psychoses, certain personality disorders, and, at times, other psychosexual dysfunctions.

Case Example

Rita, a 22-year-old bride of three months, contacted a marital therapist because of concerns about her marriage. She appeared for the first interview alone, stating that her 23-year-old husband, Sol, refused to accompany her and felt that he had no problems and needed no help. Rita had become concerned over a period of several weeks during which Sol had been acting strangely. She reported that he had failed to come home on several evenings and had subsequently told her, in unabashed fashion, that he had spent these nights with prostitutes or other women that he had picked up at bars. In addition to this, Sol had started making constant sexual demands on Rita in a manner she had never seen him exhibit previously. He was very talkative, slept very little when he was home at night, ate very little, and his mind seemed to go from one idea to another with tremendous rapidity.

At the end of the session, the therapist gave Rita some suggestions that helped her persuade Sol to come to a second interview on the next day. At that time, Sol was much as Rita had described him and talked almost incessantly throughout the sessions. He seemed excited almost to a point of elation, was physically hyperactive, and stated that he wanted "to have intercourse with every woman in the city of Philadelphia." Suspecting that Sol was suffering from a psychotic reaction, the therapist strongly urged psychiatric consultation, but Sol refused to accept this suggestion. Subsequently, however, the consultation was arranged by enlisting the aid of Sol's parents, who were apprised of the situation and helped to cajole and accompany him on a visit to the psychiatrist. This visit did indeed confirm the existence of a manic episode of bipolar disorder. In fact, it emerged that Sol had suffered previous depressive episodes, a fact he had not shared with Rita. Sol was hospitalized for a period of three weeks. Treatment with antipsychotic medication (thioridazine) and with lithium was effective, and after discharge from the hospital Sol's general and sexual behavior returned to his prepsychotic norm. Sol and Rita, however, did return to the marital therapist for some much needed follow-up counseling. Each of them harbored severe resentments because of the manic episode. Rita felt that Sol (and his parents) had deceived her by not telling her about his past psychiatric history. Moreover, even though she understood that his sexual philandering during the manic episode was induced by his psychotic excitement and lack of judgment, she found it difficult to forgive and forget this behavior. Sol, on his part, insisted that he would have been all right without the psychiatric hospitalization and for some time remained angry at Rita, his parents, and the marital therapist. He did continue to come to the conjoint counseling, however, and eventually the bilateral resentments seemed to fade and a reasonable degree of marital harmony was restored.

Manic episodes are by far the most common psychotic causes of hypersexuality, and in many instances the onset and course of the disorder are not quite as obvious or dramatic as in this case example. The diagnosis should be strongly considered whenever a person, particularly someone in the teens or twenties, shows a rather sudden emergence of sexual behavior differing from the previous norm. Sleeplessness, loss of appetite, rapid speech pattern, flights of ideas, "racing thoughts," poor social judgment, and, of course, elation or euphoria are associated symptoms commonly seen in manic states. Previous manic episodes, previous depressive episodes, and a family history of depressive or bipolar disease all lend credence to the possibility of this diagnosis.

Other psychotic causes of hypersexual behavior do exist. These include drug-induced psychotic states such as those resulting from LSD, phencyclidene or PCP, cocaine, the amphetamines, etc. Hypersexual behavior is sometimes a part of schizophrenic psychoses, but in these cases it tends to be bizarre in nature and the diagnosis is usually not difficult to make.

Of more direct pertinence for the marital or sexual therapist is the fact that hypersexuality is a not uncommon symptom among patients with certain personality disorders. It may be part of the general picture of a sociopathic, histrionic, narcissistic, or borderline personality disorder. In all these cases, it does not seem that the sexual need per se is particularly strong or prevalent. Rather it is a matter of the individual utilizing sexual intercourse and sexual behavior as a means of filling some other needs. In sociopathic personality disorders, sexual activity is used as a means of controlling and manipulating other people. Sociopaths often tend to sexualize almost all their interpersonal situations, but they do so with the aim of thereby gaining an advantage; exploitation of the other person is the almost constant concomitant of their sexual interactions. Narcissistic and histrionic individuals not uncommonly engage in very sizable amounts of sexual behavior but do so with the primary purposes of gaining attention from other people and of reassuring themselves of their attractiveness, their appeal, their "special" qualities. The classic "Don Juan" type of man probably fits best into this diagnostic category, the assumption being that a Don Juan or a Casanova is compelled to make sexual conquest after sexual conquest as a way of reassuring himself of his own irresistibility and very special masculinity.

Borderline personalities utilize excessive sexual behavior in a particularly striking fashion. They are plagued by chronic feelings of severe loneliness, emptiness, isolation, even personal "nothingness." Repetitious, frantic sexual activity then becomes an effort on their part to somehow give themselves a feeling of personal identity by fusing with another person, or to somehow fill up their inner void. The borderline person's search for a sexual partner has a markedly frenetic quality to it and often leads to involvements and sexual intercourse with some very undesirable characters. Thus, it is not at all unusual for borderline personalities and sociopathic personalities to establish sexual relationships with each other in which each partner is attempting to fulfill respective needs for fusing and filling or for dominating and manipulating. (A striking example of such a borderline-sociopathic sexual situation is presented in the book and film "Looking for Mr. Goodbar." Herein, the heroine—very probably a borderline personality—becomes sexually involved repeatedly with sociopathic personalities, culminating eventually in her murder.) It is equally common for borderline personalities and narcissistic or histrionic personalities to interact in sexual relationships that are entered into with the utmost rapidity, are pursued frenetically, and generally abandoned almost as quickly as they are initiated.

Occasionally, someone who is suffering from another form of sexual dysfunction may develop some hypersexual behavior. Rhoda L., a 32-year-old divorcee, provides an example of this phenomenon. During her eight years of marriage she suffered from an inhibition of orgasm. After the first few years of this, her husband lost interest in their sexual relationship and began to find his satisfaction in extramarital relationships. Eventually, this situation became so unsatisfactory for Rhoda that she left the marriage. Now, in her newly divorced state, she still suffers from anorgasmia, but she has begun a period of extremely intense sexual activity. She has sexual intercourse at every possible opportunity presented to her, masturbates almost incessantly, has tried lesbian relationships, and says that her desire is extreme, intense, and insatiable. Much of her behavior seems to represent a reaction formation to her orgasmic inhibition and her years of sexless marriage. Eventually, if she becomes more comfortable with her body or in some fashion is able to break through her orgasmic dysfunction, her hypersexuality may well subside.

Recently there has been a tendency to group many problems of excessive sexual desire or hypersexuality along with various sexual paraphilias and to refer to the entire aggregate as problems of "sexual addictions" (Orford, 1978). Although this concept is being viewed as new and revolutionary, it seems to be merely a relabeling of well-established and well-recognized phenomena. Thus, the term *addiction* can be used loosely to refer to any situation in which behavior is *compulsive*. Compulsive behavior is that to which an individual is driven, not necessarily for the pursuit of pleasure nor even the relief of pain. Often, the compulsive drive is a seemingly meaningless, repetitive force that grips the person. Characteristically, actions taken because of a compulsion never satisfy that drive more than very fleetingly, and so the compulsion recurs over and over. Viewing all this in terms of addiction does offer at least one important advantage. The compulsion is then seen not as a mysterious inner force gripping the person, but rather as a type of definite disease process from which the person suffers and which, with proper therapy, he can be empowered to recognize and to combat (see Table 1).

EXCESSIVE SEXUAL DESIRE AND COUPLE INTERACTION

Whatever the etiology of hypersexual behavior may be, its effects on couple interaction are profound and complex. Because of the circular nature of such interaction, both members of the couple will sooner or later feed into the causative process. This is most vividly exemplified by those not uncommon couples in which the man, for instance, will want to have sex daily, and the woman, in reaction, will not only decline the daily schedule but will retreat to a position of withholding sex almost entirely. It is obvious, then, that in such couples the sexual interaction quickly becomes an arena for playing out the struggle for power and control.

On rare occasions, a therapist may have the opportunity to intervene in a problem before interactional factors have added complexity. Marilyn, for example, was a 22-year-old woman who had been seeing a psychotherapist for individual treatment of some relatively mild neurotic problems. Shortly after finishing her treatment she married a young man she had known for some time. About three months later she called and arranged for a follow-

Table 1
Possible Causes of Hypersexuality

Hyperandrogenic states in women

Temporal lobe lesions, Pick's disease, Alzheimer's, head trauma, herpes simplex encephalitis

Disinhibiting drugs (e.g., alcohol, amphetamines, cocaine)

Psychoses (especially manic states)

Sexual dysfunctions leading to reaction formation

Drug-induced psychotic states (e.g., PCP, cocaine, amphetamines)

Personality disorders (especially sociopathic, narcissistic, histrionic, or borderline)

---

up interview with her therapist. At that interview, Marilyn was asked how the marriage was going. Her answer, although positive in content, was somewhat reserved or ambiguous in tone, so that the therapist challenged it and wondered aloud if there were severe problems occurring between Marilyn and her husband, Mike. Pressed that far, Marilyn then admitted that the sexual relationship was not going well. Mike seemed to want intercourse "all the time," and she found that she just could not keep up with his demands and still enjoy herself in the process. Did she lack pleasure in the sexual act, the therapist queried? No, Marilyn replied, once or twice a week she "really got into it," but on the other occasions she found herself just going through the motions. After some further discussion, the therapist suggested that he would be willing to meet with Mike to discuss the problem, and then to have a conjoint session with them in an attempt to be helpful. This offer was promptly accepted and the following week Mike appeared in the office. Mike radiated optimism and good feelings about the marriage. He couldn't really understand why his wife had wanted him to see the therapist, but he was glad to do anything she suggested. Moreover, he was happy for the opportunity to tell someone how pleased he was with Marilyn, with their marriage, with their wonderful sexual relationship, etc.

Listening to all this the therapist had a definite impression that Mike was protesting too much and exhibiting more than a little overcompensation. How did Mike enjoy the daily sexual activity, he asked. The answer was immediate and unequivocal: It was super! It was everything Mike had ever dreamed of and he just couldn't get enough of it. Again, the very vehemence of the answer somehow had a hollow ring, and the therapist decided to risk a questionable maneuver. Resorting to what was at best a gross oversimplification or at worst a little white lie, he mused aloud with Mike, "That's very unusual—very unusual! Most healthy young couples are really quite content having sex twice a week." "What was that you said?" Mike asked with a notable degree of agitation. The therapist repeated his statement, and as he did, Mike seemed to sit back in his chair and relax quite noticeably. A few further comments by the therapist elicited the full story. Mike, it seemed, really was finding that daily intercourse was a bit much and suspected that twice a week would be just fine. However, he worked in a large office where his co-workers were constantly kidding him about his newlywed status and referring to the gargantuan amounts of sexual activity he must be having—all of which had made Mike feel he *should* be wanting sex every day, and since Marilyn had not actually articulated any dissent from this, he presumed she wanted that level of activity. The conjoint session with this couple was held a month later, at which time the problem had disappeared and the sexual relationship was mutually satisfactory. What had started out sounding like a possible problem in excessive sexual desire turned out to be a simple case of trying to keep up with the Joneses—never a wise course and certainly not one to pursue in bed.

Even in this "easy case," however, the involvement of *both* members of the couple is very evident. Each of them *assumed* a knowledge and an understanding of the other's desires and capacities for sex, and both totally failed to articulate openly and honestly their own sexual feelings. Each of them was going along with an unsatisfactory situation in the vague hope or anticipation that it was going to somehow, spontaneously, magically improve or clear up. Needless to say, without therapeutic intervention, this desired turn of events often fails to occur and the problem becomes more entrenched, more encrusted, more complex with the passage of time.

Another common but more complicated sort of interactional setting involves couples wherein one partner's excessive sexual desire cannot be fulfilled or abated by the other partner. Sometimes this may be due largely or in part to the unsatisfactory quality of their sexual relationship and, if such is the case, couples therapy utilizing sensate focus exercises or some form of sex therapy is appropriate. At other times, the problem is very strongly reflective of problems in the general interpersonal relationship and couples therapy with emphasis on the relational aspects is indicated. Yet again, there are other instances in which neither of the preceding possibilities pertain. In these cases the quality of the sexual relationship per se appears to be at least reasonably good and the general relationship is for the most part loving and functional. Nonetheless, one partner is repeatedly driven to find sex elsewhere, a phenomenon that may or may not be known to the other partner.

In most instances, these constant seekers of extracurricular sex are reflecting some degree of inner psychopathology. This is not to say that the desire for sexual variety is abnormal. Obviously it occurs in most of us. Moreover, it is up to any given couple to decide the parameters of what is permissible in their sexual relationship and what conforms with their religious, aesthetic, and philosophical convictions. But the constant search for new and different sexual relationships is rarely compatible with the stable functioning of a couple and most often causes severe discontent both in the individual and in the relationship. Or it may be that it is a *symptom* of severe discontent in the individual and then causes severe discontent within the relationship.

Allen, a very successful lawyer in his forties, is a case in point. He and his wife, Judy, consulted a marital therapist for help after a dozen years of marriage. These years had been basically rather satisfactory for both of them, with the exception of one problem: Allen's constant search for sex outside the marriage. Their own sexual relationship met most criteria for normality. It was frequent (about three times a week), both affectionate and passionate, and almost always resulted in climaxes for both of them. Despite all this, however, Allen was always looking for—and very frequently finding—other women. He would encounter them among his clients, among the women attorneys, paralegals, and secretaries at his work, in bars and nightclubs, etc. He was extremely adept at the quick conquest; his own involvement was always superficial and soon ended once the novelty of the situation faded. During the first four or five years of marriage, Allen had somehow been able to hide his outside activities from Judy. This was not an easy process, however, and those years were clouded for him with guilt, shame, and worry. Finally, a combination of circumstances led to his being detected by his wife, not once but on repeated occasions. Matters were then out in the open, and Allen had originally felt some relief. Subsequent events were not pleasant, however. Promise after promise to change his behavior was elicited by Judy from him and promise after promise was broken. They tried increasing the tempo of their own sexual activity even further and, oddly enough, this only resulted in an even stronger drive for more extramarital sex on Allen's part.

There is little question that Judy played a significant role in this problem. It could be argued that she contributed to Allen's behavior by hiding it from her conscious awareness for years and then by tolerating it after she could no longer deny its existence. Nevertheless, in the course of a number of conjoint marital sessions the therapist gained a strong impression that the sexual problem was primarily a symptom and a reflection of deep intrapsychic pathology within Allen. He was referred for intensive individual psychotherapy and was subsequently diagnosed as having a narcissistic personality disorder, which contributed largely to his need for constant sexual conquests. These seemed to represent repeated acting-out of a need to reassure himself as to his masculinity and also of a need to possess, to dominate, and to inflict pain through rejection of women. (Obviously, Allen's sexual peccadilloes simultaneously expressed this possession, domination, and rejection of his wife.) Conjoint marital sessions with the original therapist continued on an occasional basis, and with this combination of individual and conjoint help, Allen and Judy were able to bring about significant changes after a period of about two year's work. Since that time, Allen's extramarital sexual activities have been given up, the marital sexual relationship has remained active, and in fact it is now apparently satisfying both physically and emotionally to each of them.

The previously mentioned concepts of *obsession* and compulsion are useful in understanding cases such as that of Allen and Judy as well as many others. Through his psychotherapy Allen learned that he did not have a need for daily orgasms, although he was obsessed with the idea of such a need. In actuality, Judy and he had always been easily able to satisfy his purely sexual needs, but the *compulsion* to conquer and then reject woman after woman had gone on and on. Like all compulsive behavior it produced only very transitory psychic relief and often left Allen feeling angry and disgusted with himself. Like all compulsive behavior it was really an attempt to relive and relieve the distress of the dim past, an attempt that is perforce doomed to failure. All sorts of compulsive behaviors may be manifested as part of a sexual pattern or sexual interaction. George and Hanna, for instance, have a situation that sounds at first remarkably similar to that of Allen and Judy. They have the same sort of generally satisfactory sexual relationship between themselves and the same sort of functioning marriage. And George is constantly chasing after and seducing other sexual partners. The one difference is that George's extra-marital sex is all achieved with other men. Rarely does a day go by that he does not have a brief and hurried homosexual encounter, all of which is about as satisfying to him as were Allen's heterosexual dalliances. More does not need to be said about this case other than to recognize that despite the homosexual trappings, it simply represents another problem in compulsive sexuality.

Some couples may become jointly obsessed in a hypersexual manner and may share compulsive behavior. Such, for example, is the case with some self-avowed "swingers": couples who devote enormous amounts of time and energy to finding and interacting sexually with other couples of like per-suasion. Probably far more common are those instances in which couples develop more moderate forms of sexual obsessions that compel their actions: the compulsion to have sex constantly as if there were a *Guinness Book of World Records* goal to be attained, the compulsion to prolong the sex act for remarkable lengths of time, the compulsion to have simultaneous mutual orgasms, the compulsion to have "perfect sex." All of these compulsions may be viewed as less intrusive and dysfunctional in nature, but all are capable of taking the joy and gratification out of sex and turning it into work.

Yet another interactional setting that may be conducive to hypersexual behavior is that commonest of all phenomena, the struggle for power and control. This may play itself out in several possible scripts. When each mem-ber of a couple is firmly convinced that his way and only his way is "right" or "normal" or healthy, any other way must perforce be labeled as wrong or abnormal. Under such circumstances, it is easy for one partner to brand the other's sexual desire or sexual behavior as excessive. (it is of course equally easy in this manner to affix the label of *inhibited* to sexual desire or behavior). Another possibility involves denial of a problem on the part of one partner with the subsequent projection of the difficulty onto the other. Thus, a sexually inhibited wife may protest that her level of desire is quite normal and that her husband is hypersexual because he desires sex so much more than she does. Or a husband with excessive sexual desire may deny that he has any problem and choose to label his wife as "frigid" or inhibited. In all these various instances, the therapist's stance, of necessity, must be nonjudgmental. Rather than affixing or going along with labels such as *excessive* or *inhibited*, the therapist can best view the problem as a conflict over quantitative and qualitative aspects of interpersonal behavior and can then proceed to deal with this in terms of the total interaction of the couple: how they share or struggle for power, how they are able or unable to give to each other, how well or how poorly they accept differences, whose needs are given priority and when, etc.

TREATMENT OF HYPERSEXUALITY

Obviously the treatment of excessive sexual desire is dependent on those etiological factors which are identified as being causative of the problem. Careful elucidation and evaluation of the past and present sexual history, the family history, and the personal developmental history is required. The identified patient should be interviewed individually as should the spouse or significant other; in addition, one or more conjoint interviews should be carried out as part of the diagnostic workup. This gives the therapist a much needed opportunity to directly observe the interpersonal relationship and to calculate its effects on the sexual relationship and problem.

As part of the individual assessment of the patient, a careful psychological evaluation and psychiatric history should be carried out. Particular attention should be paid to obtaining a thorough history of any drug usage and of head trauma, sleeping sickness, mental confusion, epileptic seizures, or other neurological signs or symptoms. When it is not possible to rule out the existence of underlying organic disorders, a thorough neurological examination and endocrine evaluation are indicated. In general, when etiological factors within the individual are found to be predominant, therapeutic attention must be focused on these. This applies equally to organic factors such as brain tumors or endocrine abnormalities, to psychological factors such as severe personality disorders, and to truly biopsychosocial factors such as bipolar disorders. Thus, appropriate individual psychotherapy of a borderline or narcissistic personality disorder or appropriate psychiatric and psychopharmacological treatment of a bipolar affective disorder may be the primary means of treatment for a given patient suffering from excessive sexual desire, as may be the removal of a brain tumor or the correction of some other neurologically disinhibiting factor. With all these possibilities, it is also true that conjoint treatment of the identified patient along with the significant other, *combined with* the appropriate individual approach, is likely to make for a surer and greater degree of success.

The treatment of hypersexuality by use of medication has been attempted. Antiandrogen drugs such as CPA (cyproterone acetate) and medroxyprogesterone have been used both alone and in combination with various forms of psychotherapy (Cordoba & Chapel, 1983; Moore, 1980; Neuman, 1983). Such treatments have most often been used with sex offenders or paraphiliacs, in whom good degrees of efficacy have been reported. Most probably, any success represents the effects of decreasing normal testosterone levels to levels so low that sexual appetite is impaired. The complexities of such "chemical castration," as the treatment is sometimes termed, are very considerable in terms of legal, moral, and ethical issues, and the effects on couple interaction would have to be regarded as highly problematic at best.

THE COUPLES-THERAPY APPROACH
TO PROBLEMS OF EXCESSIVE SEXUAL DESIRE

This approach is based on a number of principles and concepts that apply to most or all types of couples therapy.

1. Major attention in the therapy is focused on the interaction within the couple, including those parts that are obvious and accessible to the couple's awareness and those parts that are unconscious or hidden from the couple, but are observed or detected by the therapist.

2. Each member of the couple is encouraged to look at ways of relating that he or she may have developed within the interactions of the family of origin and then carried into the present relationship. Thus, early life attitudes and family attitudes about sexuality, about sensuality, about levels of sexual desire, etc., are examined and scrutinized for their effects on the current problem.

3. Attention is not limited to the sexual interaction, but includes all aspects of the couple's relationship, since any or all of these may be highly relevant to the sexual symptomatology. For example, a man who is always demanding his wife's attention and expects her to cater to his every whim may demand sex several times a day. Moreover, a wife who submits passively to his demands in general will be likely to go along, albeit grudgingly, with his sexual

requests. For change to occur, such a couple will need to look at their total relationship and the dominant/submissive roles that are being played out in it.

4. Therapeutic interventions may be based on behavioral, strategic, psychodynamic, and other approaches. The therapist's approach in the case of Marilyn and Mike, previously mentioned, could probably be considered strategic in nature. Whatever the nature of the intervention, however, it should be applied to the system, which in these cases means *conjointly*.

5. The most generally applicable form of behavioral intervention consists of the use of some form or adaptation of sensate focus exercises. At first blush, it might seem that these exercises would serve only to intensify the overly mechanistic, compulsive, perfectionistic approach that is so often associated with problems of hypersexuality. If the exercises are properly prescribed and properly carried out, such is not the case. In fact, the abstinence from sexual intercourse, the deemphasis on orgasm seeking, and the encouragement of greater degrees of bodily relaxation and sensuality are all aspects of sensate focus that may be quite helpful to the couple struggling with hypersexuality. The key problem from the therapist's standpoint is to enlist the couple's genuine cooperation and wholehearted participation in the program. This may be particularly difficult in terms of obtaining a prolonged period of sexual abstinence during which the exercises are utilized. Generally the therapist will do best by developing a sound and solid therapeutic working alliance with both members of the couple *before* making any attempt to prescribe sensate focus or any other form of behavioral therapy.

6. Throughout the therapy, each member of the couple is repeatedly encouraged and assisted to recognize *his or her own part* in the problem and to concentrate his/her efforts on changing his/her own behavior and reactions, rather than those of the partner.

7. Where and when necessary the couple therapy is combined with individual psychotherapy, psychopharmacological treatment, or whatever may be indicated. The couples therapist is well advised, however, not to simultaneously attempt to also function in the role of individual therapist, but to refer the patient elsewhere for such help. When a therapist does try to be all things to his patients—conjoint therapist, individual therapist, etc.—the boundaries between these roles get badly blurred, and the therapy almost inevitably suffers.

8. Use of nonprescribed drugs is frowned upon, abuse of drugs is forbidden. This dictum is of major importance in the couple's treatment of hypersexuality. As we have repeatedly observed, hypersexual behavior is very often the result of *disinhibition*, rather than of excessive sexual desire. And the most common cause of disinhibition of the central nervous system is undoubtedly alcohol. Many other drugs are equally capable of producing this effect, including barbiturates, amphetamines, cocaine, Quaalude, etc. (In fact,

Quaalude originally became an immensely popular street drug because of its reputed aphrodisiac qualities. Aphrodisiac it is not, but sedative it is, and central nervous system sedatives produce disinhibition.)

Because of these facts, it is wise to encourage any couple who are experiencing problems of hypersexuality to minimize their drug usage. This very definitely means recommending abstinence or minimal consumption of alcoholic beverages. In some instances, this program of minimizing drug intake will in and of itself clear up the hypersexual problems.

When drug abuse exists in one or both members of the couple, it *must* be dealt with before any attempt at working with the hypersexuality can reasonably be made. This means that the drug abuser must accept commitment to recovery through a program of abstinence such as Alcoholics Anonymous or Narcotics Anonymous. Only then is it feasible to proceed with couples therapy and to deal directly with the hypersexuality.

In devising and carrying out a treatment strategy for hypersexuality, it is of utmost importance for the couple's therapist to elicit the chronology of the disorder. A key question is whether the hypersexual partner has exhibited such behavior in *all* relationships (previous marriages, etc.), in which case the disorder can be regarded as *generalized hypersexuality*, or whether it is *selective hypersexuality*, which has only been evidenced as a part of the present relationship. Selective hypersexuality, as might be expected, is more often readily responsive to conjoint therapy; generalized hypersexuality is likely to require lengthy periods of treatment, often involving a combination of individual and conjoint modalities.

In the course of treatment, it is not unusual to encounter certain other symptomatology which may break through as the hypersexual behavior abates. For example, the nonhypersexual spouse may begin to show inhibited sexual desire or, in rare instances, excessive sexual desire, *after* the other spouse's desire has receded to normal levels. Such a development is, of course, very likely to represent a resistance based on the need of the couple to remain in a struggle for power and control. Far more common is the situation in which a person whose hypersexual behavior is abating begins to show increasing evidence of anxiety and depression. This is precisely parallel to what generally happens when an individual first gives up compulsive behavior of any sort (overeating, smoking, etc.), and it should not be allowed to slow or sidetrack the ongoing conjoint therapy. Rather, it should be explained to the couple that this is a usual development, that it signals *progress*, and that it will pass in due time as new behavior patterns become established.

In fighting the compulsive nature of many cases of hypersexuality, it is of particular value for the hypersexual individual to develop what might be called *healthy compulsions*. For instance, the therapist may strongly recommend an organized, regular approach to physical exercise involving the long muscles of the body, such as running, walking, swimming, tennis, squash, or racquetball. Obviously, any or all of these exercise modalities can be approached as joint activities by the couple, which will in some cases be highly desirable. In other instances it is clearly best for the exercise program to be an individual matter, since one of the prime purposes it may serve will be that of giving the individual an innocuous and constructive way of "doing his (or her) own thing." Admittedly, the concept of an exercise program being valuable in the treatment of hypersexuality may have the ring of age-old advice to "take cold showers." Exercise is, of course, no cure-all, but it can be an important part of an overall program for promoting change. Exercise, sports, and various games—vigorously and competitively pursued—can help to provide a healthier outlet for some of the competitive drives, drives for conquest, and urges to excel that are often misdirected in sexual behavior.

Along with the concept of *sexual addiction*, now achieving some popularity, comes the idea of treating people troubled with hypersexuality by methods and techniques that have been traditionally used for battling addictions. Such programs are modeled very closely or entirely on the Alcoholics Anonymous approach and emphasize the disease concept, the group approach, strong peer support, a definite religious element, etc., in much the same manner as does AA. Whether or not hypersexuality really is an addiction in the sense that alcoholism is, there seems to be little doubt that this therapeutic approach is likely to be helpful if the patient subscribes to it with enthusiasm and accepts the program in full. (Indeed, the patient can become healthily obsessed and healthily compulsive about the program, as a way of replacing troublesome sexual obsessions and compulsions.) It is, of course, possible and at times may be quite helpful to recommend a group "sexual addiction" recovery program as a concomitant or as a precursor to conjoint couples therapy.

In summary, a strong case could be made for the concept that the most effective therapy for hypersexuality—individual, conjoint, or otherwise—should be custom-designed, in effect, by the therapist to provide a reasonable and comfortable fit for the individual and for the couple, which will maximize the possibilities for change.

Clearly, change is not always possible, however—for a variety of reasons. When such is the case, the therapist has an additional delicate and difficult task: to help the couple examine the alternatives for other action. That means considering whether there is some way to accept the behavior within the marriage, whether separation and/or divorce is the wisest course, or whether there are any other alternatives between these two extremes that can be pursued fruitfully.

REFERENCES

American Psychiatric Association. (1980). *Diagnostic and statistical manual of mental disorders (DSM-III)* (3rd ed.). Washington, DC: Author.

Bancroft, J. (1984). Hormones and human sexual behavior. *Journal of Sex and Marital Therapy, 10*(1), 3-21.

Cogen, P. H., Antunes, J. L., & Correll, J. W. (1979). Reproductive function in temporal lobe epilepsy: The effect of temporal lobectomy. *Surgery-Neurology, 12*, 243-246.

Cordoba, O. A., & Chapel, J. L. (1983). Medroxyprogesterone acetate antiandrogen treatment of hypersexuality in a pedophiliac sex offender. *American Journal of Psychiatry, 140*, 1036-1039.

Cummings, J. L., & Duchen, L. W. (1981). Kluver-Bucy syndrome in Pick's disease: Clinical and pathological correlations. *Neurology (NY), 31*, 1415-1422.

Gerstenbrand, F., Poewe, W., Aichner, F., & Salturai, L. (1983). Kluver-Bucy syndrome in man: Experiences with post-traumatic cases. *Neuroscience-Biobehavioral Review, 7*, 413-417.

Levine, S. B. (1982). A modern perspective on nymphomania. *Journal of Sex and Marital Therapy, 8*(4), 316-324.

Levine, S. B. (1984). An essay on the nature of sexual desire. *Journal of Sex and Marital Therapy, 10*(2), 83-96.

Lilly, R., Cummings, J. L., Benson, D. F., & Frankel, M. (1983). The human Kluver-Bucy syndrome. *Neurology (NY), 33*, 1141-1145.

Moore, S. L. (1980). Satyriasis: A case study. *Journal of Clinical Psychiatry, 41*(8), 279-281.

Nakada, T., Lee, H., Kwee, Q. L., & Lerner, A. M. (1984). Epileptic Kluver-Bucy syndrome: Case report. *Journal of Clinical Psychiatry, 41*(8), 279-281.

Neuman, F. (1983). Pharmacological basis for clinical use of antiandrogens. *Journal of Steroid Biochemistry, 19*, 391-402.

Orford, J. (1978). Hypersexuality: Implications for a theory of dependence. *British Journal of Addictions, 73*, 299-310.

Vogel, H. P., & Schiffter, R. (1983). Hypersexuality: A complication of dopaminergic therapy in Parkinson's disease. *Pharmacopsychiatria, 16*(4), 107-110.

Chapter 12

Marital and Sexual Counseling of Elderly Couples

Jacob D. Stone

INTRODUCTION

Older and younger couples are not qualitatively different from each other. The theoretical formulations, assessment processes, and approaches to counseling are *structurally* identical in both cases. Older couples experience the same interactional and sexual dysfunctions as younger couples and are generally seeking the same types of remediation.

Why, then, a chapter on counseling the older couple? The answer lies in the fact that the aging process often disrupts whatever marital homeostasis a couple may have achieved, and this disruption may precipitate their seeking marital therapy. The social, psychological, and physical effects of aging can influence the *content* of a counseling relationship, and thus a discussion of therapy with the elderly couple is important insofar as it addresses these functional correlates of aging.

This approach suggests a practical definition of the "elderly couple." For purposes of this discussion, the elderly couple can be considered any couple whose marital distress is caused or exacerbated by the changes and losses that come with aging. The helping professional will want to carry out a careful investigation to determine whether these changes and losses have occurred, and what effect they have had, but beyond this we need to remember that aging couples are not a separate category of client.

Beyond this practical definition, it is useful to define the elderly in more concrete terms. Each program of services to the elderly seems to generate its own definition. Some definitions focus on 55 years of age, and others target people over 60 or over 65. There are even definitions that categorize people into young-old and old-old. For the purposes of this discussion, however, 65 is a useful but necessarily arbitrary demarcation line. Sixty-five is an age at which significant changes have occurred, are occurring, or will soon occur in the life-style of an aging couple. When one begins to work with aging couples, he or she will find that people at or near this age will be undergoing sufficient transitions that some aging-related changes will often be evident.

There has been very little research on how aging affects marital and sexual relationships. The demographic reasons for this are clear: it is only in recent years that there have been significant numbers of couples in which both partners reached old age. The dramatic improvement in the health and financial security of these elderly couples gives them for the first time the luxury of seeking satisfying relationships. Population projections for the remainder of the century and beyond suggest that the need for marital counseling of the elderly will become increasingly common as the percentage of elderly in our population reaches 20%. This increase will be accompanied by continuing improvements in the physical and mental health capacities of this group. Furthermore, this group, raised in an era conversant with psychoanalytic and psychological thought, will expect and hope for satisfying relationships and will be increasingly comfortable with the vernacular of marital and sexual therapy. It seems a certainty that helping professionals will find themselves working more and more with elderly couples.

THE AGING PROCESS

The therapist working with an older couple must be alert to three areas of loss and change that affect people as they age. They are: changes in mental status, changes in physical capabilities, and changes in role and life expectations. These changes can impact on couples in several ways:

1. By introducing a change in the dependency relationship that has been established in the past. The wife suddenly having to care for her husband after he suffers a stroke might encounter considerable distress as a result of finding herself in the caregiver's role; similarly, the husband might be very resentful of his need for assistance.

Closely related to this situation is the potential for a change in the frequency and intensity of contacts between the two parties. As we age, we find ourselves increasingly dependent on our primary relationships. Whether or not the primary relationship can withstand this closeness is a significant issue for the counselor. It is similar to the situation that newlyweds experience, when their time together is dramatically increased and they find that previously tolerable stylistic quirks of a spouse become intolerable. In an otherwise stable relationship this adjustment will probably be accomplished smoothly. However, in a relationship already defined as "problematic" this adjustment may be a significant hurdle.

2. As one partner undergoes a transient or chronic disturbance the distress generated may impact on the marital relationship. The prior stability of the relationship has a bearing on how well the couple withstands this disorder. Aging-related sexual problems fall into this category. For example, the husband who begins to experience an increase in erectile dysfunction due to increasing age may isolate himself from his spouse or may blame her for the problem. The wife who begins to experience painful intercourse may resist sexual contact. Although this is an easily resolvable problem, ineffective marital communications can make this problem loom large.

Problems other than sexual can occur as a result of these disturbances. An example is that of the spouse whose depression resulting from role changes seriously disrupts the relationship with his or her spouse. The first signs of organically based dementia in one spouse can be a major precipitant of marital distress and in an otherwise strained relationship this can be extremely divisive.

After a brief discussion of theoretical formulations, this chapter will consider these elements from the perspectives of *assessment, goal planning*, and *treatment considerations*. The intent will be to integrate information about the elderly couple into the more general field of marital and sexual therapy.

A NOTE ABOUT THEORETICAL FORMULATIONS

The elderly couple need not be examined through any special theoretical contrivance. Their needs, goals, and problems do not differ from those of other families and couples, and any theory of family systems can be applicable. However, these approaches can be enhanced through the addition of a theoretical and value base that directly addresses the losses and changes of the aging process.

A prominent and controversial theory of aging is the disengagement theory (Cumming & Henry, 1961), which postulates that a withdrawal from social involvement and participation is a normal, necessary, and even desirable correlate of aging. It suggests that many of the intrapersonal and interpersonal problems that befall elderly persons result from resisting this inexorable process of disengagement.

In describing the disengagement theory, its authors articulated the "activity" theory, more as a counterpoint to the disengagement theory than as a free-standing theoretical construct. The activity theory, which they believe has reflected implicit values of our society and of researchers in aging, argues that "successful aging consists in being as much like a middle-aged person as possible" (Cumming & Henry, 1961, p. 18), and that "the individual is seen as unfolding and expanding in such a way that every time a role or relationship is lost, a new one fills its place — perhaps even more than fills it" (Cumming & Henry, 1961, p. 18).

From the perspective of the marital therapist, neither model is ideal since the behavioral manifestations of each limit the repertoire of possible goals and plans. A more useful model would be one that provides a full range of options for the therapist and clients but also alerts the therapist to the aging-specific obstacles that might be encountered.

One particularly relevant model of aging is the compensatory model (Hussian, 1981). Originally a behaviorally oriented model used in developing aproaches to specific behavioral problems, it easily adapts as a useful model for marital and sexual therapy with the elderly. The compensatory model suggests that successful aging is a product of appropriate "adaptation to the natural changes occurring in aging . . . " (Hussian, 1981, p. 22). However, this is viewed as a particularly difficult task for the elderly individual:

> . . . the deterioration which normally accompanies aging not only reduces adaptive proficiency, but also requires the use of adaptive behavior more than at any other time in order to compensate for such decreases in proficiency. The elderly person, then, is in a double bind. He or she must compensate for the loss of adaptive ability and for the decrease in sensory acuity, memory deficits, and slower response times. He or she must also compensate for the environmental and social changes which are imposed (Hussian, 1981, pp. 22-23).

For the helping professional whose clients exhibit aging-related changes, this model provides a useful approach. It suggests that the counselor needs to help define those losses for which the person might be able to compensate. It also suggests that some attention be paid to the effectiveness of the adaptive strategies that are being used, since the older individual may be experiencing diminished compensatory ability. The task of compensation can encompass elements of both the disengagement and the activity theories. We may help the elderly client come to terms with some changes and attempt to preserve or recapture other aspects that have been lost. In other cases we will want to help them develop effective substitutions, modifications, and compensations and help them discover new ways of accomplishing these adjustments.

ASSESSMENT

Working with an elderly couple requires certain additions to the assessment processes that begin any counseling relationship. The therapist should look for changes that have occurred as a result of aging. These changes may be pivotal indicators of the source of the marital distress. The two areas of functioning that must be thoroughly addressed with elderly clients are mental acuity and physical functioning as they relate to activities of daily living. These areas should be evaluated in addition to the usual intake, which includes a study of presenting problems, personality typology, and interactional issues.

Mental Acuity

The popular view that all elderly persons suffer from dementia is not at all accurate. The percentage of elderly persons who suffer from a dementing condition is small, estimated at between 2 and 12% depending on the criteria used. However, this is a significant percentage and becomes even more significant in view of the fact that changes in mental functioning are precipitants of marital and sexual discord among the elderly. Changes in mental process can dramatically alter the individual's personality and affect as well as his or her cognitive functioning. These changes are often difficult for a spouse to understand or accept.

Organic mental changes of a dramatic nature will virtually always preclude the possibility of any significant marital or sexual therapy (although severe changes on the part of one spouse may suggest the need for supportive counseling for the unimpaired mate). However, an important element in the disruption of marital stability among older persons is the early and insidious onset of a debilitating dementia. During these early stages a person may be generally well compensated except for certain indicators of the condition. Making the situation even more difficult for both spouses is the fact that persons suffering from early dementing conditions often experience significant episodes of functional depression and anxiety.

The *Diagnostic and Statistical Manual of Mental Disorders* (DSM-III) (American Psychiatric Association, 1980) notes that the diagnostic criteria for dementia are:

1. A loss of intellectual abilities of sufficient severity to interfere with social or occupational functioning.
2. Memory impairment.
3. At least one of the following: impairment of abstract thinking; impaired judgment; aphasia, apraxia, agnosia, or constructional difficulty.
4. No clouded consciousness.
5. Evidence of a specific organic etiology or, in the absence of such evidence, the elimination of other etiological factors. (American Psychiatric Association, 1980, pp. 111–112.)

There are two major categories of dementing condition: multi-infarct dementia and primary degenerative dementia. Multi-infarct dementia is characterized by sudden and relatively dramatic change in cognitive capacity and therefore will not usually become an assessment issue within the context of marital or sexual therapy. On the other hand, primary degenerative dementia can often be a significant element in the breakdown of a couple's functioning because of its gradual and insidious onset. It is common for spouses of individuals suffering from a primary dementia to report that although they saw signs of the dementia for months or years, they did not accept that this was anything more than normal aging or even an attempt at manipulation by the individual in question. During the time that the condition has manifested itself, but has not yet been recognized as such, a couple may well report marital and/or sexual stress. The affected individual, for example, may be experiencing diminished impulse control that manifests itself in unusual sexual behavior distressing to the spouse; similarly, the affective lability that often accompanies organic changes may cause sexual encounters to be so distressing that they are minimized or discontinued.

The diagnostic puzzle is made more complex by the frequent presence of two further diagnostic categories that frequently accompany the irreversible dementias: organic personality syndrome (OPS) and organic affective syndrome (OAS). OPS describes changes in personality that are organically derived, and OAS describes affective changes with the same etiology. Although these diagnoses are not formally given in the presence of a diagnosis of an organic dementia, they are often early manifestations of an irreversible dementia.

The counselor should also be alert to what is commonly known as pseudodementia, a dementialike condition that is caused by any of a number of factors but which does not cause irreversible confusion. Among older persons a depressive episode can often appear to be an irreversible dementia. Similarly, sensory impairment, malnutrition, relocation, inadvertent misuse of medications, dehydration, and any of a number of metabolic conditions can trigger a reversible dementialike condition. This can be a particularly gratifying discovery for a therapist, since recovery from these pseudodementias is sometimes dramatic and can point to exciting possibilities for successful functioning. Close work with the individual's physician is needed in these cases, since most pseudodementias are chemically based. However, the therapist's facility at interviewing may be useful in discovering life-style issues such as eating and drinking habits, use and misuse of medications, recent life disruptions, and other environmental stressors.

Even more complicating is the fact that many cases of dementia combine two or three causative factors. It is entirely possible — even probable — to be presented with someone who is suffering from both a primary dementia and a functional depression, or who has both primary dementia and multi-infarct dementia. The task of differential diagnosis becomes substantially more difficult in this case, with the goal being to resolve those pathologies that can be resolved in order to ascertain what impairments have been wrought by the irreversible elements of the clinical picture.

When working with the elderly, the therapist should also be aware of the possible presence of benign senescent forgetfulness. This is a condition that affects most people as they age. It is characterized by a forgetfulness for names of people and places in the presence of intact memory for the events and situations themselves. It is a benign condition not indicative of dementia and is mentioned here so that the professional can effectively make a differential diagnosis, and so that the therapist can reassure clients with this condition that it is not the "senility" that they fear.

Exhaustive evaluation of early dementia is a complex and multidisciplinary procedure generally requiring medical evaluation, detailed history taking, and neuropsychological testing. However, the marital or sexual therapist working with the elderly will find it useful to develop a facility at preliminary screening in order to help with his or her own treatment planning.

When beginning work with any middle-aged or elderly individual, the professional will want to remain alert for impairments of memory (most notably short-term memory), judgment, reasoning ability, conceptual ability, computational ability, or language and motor facility. If the professional suspects that any of these are present, he or she will want to explore this in much greater depth.

It is important for the therapist to determine the precise history of the impairment; crucial clues can be found in the nature of the onset and progress of the impairments. An exhaustive history will virtually always require discussion with reliable informants as well as with the person being assessed. In many cases a good history alone is enough to help differentiate between an organic dementia and a treatable pseudodementia.

A concurrent step is to verify and objectify the initial impressions through the application of a mental status examination that focuses on cognitive functioning. A rich body of testing resources has been developed in recent years, much of which is accessible and easily utilized by professionals even without extensive experience in gerontology.

The instrument most widely used during the past 20 years or more is the Mental Status Questionnaire (Kahn et al., 1960), which evaluates responses to 10 questions regarding present location, date, month, year, personal history, and awareness of major news events. A very similar instrument is the Short Portable Mental Status Questionnaire (Duke University Center for the Study of Aging and Human Development, 1978). Both of these are particularly useful for assessing major deficits, but to ascertain more subtle deficits one might want to consider the Mini-Mental State Examination (Folstein et al., 1975), which examines orientation, memory, attention, conceptual ability, computational ability, and language ability. Other tests that have proven particularly useful are the Face-Hand Test (Fink, Green, & Bender, 1952), which specifically tests for organic impairment, and the Set Test (Isaacs & Kennie, 1973), which tests for the intactness of conceptual ability, one of the abilities lost in cases of senile dementia.

An exhaustive discussion of assessment procedures is beyond the scope of this chapter. The professional undertaking work with the elderly will be well served by the discussions of this process in two definitive works, by Kane and Kane (1981) and by Zarit, Orr, and Zarit (1985). Both these works provide accessible and useful guidelines for the practitioner.

When the therapist has well-documented concern about an individual's mental functioning, he or she will want to facilitate a definitive diagnosis through contact with the individual's physician and appropriate specialists, most often a neurologist, neuropsychologist, or psychiatrist. The author has found it particularly useful to use a neuropsychologist, who is a psychologist specializing in the determination and specification of organic etiology in mental disorders through the application of a wide range of testing procedures.

Physical Changes

As persons age they inevitably encounter changes in their physical health. Their cardiovascular health may decline, significantly reducing their strength and stamina. Sensory impairment may occur, and neurological problems may impede mobility and independence. Arthritis may impair movement. Respiratory difficulties may also impact on the elderly, and bladder and bowel difficulties may also have a severe effect.

The mental health professional counseling an elderly couple must also be alert for physical changes that are affecting the couple's interaction or sexual functioning. Changes in physical capacity have their most significant effect when they change what may have been long-standing roles within the relationship. The elderly couple and the professional alike can usually identify these changes easily, since they are major precipitants of stress. The residual of a cardiovascular accident, for example, can be a significant stressor; the affected spouse may experience deficits of speech, mobility, independence in activities of daily living, and impulse control, among other possible effects. The unaffected spouse will have to make major adjustments to accommodate these new needs, and there may be significant emotional trauma accompanying this change.

Beyond assuring that the affected person is under appropriate medical care, knowing the precise nature of these conditions is less important than understanding the functional impairments that they cause. The counselor will want to examine the changes in life-style that have resulted from the medical situation. A useful way to do this is to borrow from the field of occupational therapy, in which assessment of capacity to perform activities of daily living (ADL) has been brought to a high level of sophistication. Numerous assessment instruments have been devised, and the professional seeking to structure this aspect of functional assessment will find many choices in the occupational therapy literature. One particularly useful and comprehensive model is the activities of daily living section of the OARS model developed at Duke University (Duke University Center for the Study of Aging and Human Development, 1978). A detailed questionnaire examines the following items: telephone use, traveling to places out of walking distance, shopping, meal preparation, housework, taking medication, handling money, eating, dressing and undressing, personal hygiene, walking, transferring in and out of bed, bathing, and toilet independence.

It is also important to assess what the unaffected spouse is doing, and what effect this is having on their relationship. It is useful, when possible, to conduct the ADL segment of an assessment separately with each spouse, to determine their adjustment to these new roles in their relationship.

Another step that is particularly important when beginning to work with aging couples is the need to contact their physician(s) to determine their physical status. This can be an important element in determining what losses and changes they have encountered, as this may well impact on their treatment.

A particularly important aspect of change in physical functioning is that of change in sexual functioning. When evaluating an aging couple, the counselor should be aware of two elements. First, there are the normal aging-related changes in sexual function, which are often interpreted as sexual dysfunction. Second, aging individuals and couples continue to be susceptible to sexual dysfunction unrelated to their aging. An important task for the practitioner assessing an elderly couple is to evaluate their sexual history and functioning and to categorize sexual dysfunctions into these two categories. This categorization will directly impact on the development of goals and plans for treatment.

Aging-related changes in sexual functioning affect both males and females. Men can naturally expect to need more stimulation to achieve erection, increased stimulation to achieve orgasm (a change often perceived as positive!), and increased refractory time; they may also experience less firm erections, episodes of absent ejaculation, and reduced intensity of ejaculation, as well as changes in the intensity and frequency of sexual desire.

Although there is a clear diminishing of testosterone levels with aging, sexual capacity and desire generally continue well into old age in the absence of other disabilities that affect sexuality. However, in some cases there may be what Kolodny et al. characterize as a male climacteric, precipitated by an extremely subnormal testosterone level. The diagnostic criteria are positive findings for at least four of the following: listlessness; weight loss or poor appetite, or both; depressed libido, usually accompanied by loss of potency; impaired ability to concentrate; weakness and easy fatigability; and irritability. Since these symptoms can relate to many other conditions, the diagnosis only applies if there is a remission of symptoms within two months of initiating testosterone replacement therapy (Kolodny et al., 1979, pp. 107–108).

Aging males confront prostate difficulties with a frequency so high that it can almost be considered a normal concomitant of aging. One study notes that 50 to 75% of all men aged 80 or over experience benign prostatic hypertrophy, and that even men between 41 and 50 experience it at a rate of 30%. Also, the likelihood of prostatic cancer increases with aging.

Although benign prostatic hypertrophy does not directly affect sexuality, certain of the surgical procedures employed for this and for prostatic cancer can increase erectile dysfunction. However, the situation is greatly complicated by the frequent presence of psychogenic dysfunction following the surgery, and very careful assessment of this problem is necessary in cases of postsurgical erectile dysfunction.

Natural aging-related changes in women include alterations in natural patterns of lubrication and physical comfort during intercourse, with a noticeable decrease in natural lubrication and a reduction in vaginal elasticity. Occasional discomfort during orgasm has also been noted. Research also indicates that the effect of aging-related functions in women is exacerbated by sexual inactivity. It is also important to note that these changes do not by themselves decrease the libido or the capacity for orgasm in aging women. Furthermore, these changes seem to be minimized in the case of women who have remained sexually active during their postmenopausal years.

It is essential to determine whether or not these aging-related changes in sexual functioning have occurred and whether they are the source of marital or sexual distress. If these factors have precipitated problems, they are often amenable to quick amelioration through a process that is more educational than therapeutic, as discussed below. In addition, there are some medical interventions available, ranging from simple instruction in use of lubricants to penile implants for otherwise unresolvable erectile dysfunction.

Another common problem of the elderly couple is that of sexual feelings being incongruent with sexual attitudes. Counselors may find their elderly clients distressed that they have intense sexual feelings at a time in their lives when they should be "past all that." A related problem is that of one spouse believing that they should both be "past all that" while the other spouse is still very much in touch with his or her sexuality. In both cases these are sharply aging-related issues in which the aging process and the attitudes that accompany it have precipitated a problem in effective sexual functioning.

It is also important to remember that older couples may be experiencing sexual problems that are unrelated to their age. Problems relating to female orgasmic dysfunction, for example, are usually not age-specific. Incongruence of levels of sexual desire in a relationship may be precipitated by elements of the aging process, but is often of long duration and antedates the attainment of old age. Disagreements about sexual practices generally are not age-specific. Even cases of erectile dysfunction may be psychogenic and not at all related to aging. These cases require the same treatment that would be provided for younger couples, as long as the therapist is assured that there are not any intervening factors that are clearly aging-related.

Other Assessment Issues

In addition to examining the issues of mental and physical changes, the therapist must also examine the backdrop against which these new problems present themselves. Older couples require the same comprehensive assessment that is provided to couples of any age, but four further elements should be examined as well: their responses to aging-related role changes, the personality styles of the two individuals, their expectations in marriage, and their interactional style prior to aging.

The individual's acceptance of, and adjustment to, role changes can be a major factor in marital and sexual adjustment. Erikson's paradigm of the last developmental task is particularly apt: ego integrity versus despair (Erikson, 1959). If the individual can accept that his or her life has been meaningful and satisfying, the result will be ego integrity and a sense that life was "something that had to be and that, by necessity, permitted of no substitutions. . . . It is a sense of comradeship with men and women of distant times and of different pursuits, who have created orders and objects and sayings conveying human dignity and love" (Erikson, 1959, p. 98). Failure at this task leaves one with a despair that "the time is now short, too short for the attempt to start another life and to try out alternate roads to integrity" (Erikson, 1959, p. 98).

The need for successful completion of this last task becomes very clear to the marital and sexual counselor working with an elderly couple. As social and marital roles change, those who see the changes as a sign of failure will experience a sense of despair. The clinical manifestations of this despair are found in the category of adjustment disorders and in significant impairments of social, occupational, marital, and sexual functioning.

When assessing an elderly individual, it is important to evaluate his or her perspective on the past and its relationship to the future, in a sense determining the person's place in the Eriksonian paradigm. The person with a positive view of his or her past is generally more able to cope with changes and losses, whereas the person who believes that life has not dealt fairly with him or her will be far more susceptible to change-induced trauma. In terms of developing goals and strategies this line of inquiry is particularly important and fertile for the counselor beginning work with an elderly couple. The counselor's knowledge of the person's view of his or her past and future can be the single most important indicator of the individual's ability to make positive change. If the person has an essentially negative view of life and is moving toward the "despair" side of the paradigm, the counselor may find that this presents an obstacle that must be overcome before further progress can be made. Sadly, it often represents a long-term pattern of functioning that is not easily modified.

Assessment of an individual's place in this paradigm is an uncomplicated process. The information is usually apparent in any significant interview with the client. It is also quite feasible to simply ask the client for his or her assessment of how successful his or her life has been, and to seek evaluations of childhood, marriage, career, and parenthood. This information is virtually always in the consciousness of the older client, and the therapist will generally be able to discern easily the person's perspective on his or her past and future.

Measurements of personality can be as implicit or objective as the counselor feels is warranted and can be carried out through any standard approach that seems appropriate. If objective testing is going to be used, The 16PF test (Cattell, 1949) seems to be particularly useful for elderly persons whose cognition is generally intact. However, the counselor will want to explore carefully the client's level of comfort with objective testing. Older persons may be more intimidated by testing than by clinical interviews.

Another factor that must be carefully evaluated is the set of expectations that each partner brings to marriage. This is less important in a long-term marriage, which is often based on a philosophy of "'til death do us part." However, with increased life-spans late-life marriages of convenience have become common. In these relationships the therapist may find far weaker bonding than in a long-term marriage. The spouses may not consider it their duty to be a caretaker to an impaired partner, and they may not be highly motivated to resolve interpersonal or sexual issues. This relationship style is not particularly problematic if the expectations have been explicit, but it is crucial for the counselor to ascertain whether there is dissonance of expectations in the relationship. This dissonance may relate to caring for an invalid partner, or it may relate to sexual contact or to sharing of expenses and income. Regardless of the issue at hand, a frequent cause of tension is this dissimilarity of expectations in late-life marriages.

It is important to develop the baseline information about the couple's relationship before aging-related changes occurred. The distant but cordial couple who are now thrown together will experience problems that will not occur in the case of the couple who have been extremely close in the past.

When a formerly dominant husband finds himself incapacitated and cared for by his wife, he will probably be more upset than a man who has always been cared for by the wife. The couple with a previously inactive sex life may not be significantly disrupted by changes in sexual capacity or appetite, but a couple for whom sex loomed large will find these changes introducing a significant dislocation. Only through the development of this baseline data can the counselor determine what changes the aging process has wrought.

In summary, the therapist is advised to make some additions to the assessment process that will facilitate the examination of aging-related changes. A significant goal of the assessment process is to ascertain how (if at all) the advancing years have been the operational variable in causing or exacerbating marital or sexual stress. The reader is reminded that the elderly couple is much more similar to than different from younger couples, and unless aging is clearly a factor, these issues are essentially tangential to the counseling process.

GOAL PLANNING

The process of goal planning can often be frustrating for the counselor working with elderly couples. After many years of marriage, a couple may wish only to return to a homeostatic point rather than make major structural adjustments. This need may suggest therapeutic goals that are less ambitious than the counselor would consider ideal. The goals of aging clients will often be expressed in extremely concrete and behavioral terms, and this may be all that the couple is seeking or is able to consider. For example, a couple at odds with each other because they are spending too much time together following retirement may be unable to resolve the basic differences between them and may benefit from the counselor's help in negotiating an agreement about time apart from each other. This need may not require comprehensive marital and sexual therapy. It may be the only change that the couple can contemplate or that they desire. If conflict management will meet their perceived needs, then that may be the only feasible and desirable goal of treatment.

We must also remember that an elderly couple's image of an ideal marriage may be dramatically different from that of the therapist. Persons socialized early in this century may have firmly rooted ideas about marriage and sexuality that others might consider outmoded or even repressive. Rather than effect any changes in their belief systems, the couple may only want to bring their present functioning into conformity with their long-standing beliefs. For example, the writer remembers one extreme example of this, a woman whose goal in treatment was to have her husband hit her less severely. Physical violence had been an integral part of her and her husband's families of origin, and throughout their 50-year marriage he had communicated with her through physical violence. The passage of time had made her more frail and had significantly impaired her husband's judgment and impulse control, so the physical violence had become more severe and less tolerable to her weakened body. However, all she sought in counseling was a method of making him hit her less severely. It appeared that she perceived the physical abuse prior to the increase in severity as a form of ongoing communication, and it represented the norm for her relationship. The woman rejected or ignored all attempts to realign her perceptions about the appropriateness of physical violence in marriage.

It is also important when developing goals for counseling to allow for the fact that many elderly couples will not be able to participate effectively in a counseling process that depends a great deal on insight and discussion of feelings. Although this is not universally true, and will be decreasingly true in the future, the present-day counselor working with elderly couples may find among many clients a hesitance to work in the area of emotions. They are seeking to solve their problems, not to develop problem-solving insights.

A practical and tangible approach to goal setting can be quite appropriate in working with elderly couples. They often need help in learning new activities and compensating for what they have lost. The setting of very tangible goals is particularly useful because the process is accessible and understandable to the elderly couple. In one case, a couple were at odds because the wife's sexual needs and "tolerance" (in her phraseology) had declined, but the husband continued to feel the need for sexual contact. They rejected any suggestion that the wife's changes in sexuality could be ameliorated. Discussion of some of the approaches used in modern sex therapy began to alienate them because it necessitated open discussion of details of their sexual functioning with the counselor, something that they could not do. Ultimately the couple negotiated an agreement that consisted of an increase in nonsexual intimacy and sexual contact at a reduced frequency. The problems still remained, but the couple was quite satisfied to deal with its most problematic manifestation.

Goal planning can be facilitated by consideration of the compensatory model of aging. Three options for planning are available in this model: adjustment to inexorable changes, restoration of aspects lost but restorable, and substitution and compensation for losses to the extent possible. Throughout this process, the counselor must also remain focused on the overriding goal of helping the elderly couple remain proficient at making changes.

TREATMENT CONSIDERATIONS

As in assessment and goal planning, the treatment phase of working with an elderly couple is more similar to than different from work with couples of other ages. One of the reasons that a separate body of knowledge about counseling the elderly does not exist is simply that it is not needed. The elderly are not *similar* to us; they *are* us.

There are some approaches to marital therapy that can increase the counselor's potential for effectiveness with older couples. These approaches are based on characteristics of elderly couples that the therapist is likely to encounter, some of which have already been noted:

1. A hesitance about marital and sexual therapy, and some questioning of its possible efficacy. Many elderly persons were socialized in an era when psychotherapy was virtually nonexistent except for the treatment of "madness."
2. Possible discomfort in making full disclosure about feelings to the counselor and/or in front of the spouse. This may include a clear inability to express these feelings and may also reflect a lack of personal familiarity with the language of emotions.
3. The possibility that organic mental changes have impaired the ability to participate effectively in the counseling process.
4. The potential for discomfort with behavioral sex therapy.
5. An unwillingness or inability to contract for long-term therapy, even when it is indicated.
6. The fact that elderly couples often have significant others in their lives, most often adult children. These others can be useful or deleterious in the counseling process. Other significant relationships are often those with physicians and clergymen.
7. The likelihood that one or both partners in the relationship will be experiencing reduced vitality and stamina.
8. The likelihood that there will be significant sensory impairments on the part of one or both partners.

It is important to remember that no stereotype fits every elderly couple. These characteristics are those which the counselor may find, and it is necessary to remain alert to the possibility of their presence. However, no case will present all of these characteristics, and it is entirely possible that a particularly vital elderly couple will present none of them. These should be utilized as guidelines for exploration rather than as inflexible descriptors.

However, the counselor working with elderly couples will encounter enough of these, and with sufficient frequency, that it is worthwhile to consider ways that the treatment process can effectively integrate the needs and limitations of the elderly couple. There are three aspects of treatment considerations that need to be reviewed: *opening treatment, effective approaches to counseling,* and *logistical considerations.*

Opening Treatment

The beginning of any treatment process requires the building of trust between the clients and the therapist. The elderly couple may require special attention to the establishment of an effective working relationship.

The counselor should be particularly attentive to the process by which the couple made contact. This writer's experience has been that elderly couples do not decide to seek counseling and then shop for a counselor. Almost always, they present their problems to a physician, a clergyman, or—less frequently—a friend or family member. These others may suggest marital or sexual therapy and help the couple make contact with a counselor. At this point, the couple may feel themselves caught in a process from which they cannot escape, especially if the person recommending counseling is an authority figure in their lives, most often a clergyman or physician.

As the counselor determines what hesitance if any is present, the early sessions may need to be devoted, at least in part, to discussion of the process of counseling, with special attention paid to the right of the clients to self-determination in the process. Some elderly individuals and couples have expressed fear of involuntary institutionalization, and it has been necessary to reassure them that this will not happen as a result of counseling.

There may also be a need to explain some of the techniques that are used in marital and sexual therapy. For many elderly couples this is an alien area, and they are often reassured to learn that the techniques are not mysterious. The image of the classical psychoanalyst persists as well, and it is very helpful for elderly couples to learn that counseling as it is presently practiced is often quite different from that style.

The behavioral techniques of sex therapy can be quite problematic for older couples. The counselor will want to explore the couple's perceptions about these techniques early in the process, to either help them overcome their hesitance about them or reassure them that they will not be pressured into practices that make them uncomfortable. In one case, for example, a woman anxious to increase her orgasmic responsiveness felt extremely diffident about using the self-pleasuring techniques that have become part of the standard treatment for this dysfunction. Her discomfort was in part because the therapist was male, but was more because of lifelong proscriptions about "self-abuse." The situation was salvaged by quickly transferring her to a female therapist who deferred all behavioral work until they had spent several months developing a high level of trust and overcoming her feelings about self-pleasuring as opposed to "self-abuse."

In another situation, a middle-aged man was experiencing some difficulty with premature ejaculation. He sought counseling, and his wife accompanied him but made it clear that her husband was the "patient" and that she was there as an interested bystander. Assessment of their marriage showed it to be stable. The therapist perceived very quickly that the "squeeze technique" might well be utilized, so he discussed behavioral therapies with them soon after the initial assessment sessions. When it was explained, along with the advisability of spouse participation, they both agreed that the treatment was not something they could share. In order to maintain the trust of the clients, the therapist had to reorient his approach based on this discomfort, and he worked with the husband after failing to increase the wife's participation. A modified "stop-start" approach was used successfully in this case.

The therapist should not be diffident about dispelling some of the more florid myths about sex therapy. The author has had to reassure clients that there would be no sex in the office, and that they would not be asked to participate in surrogate therapy.

The need to carry out a thorough assessment of mental and physical functioning has already been discussed, and this, of course, should be done during the early stages of the treatment process. However, it should be noted that a formal examination of cognitive functioning can be distressing for an aging individual, especially if he or she suspects some impairment. If the individual perceives the therapist's suspicion of cognitive impairment, the iatrogenic upset will often guarantee a poor showing of cognitive capacity. In addition, the upset caused by this revelation may make it impossible to continue with marital, sexual, or other therapy. Therefore, the counselor may want to make the screening process a covert part of the assessment and treatment.

Fortunately, many of the questions that are asked in a mental status examination can be asked as part of a normal intake interview. For example, it is entirely reasonable to ask a person what year he was born, how old he is, and his birthday. One can ask a client to compute his grandchildren's age by subtracting the year of their birth from the present year, a process that gives insight into memory and computational ability.

Another way to move gently into this area of inquiry is to respond to the client's expressed concerns about his own mental acuity. This is a very common concern among the elderly, especially those who have experienced benign senescent forgetfulness. The therapist can respond to the client's concern by offering to do a quick screening, an offer that is usually accepted.

Except for the specific additions to information gathering that have been discussed, a standard approach to history taking is generally appropriate. This model, a familiar one to many therapists, consists of one or two initial joint interviews followed by individual sessions with each spouse, followed again by one or more joint sessions.

The counselor must also be aware that the taking of a sexual history may be extremely discomforting for an elderly couple or individual, and if this becomes too intense, the counselor may need to defer this segment until a greater level of trust has been established unless the major presenting problem is clearly of a sexual nature. This discomfort may be increased if the interviewer and the client are of opposite genders. The counselor might then want to consider working with an opposite sex cotherapist or transferring the case to a counselor of the appropriate gender.

Counseling Approaches

During the past 20 years conjoint therapy has been the modality of choice in marital and sexual therapy. It fosters enhanced communication between the clients and develops a sense of shared commitment to solving the problems. However, the therapist may encounter times when maintaining a conjoint approach is too intense and intimidating for one or both parties in the couple. If the norm in their relationship has been one of minimal communication, then the intensity of communication that is a hallmark of the conjoint approach may offer heightened feelings that are too intense to allow productive work to be done.

This discomfort with the intensity of conjoint marital counseling may be particularly true for couples who are seeking sharply limited solutions to their problems. The counselor may want to consider utilizing a concurrent style of treatment in which he or she sees each member of the dyad separately, with conjoint sessions as appropriate. If gender issues become an ongoing problem, one might want to consider utilizing a collaborative model of counseling, with cotherapists of the appropriate genders working with the respective members of the couple, allowing for conjoint sessions as needed.

The concurrent approach will often be less threatening for an older person and may help to develop an effective working relationship with the counselor. However, the counselor should also be alert for opportunities to bring the couple into conjoint efforts. The safety of the concurrent approach also denotes less opportunity for growth and change.

In one case, a couple was at odds over the frequency with which they had sexual relations, with the husband seeking sexual activity far more frequently than the wife. The wife perceived that the husband's demands had increased dramatically during the previous two years, but her need and desire had remained stable and perhaps had even declined in response to his demands. They sought counseling at the request and even insistence of their adult son, who was aware of some stress between them but did not know that the problem was sexually related. They acknowledged the problem to the therapist, but the husband seemed resistant to discussing it in any depth, making frequent attempts to change the topic. Two conjoint sessions produced no movement whatever, and the therapist decided to see the husband alone for several sessions. During these sessions he quickly revealed that he had developed an infatuation for a younger woman, although he had never acted on it or even acknowledged to the younger woman that he had these feelings for her. He felt a great deal of guilt about these feelings. In these private discussions he suggested on his own that perhaps his sexual demands were a way to overcompensate for what he perceived as "mental philandering," to prove to himself that he still found his wife attractive. (The accuracy of his insight was irrelevant; it was, however, extremely useful because it allowed him to resolve his dilemma.) Also, the therapist was able to discuss with him the fact that fantasies and infatuations are usually quite harmless. Once these hurdles were overcome, several conjoint sessions were all that were necessary to resolve the issue. After a one-month follow-up both husband and wife reported that they had once again achieved a mutually comfortable balance in their sexual relations. In this instance, the use of a concurrent model was instrumental in resolving problems efficiently and effectively, and it should be considered a useful modality in working with older couples.

These variations of approach will be particularly effective when the goals of treatment are limited to education and the teaching of skills, rather than to the development of significant insights about the relationship. As discussed above, some couples may have expectations for their relationship that preclude dramatic changes in style of interaction. The counselor will do well to focus on approaches that meet the expressed desires of the couple.

The educational-skills development approach is a particularly apt one for the elderly client precisely because it is not perceived as a threatening endeavor. The development of improved communication skills and some information about assertiveness is often accepted and integrated rapidly, precisely because it is the tangible sort of information that is most palatable to older persons.

Similarly, the therapist may find himself or herself in the role of coach and mediator. Although this may require a change in the traditional counseling mindset that seeks growth following insight, this new role may, like the educational approaches, be precisely what the couple is willing and able to accept. Coaching and mediation focus on behaviors and not on the reasons underlying the behaviors.

The author's work with one aging couple illustrates this concept. The couple was referred for counseling by their minister because the wife was finding fault with everything that the husband did or said. The husband was being criticized several hundred times a day, and no friendly words had been exchanged between them for weeks at a time. Sexual contact had not occurred for several years, although they reported that until this increase in hostility they had continued with modified physical contact, including hand holding and hugging. The lack of more intimate sexual contact was not considered a problem for either of them, since they both felt that "that's for younger people."

It became clear in interviews with the wife that the criticisms of the husband were related to her lack of self-esteem and to a desire to receive some attention from him. The increase in anger at the husband had followed closely a bout with cancer from which the wife was making an excellent recovery. The husband presented himself as a very quiet and reserved individual whose response to her attacks was to withdraw even more than he had. He could offer no insight into the reasons for his wife's change in behavior.

Although it was easy for the counselor to develop some explanations for the behavior, it was interesting as well as discouraging to observe how little impact was made by the discussion of these insights with the couple. The information was accepted as interesting but academic, and they continued to ask how they could change the pattern in which they found themselves. Although the wife was an excellent candidate for individual psychotherapy, she was unwilling to undertake it. She indicated that "I just want my days to be more peaceful; I don't want to spend a lot of time discussing my past."

On this note we entered into a mediation process that lasted several sessions, and which was highly successful in developing some guidelines for daily coexistence. Although the couple wanted the counselor to dictate these guidelines, they participated in the development process to the best of their ability. The guidelines focused on clear mandates for the behavior of each partner, including some concessions on the part of each partner about certain behaviors and a structured communication time every few days using communication skills taught by the counselor, including active listening and "I" messages. Resumption of physical intimacy was negotiated, although this behavior was limited by mutual choice to hugging and hand holding.

At follow-up they reported a substantial decrease in the intensity of hostilities between them. They were able to follow the guidelines with great exactitude and found that the structure was very comfortable for them. Follow-up contact over several months showed continued improvement. They expressed complete satisfaction with the results of the treatment even though from the counselor's perspective the continuing level of hostility seemed high. They were clearly unwilling to proceed with counseling beyond the point they had reached. However, they were very pleased to authorize the reporting of case information to their minister, who agreed to remain in regular touch with them for monitoring and follow-up.

The major point of this vignette is that a simple educational and "coaching" approach was all that would be accepted by the clients and was successful within their framework. In addition, two other therapeutic elements are illustrated. One is the use of authority figures by both clients and counselors, and the other is an apparent preference for short-term therapy on the part of many older couples.

Authority figures are often useful in working with aging couples. As couples age there is often an increase in their dependency on others, and when this dependency is comfortable for the couple, it can be used effectively. The couple was willing, even pleased, to have their minister take over the role of monitor and expressed that they felt this would help them remain within the guidelines that had been devised.

The minister had also served as an authority figure in urging the couple to seek counseling. The couple themselves never considered counseling until the minister suggested it and were able to overcome their hesitance only because of the urging of their trusted clergyman. During the early days of counseling, the minister's support was important in helping them continue with this strange process. When it was time to terminate, the minister again helped maintain the progress.

The most common authority figures are clergymen, physicians, and sometimes adult children. Authority figures can become important adjuncts in working with an elderly couple and can help the couple continue in and invest themselves fully in a process. Counselors will find that there are often times in working with the elderly that a mutual effort with an authority figure can move the situation past an impasse.

A further point is that older couples may not have the desire, stamina, or even financial resources to manage long-term counseling, even when it is clearly indicated. The writer's experience has been that elderly couples are often seeking specific and rapid amelioration of their concerns, and the counselor may often have to work within this limitation. However, it is also common among the elderly to seek episodic counseling as difficult times arise. In this way the elderly and many younger couples have a great deal in common. As further contacts occur, the counselor might have further opportunities to influence the goals of the couple, and perhaps more substantial structural change can be implemented.

Older couples may also resist participating in dramatic forms of therapy. Although the technique of addressing an empty chair, for example, may be comfortable for someone familiar with the vernacular of modern therapies, it may not be comfortable for an older person. The writer is familiar with an elderly couple who were urged by a friend to attend a weekend-long human growth seminar. Rather than being helped, they both found it extremely distressing and remained for the entire weekend only because of pressure from those around them. In another instance, an elderly lady described a group therapy leader as "crazier than me!"

The reader is reminded that these caveats do not hold true for every older couple. This examination is of the ways that the therapist may have to modify counseling techniques to fit the particular needs of elderly clients. Each couple will present a unique set of needs and capabilities, and no doubt there will be older clients who are able to participate in the most intensive therapeutic effort that the counselor can provide.

Logistical Considerations

There are some logistical elements to counseling the elderly, elements that can make the counseling far more accessible and acceptable to them. These are simple but significant matters.

One factor to consider is the stamina that is required to participate in a typical therapeutic hour. An older couple may find that it is simply too long for them, and the counselor may want to experiment with shorter sessions. The writer has been working successfully with two individuals in long-term counseling through the provision of 15-minute sessions twice a week. Although this is not an efficient form of work from the perspective of the professional, it has proven to be quite effective from the clients' perspectives, enhancing their comfort with the counseling relationship.

Home visits are sometimes advisable. Mobility limitations may make counseling inaccessible except through home visits, and professionals may find that this is a viable format for counseling. The therapist may also find that observing the clients *in vivo* will be a useful diagnostic tool.

An interesting phenomenon that this writer has noticed is the desire and insistence of older clients to maintain a "cash-and-carry" relationship. The author's normal practice is to bill clients on a monthly basis, to simplify bookkeeping. However, an astonishing number of older clients have resisted this technique and insist on paying immediately after each session, often in cash. At this point we have adjusted the flexibility of our bookkeeping procedures to facilitate this, realizing that this serves an important need of the client.

The last and most significant logistical element is that of compensating for sensory limitations and other physical deficits in the counseling context. One simple factor is the need to allow for hearing limitations in working with the elderly. The presence of background music in an office, for example, can be an immense obstacle to someone with a hearing loss, especially to someone with a hearing aid. This is because many hearing losses diminish the ability to automatically distinguish between primary and background noises.

The therapist also needs to provide a glare-free space. Having an elderly person face a bright window will effectively render him temporarily blind, since the effects of glare on older persons are vastly more severe than on younger people.

Appropriate seating is also essential if the older person is going to effectively participate in the counseling program. Low and soft chairs can be difficult and uncomfortable for older persons to use and can become a significant obstacle to effective participation in counseling. The writer remembers numerous clients who could be comfortable in his office only when they were sitting in an uncushioned, high-backed chair.

It is impossible to predict what logistical problems one will confront when working with older couples, and aside from those which are clear to the counselor, others may well be present. Some older persons are reluctant to discuss their impairments and instead will simply struggle along within whatever limitations they encounter. Therefore, the therapist will want to explore these issues with the clients early in the relationship and perhaps check from time to time that the counseling environment is adequate.

SUMMARY

The marital and sexual upsets of older couples are not that much different from those of younger couples. However, because of the physical, psychological, and social losses that are experienced by older people, counseling professionals may have to adjust their approaches to the specific needs of the elderly couple. We need to be clear about the goals that we establish in concert with our clients and carefully avoid establishing goals that reflect our hopes for the clients rather than the clients' hopes for themselves. This may be especially difficult when the goals that the clients express seem to be parochial; yet, this is what they want and is within their capability to achieve. We must also assess the older couple's functional capacity with great care and with attention to the deficits that aging often produces. It is in this area that we will find the most significant difference between the younger and older couple. Finally, we must remember that similarities far outweigh differences, and the elderly are entitled, just as are younger people, to have rewarding relationships.

REFERENCES

American Psychiatric Association (1980). *Diagnostic and statistical manual of mental disorders* (3rd ed.). Washington, DC: Author.

Cattell, R. (1949–1982). *Sixteen Personality Factor Questionnaire*. Champaign, IL: Institute for Personality and Ability Testing, Inc.

Cumming, E., & Henry, W. (1961). *Growing old: The process of disengagement*. New York: Basic Books.

Duke University Center for the Study of Aging and Human Development (1978). *Multidimensional functional assessment: The OARS methodology; A manual*. Durham, NC: Author.

Erikson, E. (1959). The healthy personality. In Identity and the life cycle: Selected Papers by Erik H. Erikson, *Psychological Issues, 1*(1), 50–100.

Fink, M., Green, M., & Bender, M. (1952). The face-hand test as a diagnostic sign of organic mental syndrome. *Neurology, 2*, 46–59.

Folstein, M., Folstein, S., & McHugh, P. (1975). Mini-mental state: A practical method for grading the cognitive status of patients for the clinician. *Journal of Psychiatric Research, 12*, 189–198.

Hussian, R. (1981). *Geriatric psychology: A behavioral perspective*. New York: Van Nostrand Reinhold Company.

Isaacs, B., & Kennie, A. (1973). The set test as an aid to the detection of dementia in old people. *British Journal of Psychiatry, 132*, 467–470.

Kahn, R., Goldfarb, A., Pollack, M., & Peck, A. (1960). Brief objective measures

for the determination of mental status in the aged. *American Journal of Psychiatry,*
117, 326–328.

Kalodny, R., Masters, W., & Johnson, V. (1979). *Textbook of Sexual Medicine.*
Boston: Little, Brown.

Kane, R., & Kane, R. (1981). *Assessing the elderly: A practical guide to measurement.*
Lexington, MA: D. C. Heath and Co.

Zarit, S., Orr, N., & Zarit, J. (1985). How to assess for dementia. In S. Zarit, N.
Orr, & J. Zarit (Eds.), *The hidden victims of Alzheimer's disease.* New York: New
York University Press.

Name Index

Subject Index